THE MAXWELL HOUSE COFFEE COOKBOOK

The recipes in this book were prepared in General Foods Kitchens, one of America's leading test kitchens, for Maxwell House Division, GENERAL FOODS CORPORATION. Some of the recipes in this book were supplied by the Coffee Brewing Institute, Inc.

THE MAXWELL HOUSE COFFEE COOKBOOK

Consulting Editor
Ellen Saltonstall
Coffee Brewing Institute, Inc.

Executive Editor
Doris McFerran Townsend

CASTLE BOOKS ★ NEW YORK

This Edition Published By Arrangement
With Thomas Nelson & Sons

Prepared by Specialized Publishing Company
Published by Thomas Nelson & Sons
Library of Congress Catalog Card Number: 65-20630
Printed in the United States of America

Coffee . . .

Noir comme le diable,
Chaud comme l'enfer,
Pur comme un ange,
Doux comme l'amour.

Black as the devil,
Hot as hell,
Pure as an angel,
Sweet as love.

—TALLEYRAND

Contents

THE MAXWELL HOUSE COFFEE COOKBOOK

The Coffee Story:

Coffee Customs Around the World

Long ago, the legend runs, in the hills of Ethiopia, lived a young goatherd. While tending his flock, he noticed that the goats became very playful after eating the berries of a plant that grew wild on the grazing range. The boy reasoned: if the fruit gave the goats such a joyous sense of well-being, might not those berries affect humans in the same way?

The year was about A.D. 500. The goats were eating coffee berries. And the answer to his question, the boy discovered, was *yes*. . . .

Communications being what they were, coffee remained Ethiopia's secret for many years. But by the Fourteenth Century, coffee plants were grown in Arabia. The beans, pulverized and cooked in water, produced a hot, black beverage so stimulating that a man could stay up all night on a few cupfuls of it. The Arabians called it *qahwah,* which means "that which gives strength." They still drink it blacker and stronger than the rest of the world likes it, but it was, and is, essentially the coffee that we know today.

From *qahwah,* and its Turkish derivative, *kahveh,* come the names for coffee in almost every country of the world. The French and the Spanish both call it *café*. The Italian version is *caffè,* and the German, *Kaffee*. The Finns say *kahvi,* the Dutch *koffie,* the Greeks *kafeo*. Even in English, coffee hasn't always been the same term. In 1590 it was spelled *chaoua;* by 1610 it had become *cahoa;* five years later the spelling had become *cahue;* by 1640 it had been simplified to *coho*. Ten more years, two more spellings: *coffey* and *coffee*. By 1700, the word had become stabilized as *coffee,* and so it has remained.

In Turkey, almost a thousand years ago, when a man wished to marry, he was required to promise, among other things, that his wife would never want for coffee. In the streets of Damascus and Cairo, vendors sold tiny cups of coffee: a kind of on-the-move coffee break.

Traveling Europeans sampled the thick black brew the coffee peddlers carried in copper vessels, heated by spirit lamps. About 1600, the adventurous, seafaring Venetians brought the beans—the seeds inside the coffee fruit—back home with them. At first, the Church opposed coffee as "a drink of the infidels," but after Pope Clement VIII "Christianized" the beverage, the use of coffee spread rapidly. Other European countries took up this new, stimulating beverage—and wherever coffee was introduced, along came the coffee peddler to help make it popular.

The first peddler in Paris was an Armenian who set up a tent at the Fair of Saint-Germain in 1672 and hired Turkish waiters to serve coffee. He did a brisk business, and so, after the fair closed, he opened a coffee shop in Paris, continuing to send his waiters through the streets. People flocked to buy the steaming little cupfuls, called *petit noir*.

The first Parisian coffeehouses were Oriental in style. But in 1689 François Procope, who had been a street coffee peddler, opened a new kind of coffeehouse—elegant, gracious, very French—and called it the Café de Procope. About the same time, another former vendor opened the Café de la Regence. Both coffeehouses are still serving regular customers and visitors to Paris.

Coffee, by this time, had come to Vienna, too—in a spectacular way. In 1863, the city was in danger of falling into the hands of besieging Turks. A Turkish-speaking Pole named Kolschitzky volunteered as a spy, and his cloak-and-dagger efforts changed the course of the battle. The retreating Turks left behind a large supply of coffee. Kolschitzky claimed it as his reward. He first peddled the exotic brew from door to door, later opened Vienna's first coffeehouse, the Blue Bottle.

Coffeehouses had come into lively existence in London, as

well. The great minds of the times gathered in them to exchange ideas, trade impertinences, argue the hours away. Johnson, Addison and Steele, Sheridan, Swift, Hogarth—men like these were the centers of such groups in the coffeehouses they favored. An entry in the diary of Samuel Pepys, dated February 3, 1663: "I just looked in, on my way home from Covent Garden, at the great coffeehouse there where I never was before; where Dryden, the poet I knew at Cambridge, and all the wits of the town were assembled."

In America, the first coffee peddler on record was a woman, Dorothy Jones of Boston, licensed in 1670. Coffeehouses came into being in this country about twenty years later, but it was not until after the Boston Tea Party in 1773 that coffee became a staple beverage in American homes. By the time of the Civil War, coffee was very much a part of the American way of life, and a coffee break, with its accompanying stimulation and comfort and easing of tension, was as important to the morale of soldiers of the North and South as it is to the modern-day GI.

Each Union soldier's haversack contained, along with his staples of hardtack and salt pork, his rations of coffee and sugar. According to a book called *Hardtack and Coffee,* written after the Civil War by John D. Billings, who served in the Union Army, each soldier made himself a campfire at the end of the day. He got out his tin dipper, filled it with roasted coffee and water, and brewed a comforting, relaxing cup. Billings wrote: "The little campfires, rapidly increasing to hundreds in number, would shoot up along the hills and plains, and as if by magic, acres of territory would be luminous with them."

And so, century by century, coffee—and the enjoyment of the coffee break—spread around the world. In Germany, the home-style coffee break, the *Kaffeeklatsch,* had come into being by the early 1800's. The German *Hausfrau* served the beverage to her neighbors, along with freshly baked cookies or a delicious coffee cake. And, of course, a liberal helping of *Klatsch*—gossip. This gathering meant more than a new kind of socializing—it signified the German woman's assertion of her right to exchange ideas and to think and speak for herself.

Naturally, it took a while for the coffee break to reach the African jungles. But if the following story can be believed—and there is documentary evidence to support it—a break for coffee and relaxation had become a custom among the intrepid explorers of the area by 1871. Everyone knows, of course, what Sir Henry Morton Stanley said on the occasion of his famous encounter: "Dr. Livingstone, I presume?" The doctor's reply, not nearly so widely known, is said to have been: "Just in time for coffee, Stanley."

Today, the coffee break is an institution, firmly rooted in the way of life of many peoples in many countries. Here in the United States, in offices and stores and factories, employees go out to a nearby café or gather around the itinerant coffee wagon or that minor modern miracle, the hot-coffee vending machine, to unwind . . . and go back to their jobs refreshed.

In pleasant, comfortable rooms in modern theaters, waiting patrons are served cups of coffee. In one of New York's splendid old hotels, the Plaza, a very special sort of coffeehouse has come into being: The Palm Court After Eight—a beautiful old room, elegantly refurbished for the serving of after-dinner coffee and dessert.

Once again coffeehouses flourish, especially in such areas as New York's Greenwich Village. Some, like London's coffeehouses of old, are gathering places for the exchange of philosophies; some dispense avant-garde music and poetry in dimly lighted rooms so filled with "atmosphere" that you are hard put to find the coffee.

And all over the fifty states, this morning and every morning, housewives call each other—on the phone, over the back fence, across apartment-house halls—to offer the cheery suggestion, "Come on over for a cup of coffee!"

The same sort of coffee-centered socializing takes place in most other countries of the modern world, as well. Brazilians, for example, drink coffee all day long. In offices and factories in the big cities, there is usually a coffee machine on the premises. When a man is thirsty he has a *cafezinho,* for this is the way the Brazilian likes his coffee: filtered through a funnel-shaped flannel bag, heavily sugared, served in a very small cup. He may drink as many as two dozen cupfuls a day.

In other Latin American countries, the consumption of coffee is almost as high. It is the favorite drink in the home. Guests are always served coffee, no matter what the hour or the occasion. The family drinks it with every meal. Even young children have coffee in their milk, and coffee is used to flavor all kinds of dishes, all through the meal. Outside the home, too, coffee is the most popular drink. In outdoor cafés—as usual as soda fountains in the United States—people sit and chat and sip cup after cup of coffee.

When Greek meets Greek, the chances are that they'll sit down and have coffee together. Greek coffee shops are filled throughout the day and into the night with citizens downing thimble-sized cupfuls of thick, sweet Turkish coffee as an accompaniment to conversation.

If you were touring Athens, you would find it easy to fall into the local habit. You'd make several stops during a morning's sight-seeing—one of them, perhaps, at the famous Floca sidewalk café, where every other tourist in town would pass before you if you sat there long enough. In the afternoon, after the customary three-hour shutdown for lunch and rest, you would probably find your way to one of the exciting places at the foot of the Acropolis itself, to drink your coffee in the shadow of the magnificent ruins.

If your travel takes you to Denmark, you'll soon learn that Danes like to eat—whenever they have the time, a good excuse, or both. Their *Morgenkomplet* begins the day: a selection of breads or rolls, wonderful butter—and coffee. They may add eggs, bacon, porridge—and more coffee. Lunch, which is eaten early, may very well be selected from the staggering variety of a *smørrebrød* table, where meats, fish, and cheeses, arranged upon bread, can be treated as hors d'oeuvres or made into an entire meal . . . followed by coffee.

In Copenhagen, you may treat yourself to late afternoon

coffee at one of the restaurants in the famous Tivoli Gardens, and watch the lights go on over the city. The Danes' early dinner hour doesn't leave them much time for the afternoon coffee break as we know it, but it does give them a bonus which is more to their liking—a long, long evening in the course of which anyone, even if he doesn't enjoy a Danish appetite, is going to want a *little* something to eat . . . and at least one cup of coffee.

There was a time, not too long ago, when the true coffee addict had to make special plans for a trip to London. Experienced travelers packed their own supplies of coffee. Some even brought their own coffeepots, just to be on the safe side. But times have changed. Nowadays you can have a cup of coffee anywhere in England, any time you want it, and particularly at midmorning "elevenses"—the day's first coffee break.

The modern London coffee shops bear no relation to the ancient English coffeehouses. They are called "espressos" and they are an Italian importation. The coffee is good; and the tiny, brightly decorated shops make it possible for the businessman, shopper, or tourist to pause for quick refreshment and hurry on.

At afternoon "teatime," the espressos' small tables, usually at the back of the shops, accommodate those who have time to sit down for a real coffee break. The British who want to live adventurously can do it at the espressos—there they can have all sorts of French and Italian pastries, not nearly so widely known in Britain as in their home countries or here in the United States. Or the Briton can have the traditional English teatime treats with his coffee if he prefers—thin cucumber sandwiches, hot scones, plum cake. No need to carry a coffeepot to Britain any longer—it has become as unnecessary as carrying coals to Newcastle. . . .

Here's a picture to warm any traveler's heart: the dark, polished comfort of a coffeehouse, with the pastry tray brought around at regular intervals, and many, many kinds of coffee from which to choose. That's Vienna. There, in clublike atmosphere, native or tourist, businessman, shopper, or, particularly, the Viennese chess player can stop and, literally, set up shop for ten minutes or a whole afternoon. He can read a book, chat with friends, discuss business, or even plot international devilment. (Where would spy stories be without those two stand-bys, the Orient Express and the rendezvous with a mysterious stranger in a coffeehouse?)

If you like to experiment, you can spend three weeks in Vienna and drink your coffee differently each day. You can start with dark *mocha*, work your way up through *cappuccino* with boiled milk or whipped cream stirred into it, and progress, through many other stages, to *mélange*, its top mounded with stiff, rich cream and an extra dish of whipped cream on the side in case you run short. . . .

The coffee break is here—and there, and everywhere—to stay. Throughout this book, you'll find recipes for various kinds of coffee-break delicacies: pastries, tarts, sweet breads, sandwiches that are coffeetime traditions in the far corners of the globe. So, whether you tour the world in person or through the pages of books, you can have a coffee break at whatever time, in whatever style, that best suits your mood.

Which Type of Coffee Maker Is for You? The One that Makes the Coffee You Like Best!

For four hundred years, from 1300 to 1700, the accepted way—indeed, the only way—of brewing coffee was to boil it. There were differences of opinion about how the boiling should be done and how much coffee should be used, but all methods added up to the same result: a muddy, bitter beverage that, today, we would hardly recognize as coffee.

In the early 1700's, the French—always intensely interested in anything that has to do with bettering food and drink—began to steep coffee, and the bitter, boiled brew gradually disappeared. In 1800 the drip pot—again, French-designed—made its appearance. As always when something really good is invented, a rash of "improvements" followed quickly on its heels. Some of them were so unnecessarily complicated that a housewife needed a fortune to afford such a maker and a degree in chemistry to operate it. Some, though, produced acceptable refinements on the drip method, and one—the forerunner of the modern pump percolator—became standard. Shortly after that, the first vacuum pot made its appearance. Although innumerable changes have been rung on them, these three basic types of coffee makers are the ones in general use today.

MAKING PERFECT COFFEE

Start by buying the best brand of coffee—that is, the brand that makes the coffee which best suits your taste. Choose the proper grind for the coffee-making method you prefer: regular for percolators, drip grind for drip pots, and drip or fine grind for vacuum coffee makers. The right grind is important. Coffee must be fine enough for the water to circulate freely and extract all the good coffee flavor, but if it is too fine for the coffee maker in which it is used, the brewed coffee will be cloudy and may have a muddy sediment in the bottom of the cup.

Be certain that your coffee maker is always completely clean—wash all parts of it after each use in hot water, using a good detergent, and be sure to rinse thoroughly. Just before each use rinse pot again with hot water. Use your coffee maker to at least three-quarters of its capacity; you can't hope to make two cups of good, rich-tasting, satisfying coffee in an eight-cup pot. The coffee should be fresh; don't buy more than you can use within a week of opening. Keep the container tightly closed and stored in a cool, dry place—the refrigerator is ideal for coffee storage.

For each serving, use:
2 level tablespoons coffee
¾ cup (6 fluid ounces) water

Don't try to skimp—coffee can't be stretched. Coffee measures are available, and very handy. But be sure that the one you choose is the Coffee Brewing Institute's approved coffee measure—that is, one which holds exactly two level measuring tablespoons of coffee. Always use fresh, cold water—sometimes hot water pipes will deposit minerals in the water that will give coffee an off flavor.

SERVING PERFECT COFFEE

Coffee is at its very best when it's freshly prepared—always serve it piping hot, as soon as it is ready if possible. If you must keep the coffee standing for a time, place the pot or carafe—unless it's an electric maker—in a pan of hot water, or over a very low flame. *Make sure that it doesn't boil.* Just a moment of boiling will spoil the flavor.

CHOOSING A COFFEE MAKER

The "right" coffee maker is a matter of taste. Choose the one that makes the cup of coffee you like best—a percolator, drip, or vacuum pot for ground coffee or a carafe for instant coffee. Review the rules for making perfect coffee (pages 8 and 9) before making your final selection.

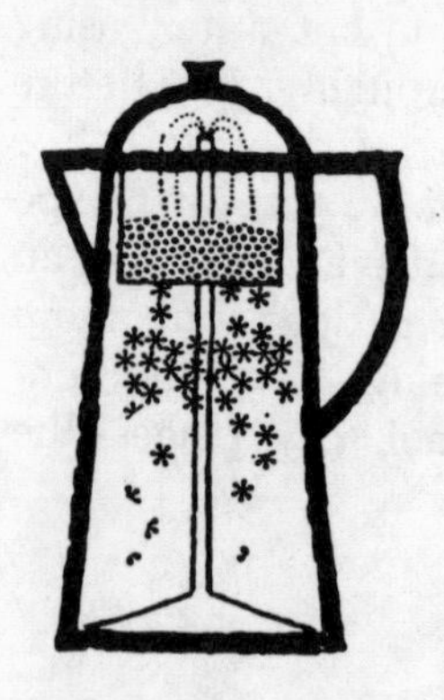

The Percolator: In this maker, water boils in the bottom part of the pot, bubbles up through a tube to spray gently over the ground coffee. The water seeps down through the coffee in the basket and then trickles back to the bottom of the pot, carrying the full flavor essence of the coffee. To start, measure fresh cold water into the bottom of the pot, and regular grind coffee, in the proper proportion, into the basket. (The water level should always be below the bottom of the basket.) Put the basket in place in the pot, cover, and heat until water starts to bubble into the top. Reduce heat. When water becomes amber-colored, start timing, and let it percolate gently six to eight minutes. Remove the basket; serve the coffee.

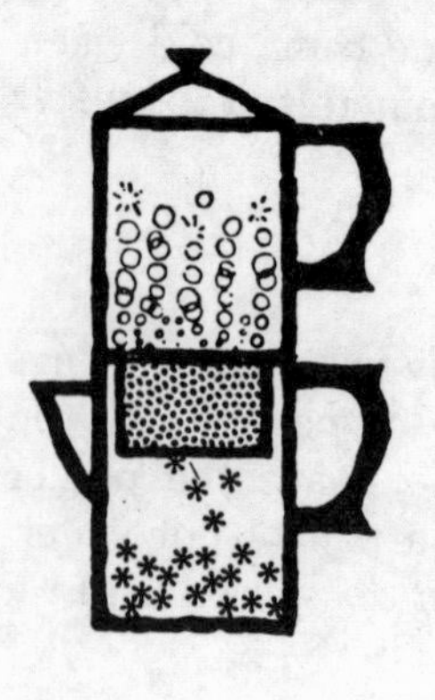

The Drip Pot: Freshly boiled water trickles slowly through the ground coffee in this method. Preheat the pot by rinsing with boiling water. Measure drip grind coffee into the filter section, and put the upper section into place. Measure fresh boiling water into upper section and cover. When all the water has dripped through the ground coffee into the lower section of the pot, remove upper and filter sections. Stir the coffee and serve.

The Vacuum Coffee Maker: By this method, steam from boiling water creates pressure which forces most of the water from the bottom bowl into the top, where it bubbles gently through the ground coffee. When removed from heat or heat is turned off, the bottom bowl cools, creating a vacuum which draws the brewed coffee through the filter and back to the lower bowl. The vacuum method calls for measuring fresh cold water into the lower bowl, set over heat. Put filter in upper bowl, and measure fine grind or drip grind coffee into it. When water boils, insert upper bowl, giving it a slight twist to make sure of a tight seal. The water—most of it—will rise into the upper bowl. When it has, reduce heat, stir thoroughly, and let the brew bubble gently two minutes. Remove from heat. In no more than three minutes the brewed coffee should have returned to the lower bowl. Remove the upper part; serve the coffee.

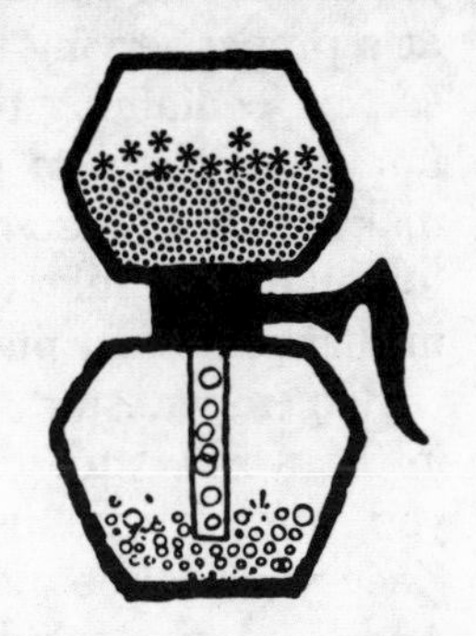

The Carafe: More and more persons are discovering the convenience and ease with which they can prepare perfect coffee every time in a simple carafe. Select a carafe that's not too large for everyday or too small when a few guests drop in —glass carafes are the easiest to keep clean and are attractive as serving containers. You can prepare instant coffee in a carafe by either of two methods. Using a rounded teaspoon of instant coffee and 5 ounces of water for each serving (or see Instant Coffee for a Crowd, page 14), measure the instant coffee into the carafe and gradually stir in cold water; then bring *just* to a boil—do not allow to boil. Or stir boiling water into the coffee, cover, and let steep a few minutes before serving. Keep the prepared coffee hot, but never allow it to boil.

ABOUT AUTOMATIC COFFEE MAKERS

There are many kinds—again, it's all a matter of taste. Some are self-timing: measure coffee and water, turn on the maker and forget it—when coffee is brewed to proper strength, the maker will automatically lower the heat and keep the coffee at a proper serving temperature. Always remove the basket or section containing the coffee grounds immediately. The most important thing to remember in buying an automatic coffee maker is to choose one that will be easy to keep clean. Then follow the manufacturer's instructions for brewing your coffee in that particular maker.

Remember, start with good coffee—the best coffee maker in the world can't give you that good, satisfying cup of coffee you want if you use an inferior blend. Measure carefully. Keep your coffee maker clean. Use freshly drawn cold water. And . . . learn to judge good coffee: it has clear color, a fresh, pleasant aroma, and full flavor, neither watery nor overstrong and bitter. Be famous for good coffee—it's a matter of taste, care, and know-how, and more than worth the small effort it takes in shopping and preparation.

Coffee for a Crowd

Church supper, fund-raising dinner, big family get-together? You'll need lots and lots of coffee. Here's the how-to for quantity coffee-making—plenty for seconds all around!

COFFEE FOR A CROWD

(Using a coffee maker)

Follow directions on your coffee maker, using the amounts given below. Always start with fresh cold water. Serve the coffee piping hot, but do not boil.

Servings (5½ ounces each)	Ground Coffee	Water
50 servings	1 pound*	2½ gallons
100 servings	2 pounds*	5 gallons
150 servings	3 pounds	7½ gallons

*To use 1 or 2 pounds of coffee from a 2- or 3-pound can, measure about 5¼ cups per pound.

COFFEE FOR A CROWD

(Using a large kettle)

Pour 1 pound regular grind quality coffee into a cheesecloth or muslin bag that is large enough to hold *at least twice* that amount of coffee. Bring 2 gallons water to a boil in a large kettle. Then drop in the bag of coffee, cover tightly, reduce heat to prevent boiling, and simmer gently 10 to 12 minutes. Plunge bag up and down in the coffee several times; then remove bag. Cover and keep coffee hot, but do not allow it to boil. Makes 45 to 50 servings, 5 to 6 ounces each.

INSTANT COFFEE FOR A CROWD

Measure instant quality coffee into a suitably large container. Stir in part of the water; blend. Then add remaining water. Bring *just* to a boil. (Do not boil.) Serve piping hot.

Servings (5 ounces each)	Instant Coffee	Water
6	¼ cup	1 quart
12	½ cup	2 quarts
25	1 cup (2-ounce jar)	1 gallon
75	about 3½ cups (6-ounce jar)	3 gallons
125	about 5½ cups (10-ounce jar)	5 gallons

ICED COFFEE FOR A CROWD

Measure instant quality coffee into a pitcher or other large container. Add small amount of water and mix well. Then gradually add remaining water, stirring constantly—stirring well as water is added helps prevent excessive foaming. Pour over ice cubes or Coffee Ice Cubes (page 22) in tall glasses. Serve with cream and sugar, if desired, or use Creamy Coffee Ice Cubes (page 22).

Servings (5 ounces each plus ice)	Instant Coffee	Water
5	1/3 cup	3½ cups
15	1 cup (2-ounce jar)	2½ quarts
45	about 3½ cups (6-ounce jar)	2 gallons

Hot and Hearty

Is there any better aroma in the world than that of hot coffee? Sometimes—when the smell is that of coffee combined with another delicious odor: chocolate, spice, fruit. Here are exotically flavored variations on the cup-of-coffee theme—to make any meal a feast, any party one your guests will remember.

CAPPUCCINO

3 or 4 tablespoons instant quality coffee
2 cups boiling water
½ cup whipped cream
Cinnamon

Dissolve coffee in boiling water. Whip the cream. Place spoonfuls of whipped cream in 5 demitasse cups. Add a dash of cinnamon. Pour hot coffee over cream. Serve with sugar, if desired. Makes 2 cups, or 5 servings, 3 ounces each plus cream.

HAWAIIAN COFFEE

1⅓ cups (about) flaked coconut
1⅓ cups milk
1¼ cups boiling water
1 to 2 tablespoons instant quality coffee

Combine coconut with milk in a saucepan. Cook and stir over low heat until foamy, about 2 minutes. Strain, reserving both coconut and milk. Spread coconut on baking sheet and toast in moderate oven (350° F.) 8 to 10 minutes, stirring occasionally. Meanwhile, combine milk, boiling water, and instant coffee, stirring until coffee is dissolved. Serve in mugs or cups. Sprinkle top with toasted coconut. Makes about 2¾ cups, or 4 servings, 6 ounces each.

Nice to know: *If your attic or storeroom harbors an old-fashioned tea wagon, bring it out, refurbish it, and put it back in service. It can have a new lease on life as a coffee cart, making the serving of coffee after dinner, or "coffee and . . ." refreshments in afternoon or evening much more attractive—and much, much easier. Roll the cart around, instead of passing cups and plates, sugar and cream, and let each person help himself.*

ARABIAN COFFEE

- ⅓ cup instant quality coffee
- 2-inch stick of cinnamon
- 3 cardamom seeds, cracked
- 4 cups water
- Sugar and cream (optional)

Measure instant coffee into a heatproof container. Tie the stick cinnamon and cardamom seeds in a piece of cheesecloth; place in the container. Pour water over coffee and spices, stirring to dissolve coffee. Cover and bring almost to a boil over medium heat. Remove from heat and let steep 10 to 12 minutes. Discard bag of spices. Reheat coffee before serving. Pour into demitasse cups. Serve with sugar and cream, if desired. Makes about 4 cups, or 8 servings, 4 ounces each.

TURKISH COFFEE

- ¾ to 1 cup instant quality coffee
- ⅓ cup honey
- 4 cups boiling water
- 5 cardamom seeds, crushed

Dissolve coffee and honey in boiling water. Add cardamom seeds, cover, and let stand 15 minutes. Strain. Bring almost to a boil. Serve in demitasse cups. Makes 4 cups, or 8 servings, 4 ounces each.

DEMITASSE COFFEE

Demitasse is extra-strong coffee served in small cups, usually after dinner and often in the living room. Traditionally served black, that is, without cream and sugar, it has recently become "correct" to add cream or sugar, or both, as preferred.

Instant Demitasse: Place 2 tablespoons instant quality coffee in small serving pot or carafe. Stir in 1 cup boiling water. Let steep 5 minutes. Makes 3 servings, about 3 ounces each.

Brewed Demitasse: Using the drip or vacuum method of brewing coffee, prepare extra-strong coffee—use 3 to 4 tablespoons ground coffee (instead of the usual 2 tablespoons) to each ¾ cup (6 ounces) water. (With many coffee makers, especially drip pots, only half the full capacity of coffee can be brewed when making Demitasse Coffee because the filter basket will not hold the amount of ground coffee that would be required for the full capacity of water.) Each ¾ cup brewed Demitasse Coffee makes 2 servings, about 3 ounces each.

MOCHA JAVA

½ cup water
½ cup milk
1 to 2 tablespoons instant quality coffee
2 tablespoons instant chocolate flavor mix
Marshmallows (optional)

Combine water and milk; bring just to a boil. Stir in coffee and chocolate flavor mix until thoroughly dissolved. Serve in a mug. Top with marshmallows, if desired. Makes 1 serving.

CAFFÈ BORGIA

½ cup instant quality coffee
½ cup instant chocolate flavor mix
4 cups boiling water
Sweetened whipped cream
Cinnamon or finely grated orange rind

Combine coffee and chocolate flavor mix in a serving pot or carafe. Add boiling water and stir to blend. Pour into demitasse cups. Top each serving with sweetened whipped cream and sprinkle with cinnamon or orange rind. Makes about 4 cups, or 12 servings, about 3 ounces each.

STEEPED COFFEE

Using 2 level tablespoons regular grind quality coffee to each ¾ cup (6 ounces) water, measure coffee into heatproof container. Bring water to a boil; pour over coffee, cover tightly, and let stand in a warm place 3 to 5 minutes. Strain into cups or mugs. Serve with sugar and cream, as desired.

Bear in mind: *Mugs—once used only on camping trips and cookouts—have come into their own. There are dozens of kinds, in dozens of price ranges, to be had today—colorful, pretty, easy to drink from, fun to use. Try them for serving these hot coffee beverages. Somehow they make the good taste even better!*

MOCHA FOAM

- 2 squares unsweetened chocolate or ⅓ cup cocoa
- 2½ cups milk
- 2 tablespoons instant quality coffee
- 1 cup water
- ⅓ cup sugar
- Dash of salt
- 8 marshmallows

Place chocolate or cocoa and ½ cup of the milk in a saucepan. Heat slowly, stirring constantly, until smooth. Blend in 2 cups milk; then add instant coffee, water, sugar, and salt. Heat thoroughly, stirring constantly. Then add marshmallows and beat until marshmallows are melted and mixture is foamy. Makes about 4½ cups, or 6 servings, 6 ounces each.

DUTCH COFFEE

Place a cinnamon stick in each cup. Pour in Demitasse Coffee (page 16). Add cream and sugar to taste. Then float butter on top.

Nice to know: *If desired, regular strength coffee may be used instead of Demitasse Coffee.*

ESPRESSO-TYPE COFFEE

In Italy and in coffeehouses throughout this country, a special roast of coffee is brewed in a special coffee maker to obtain this exotic coffee. But you can easily prepare coffee with the same unique flavor by blending instant and brewed coffees.

2 tablespoons instant quality coffee
2 cups hot brewed quality coffee

Dissolve instant coffee in the brewed coffee. Serve hot in demitasse cups. Makes 2 cups, or 6 servings, about 3 ounces each.

Coffee Neapolitan: Prepare Espresso-Type Coffee; then pour 1½ teaspoons cognac in each whisky-sour glass and fill with the hot coffee. Top with sweetened whipped cream and a sprinkle of cinnamon. Serve at once. Makes 4 servings, about 4 ounces each plus cream.

Coffee Chocolaccino: Prepare Espresso-Type Coffee, adding 4½ teaspoons sugar and 4½ teaspoons chocolate syrup. Blend. Serve in demitasse cups topped with sweetened whipped cream and shaved sweet chocolate. Makes 6 servings.

Nice to know: *To prepare Coffee Chocolaccino by the cup, measure 1 teaspoon sugar and 1 teaspoon chocolate syrup into a demitasse cup. Fill the cup with Espresso-Type Coffee, stir well, and top with sweetened whipped cream and shaved sweet chocolate.*

Bear in mind: *Of course, everyone should know how to make the easiest hot coffee beverage—just measure 1 rounded teaspoon (or more) instant quality coffee into a cup, add boiling water, stir, steep, and serve. For delicious brewed coffee, see pages 8-12.*

Flavorful and Frosty

Coffee has just one flavor? No, it has dozens—depending on the cook's ingenuity in combining favorite taste-tempters in brand new treats. Try these cool drinks and see for yourself!

ICED SPICED COFFEE

2 tablespoons instant quality coffee
3 cups hot water
2 tablespoons sugar
2 cinnamon sticks
6 whole cloves
6 whole allspice

Dissolve instant coffee in hot water. Pour over sugar and spices in large container. Cover and let steep about 1 hour. Then strain and pour over cracked ice or ice cubes in tall glasses. If desired, place a long cinnamon stick in each glass for stirring. Serve with cream, if desired. Makes about 3 cups, or 4 servings, 6 ounces each.

ICED MOCHA

⅓ cup chocolate syrup
2 cups milk
½ cup light cream
½ cup chilled brewed quality coffee
Cracked ice
Whipped cream

Combine chocolate syrup, milk, cream, and coffee. Beat or shake well. Pour over cracked ice in tall glasses. Top each serving with whipped cream. Makes about 3 cups, or 4 servings, 6 ounces each.

CAMBRIC COFFEE

Dissolve 1 to 2 teaspoons instant quality coffee in 1 glass (6 ounces) milk; then add a few drops of vanilla and sweeten to taste. Makes 1 serving.

Bear in mind: *Soda straws or sippers add to the pleasure of tall drinks. . . . Long-handled spoons are a necessity for drinks with ice cream floats—gay-colored plastic ones are inexpensive, add a festive look to drink service. . . . Cold drinks made with milk or ice cream or both can do delicious duty in place of dessert on a hot summer day.*

FROSTED MOCHA PUNCH

- 1½ cups cold water
- ¼ cup instant quality coffee
- ¼ cup chocolate syrup
- 1 cup milk
- 1 pint vanilla-fudge ice cream, softened

Add cold water to coffee; stir until coffee is dissolved. Blend in remaining ingredients. If desired, additional ice cream may be served with the punch. Makes about 1 quart, or 8 servings, 4 ounces each.

COFFEE MILK

- 1 rounded teaspoon instant quality coffee
- 1 cup milk
- Ice cubes
- Sugar

Put instant coffee in tall glass. Add small amount of milk and stir briskly until coffee is dissolved. Add remaining milk and ice cubes. Stir. Sweeten with sugar to taste. Makes 1 serving.

Coffee Maple Cooler: Prepare Coffee Milk, omitting sugar and adding 1 to 2 tablespoons maple-blended syrup. If desired, top with whipped cream and a sprinkle of nutmeg.

Coffee Malted Milk: Prepare Coffee Milk, dissolving 1 tablespoon malted milk powder and the sugar (about 1 teaspoon) with the coffee.

Coffee Float: Prepare Coffee Milk or Coffee Malted Milk, omitting ice cubes and adding 1 scoop of vanilla, coffee, chocolate, or pistachio ice cream.

COFFEE ICE CUBES

Dissolve ⅓ cup instant quality coffee in 3½ cups water. Pour into ice cube tray and freeze until firm. Use in place of regular ice cubes for iced coffee (see Iced Coffee for a Crowd, page 14) and other iced coffee beverages.

Creamy Coffee Ice Cubes: Prepare Coffee Ice Cubes, reducing water to 2½ cups and adding 1¼ cups light cream and ⅓ cup sugar.

COFFEE ICE CREAM SODA

- 2 teaspoons instant quality coffee
- 4 teaspoons sugar
- 2 tablespoons milk
- 1 bottle (7 ounces) or about 1 cup chilled club soda or ginger ale
- Vanilla, coffee, or chocolate ice cream

Dissolve instant coffee and sugar in milk in a tall glass, stirring vigorously. Stir in about half of the soda. Allow foam to settle. Then add 2 small scoops of ice cream and gradually stir in remaining soda. Makes 1 serving.

SUPER COFFEE FLOAT

- 1 package (3¾ ounces) vanilla instant pudding mix
- ¼ cup instant quality coffee
- 5 cups milk
- Sweetened whipped cream or ice cream

Combine pudding mix and coffee in a large bowl. Gradually add milk, blending well. Beat with a rotary beater 1 minute. Chill. Serve in tall glasses, topped with whipped cream or ice cream. Makes 5 cups, or 5 servings, 8 ounces each.

COFFEE EGGNOG

- 1 egg, well beaten
- 2 teaspoons instant quality coffee
- 1½ tablespoons sugar
- Dash of salt
- 1 cup chilled milk
- Few drops of vanilla

Combine egg, instant coffee, sugar, and salt. Beat until coffee and sugar are dissolved. (Or shake in a covered jar or other container until coffee and sugar are dissolved.) Then add milk and vanilla and mix well. Makes 1 serving.

For 4 servings, use 3 eggs, 2 to 3 tablespoons instant quality coffee, ⅓ cup sugar, dash of salt, 1 quart milk, and ¼ teaspoon vanilla.

CAFÉ FRAPPÉ

½ cup sugar
6 tablespoons instant quality coffee
½ cup boiling water
1½ cups cold water
¼ teaspoon vanilla
⅛ teaspoon grated lemon peel (optional)
½ cup heavy cream
1 tablespoon sugar
Cinnamon

Dissolve ½ cup sugar and coffee in boiling water. Add cold water, vanilla, and lemon peel. Pour into ice cube tray and freeze until solid. Whip cream; add 1 tablespoon sugar. Put frozen coffee mixture through an ice crusher, or place in a canvas bag and crush with hammer or mallet. Place crushed coffee ice in sherbet or old fashioned glasses. Top with whipped cream and a sprinkle of cinnamon. Garnish with a piece of lemon peel, if desired. Serve with short straw or spoon. Makes 2 cups ice, or 4 servings, 4 ounces each.

Café Crème Frappé: Prepare Café Frappé, placing crushed coffee ice in a large bowl and blending the cinnamon into the whipped cream; then swirl the cream through the ice. Serve in old fashioned glasses.

ICEBERG MOCHA MILK

¾ cup milk
Few drops vanilla
1 teaspoon instant quality coffee
1 tablespoon instant chocolate flavor mix
Vanilla ice cream

Combine milk and vanilla in a tall glass or shaker. Add instant coffee and chocolate flavor mix. Stir or shake until blended. Top with a small scoop of vanilla ice cream. Makes 1 serving.

CREAMY COFFEE PUNCH

1 cup instant quality coffee
½ cup sugar
2 quarts water
2 cups milk
1½ teaspoons vanilla
1 quart vanilla ice cream

Dissolve instant coffee and sugar in water. Then add milk and vanilla. Chill thoroughly. Pour over ice cream in punch bowl. Makes 3½ quarts or 28 servings, 4 ounces each.

COFFEE COCOA COOLER

1½ tablespoons cocoa
¼ cup sugar
¼ cup instant quality coffee
Dash of salt
2 cups water
2 cups (3 small cans) evaporated milk
⅛ teaspoon vanilla

Combine cocoa, sugar, coffee, and salt in saucepan. Blend in ⅓ cup water. Simmer gently for 2 minutes, stirring constantly. Then add remaining ingredients, blending well. Chill thoroughly. Serve with ice, if desired. Makes 1 quart, or 6 servings, about 5 ounces each.

FROSTY COFFEE SHAKE

1 to 1½ tablespoons instant quality coffee
2 teaspoons sugar
2 cups milk
1 cup vanilla or coffee ice cream

Combine ingredients in shaker, glass jar, or electric blender. Shake or blend well. Serve in tall glasses. Makes 2 servings.

Frosty Mocha Shake: Prepare Frosty Coffee Shake, adding 1 to 1½ tablespoons chocolate syrup.

Frosty Coffee-Maple Shake: Prepare Frosty Coffee Shake, substituting 2 tablespoons maple-blended syrup for the sugar.

Frosty Coffee-Scotch Shake: Prepare Frosty Coffee Shake, substituting butterscotch ice cream for the vanilla or coffee ice cream. (You can create many tasty variations of this recipe by using other ice cream flavors—try butter pecan, chocolate, and others.)

APRI-COFFEE FROST

1 cup chilled apricot nectar
1⅓ cups brewed quality coffee, chilled
½ pint coffee ice cream, softened
⅔ cup milk
½ teaspoon almond extract

Combine all ingredients; beat with rotary beater or blend in electric blender until frothy. Serve in tall glasses. Makes about 1 quart, or 4 servings, 8 ounces each.

ICED MAPLE COFFEE

½ cup heavy cream
4 cups brewed quality coffee
½ cup maple-blended syrup
Coffee Ice Cubes (page 22)

Whip the cream. Then combine coffee and syrup; mix well. Pour over Coffee Ice Cubes in tall glasses. Top with whipped cream. Makes about 5 cups, or 5 servings, 8 ounces each.

MOCHA FROST

1 cup brewed quality coffee
⅓ cup chocolate syrup
2 cups milk
½ cup vanilla or coffee ice cream
2 bottles (7 ounces each) club soda, chilled*

***Or use 1 bottle (16 ounces) low-calorie coffee soda.**

Combine coffee and chocolate syrup in a bowl; stir in milk and ice cream until blended. Just before serving, stir in club soda. Makes about 6 cups, or 6 servings, 8 ounces each.

For a Crowd: Prepare Mocha Frost, using 4 cups brewed quality coffee, 1⅓ cups chocolate syrup, 2 quarts milk, 1 pint ice cream, and two 28-ounce bottles or four 16-ounce bottles chilled club soda or low-calorie coffee soda. Makes about 6 quarts, or 24 servings, 8 ounces each.

Sip-and-Nibble Specials

Coffee and alcoholic beverages become hand-in-hand partners in these delightful drinks, some for the cocktail hour, some for after-dinner service, some just right for evening entertaining. There's a bonus of canapés and snacks to make party-giving a pleasure for you and leave your guests hoping to be invited to your house again very soon.

COFFEE CORDIAL

½ cup instant quality coffee
¼ cup sugar
4 cups boiling water
¼ cup brandy, fruit-flavor liqueur, or rum
9 strips orange peel

Dissolve instant coffee and sugar in boiling water. Reheat almost to the boiling point. Remove from heat; add brandy. Pour into demitasse cups. Twist strips of peel; add to each cup. Makes 4½ cups, or 9 servings, 4 ounces each.

COFFEE CARIOCA

2 oranges, peeled
½ cup instant quality coffee
¼ cup sugar
4 cups boiling water
¼ cup rum
Sweetened whipped cream

Remove all white membrane from oranges; cut into ¼-inch thick slices and remove seeds. Place in a large heatproof bowl with the coffee and sugar. Stir in boiling water; let stand 30 minutes. Strain coffee into saucepan. Heat almost to boiling. Remove from heat and stir in rum. Serve in demitasse cups topped with whipped cream. If desired, garnish with grated orange rind, shaved chocolate, or cinnamon. Makes 4½ cups, or 9 servings, 4 ounces each.

CAFÉ BRÛLOT

½ cup instant quality coffee
4 cups boiling water
3 sticks cinnamon
1 tablespoon whole cloves
¼ to ⅓ cup sugar
½ cup brandy
Peel from 1 orange, cut in strips
Peel from 1 lemon, cut in strips

Dissolve coffee in boiling water. Add cinnamon sticks and cloves; cover and let stand 15 minutes. Strain and reheat. Meanwhile, combine sugar, brandy, and fruit peel in chafing dish. Heat; then flame the brandy mixture. Slowly add coffee. When flame is extinguished, ladle into demitasse cups. Makes 4½ cups, or 9 servings, 4 ounces each.

IRISH COFFEE

2 tablespoons Irish whisky
1 to 2 teaspoons sugar
2 to 4 teaspoons instant quality coffee
⅔ cup boiling water
Whipped cream, chilled

In a pre-warmed 7-ounce stemmed goblet or coffee cup, combine whisky and sugar. Then combine instant coffee and boiling water. Fill goblet about two-thirds full with coffee, stirring until sugar is dissolved. Fill goblet with chilled whipped cream, letting it float on coffee—do not stir. Makes 1 serving.

BELGIAN COFFEE PUNCH

6 egg whites
1½ cups heavy cream
3 tablespoons sugar
¾ to 1½ cups instant quality coffee
3 quarts boiling water
½ cup sugar
½ cup bourbon

Beat egg whites until stiff peaks will form. Whip the cream; sweeten with 3 tablespoons sugar. Combine egg whites and whipped cream. Dissolve instant coffee and sugar in the boiling water; pour into a large bowl. Add bourbon. Top with the egg white mixture. Makes about 3 quarts punch, or 24 servings, 4 ounces each.

COFFEE MILK PUNCH

- 6 tablespoons instant quality coffee
- ⅔ cup sugar
- 2 tablespoons sherry
- 3 quarts cold milk
- Whipped cream
- Nutmeg

Combine instant coffee, sugar, sherry, and 3 cups of the milk in a bowl or electric blender. Beat with a rotary beater or blend 30 seconds at high speed. Pour into punch bowl; add remaining milk and mix well. Top each serving with whipped cream and a sprinkle of nutmeg. Makes about 3 quarts, or 24 servings, 4 ounces each.

Spanish Coffee Punch: Prepare Coffee Milk Punch, decreasing sugar to ½ cup and milk to 2 quarts and increasing sherry to ¼ cup. Makes about 2 quarts, or 16 servings, 4 ounces each.

COFFEE ALEXANDER

- ½ cup shaved or crushed ice
- ¼ cup brandy
- 3 tablespoons crème de cacao
- ½ cup heavy cream
- 2½ teaspoons instant quality coffee
- 2 teaspoons sugar

Combine all ingredients in a shaker. Shake thoroughly and strain. (Or combine ingredients in a blender and mix well.) Serve in chilled glasses. Makes about 1⅓ cups, or 4 servings, 3 ounces each.

COFFEE GROG BASE AND BEVERAGE

- 2 tablespoons butter
- 1 cup firmly packed brown sugar
- Dash of salt
- ⅛ teaspoon ground cinnamon
- ⅛ teaspoon ground nutmeg
- ⅛ teaspoon ground allspice
- ⅛ teaspoon ground cloves
- 3 tablespoons light rum
- 2 tablespoons heavy cream
- 1 strip lemon peel
- 1 strip orange peel
- ⅔ cup hot brewed quality coffee*

*Or use 1 tablespoon instant quality coffee dissolved in ⅔ cup hot water.

For grog base: Cream butter and sugar together. Add salt and spices; blend thoroughly. This grog base may be used immediately or may be covered and stored in refrigerator indefinitely. Makes 1 cup grog base, enough for 16 servings.

For each serving: Measure 1 tablespoon grog base into a mug. Add rum, cream, lemon peel, and orange peel. Then stir in ⅔ cup hot coffee.

COFFEE WITH LIQUEURS

Prepare Demitasse Coffee (page 16) and fill each demitasse cup about three-quarters full. Then add a dash of any of the following: white crème de menthe, curaçao, kümmel, anisette, or Cointreau.

CAFÉ BRÛLOT DIABOLIQUE

6 lumps sugar
8 whole cloves
1-inch cinnamon stick
1 lemon peel, cut in strips
4 jiggers cognac
4 cups hot Demitasse Coffee (page 16)

Place all ingredients except coffee in chafing dish. Ignite cognac with match and stir until flavors are well blended. After a minute or two, slowly pour in the hot coffee and continue to stir. To serve, strain into demitasse cups. Makes about 4 cups, or 8 servings, 4 ounces each.

Nice to know: In winter, heat cognac before using.

CREAMY COFFEE-RUM NOG

2 tablespoons instant quality coffee
1 cup water
1 pint vanilla ice cream, softened
1 cup milk
¼ cup light rum
Dash of nutmeg

Dissolve instant coffee in water. Add ice cream and stir until melted. Blend in milk and rum. Serve at once. Or chill; stir to blend before serving. Sprinkle each serving with nutmeg. Makes 4 cups, enough for 8 servings, 4 ounces each.

For 32 servings, use ½ cup instant quality coffee, 1 quart water,

2 quarts softened vanilla ice cream, 1 quart milk, and 1 cup light rum. Makes 4 quarts, or 32 servings, 4 ounces each.

CAFÉ CACAO FRAPPÉ

- 1 tablespoon instant quality coffee
- ½ cup cold water
- 1 cup finely shaved ice
- ½ cup crème de cacao

Dissolve instant coffee in cold water. Pour over shaved ice in cocktail shaker. Add crème de cacao; shake vigorously. Pour into well-chilled champagne or cocktail glasses. Serve with short straws. Makes about 2 cups, or 4 servings, 4 ounces each.

CREAM IN YOUR COFFEE

- 2 tablespoons instant quality coffee
- 1 tablespoon sugar
- 1 cup water
- 2 tablespoons dark rum
- ¼ teaspoon vanilla
- ⅓ cup vanilla ice cream

Dissolve coffee and sugar in the water. Add remaining ingredients, stirring until smooth. Heat and serve in demitasse cups, or chill and serve in whisky sour glasses. Makes 1⅓ cups, or 4 servings, about 3 ounces each.

CAFÉ COCKTAIL

A blend of instant and brewed coffees, making an Espresso-Type Coffee (see page 19), is the basis of this unusual cocktail.

- ½ cup brewed quality coffee
- 1½ teaspoons instant quality coffee
- ¼ cup crème de cacao
- ¼ cup cognac
- 1 to 2 teaspoons sugar
- 2 twists lemon rind
- ¼ cup light cream (optional)
- Cracked ice

Blend all ingredients except ice. Then shake with ice. Strain. Serve in whisky sour glasses. Makes 1½ cups, or 3 to 4 servings, 3 or 4 ounces each.

BLACKJACK

4 teaspoons instant quality coffee
½ cup water
¼ cup Cointreau
¼ cup brandy
¼ cup confectioners' sugar
Crushed ice

Thoroughly blend coffee, water, Cointreau, brandy, and sugar. Chill. Just before serving, stir and pour over crushed ice in whisky sour glasses. Makes about 1 cup, or 4 servings with ice.

CAFÉ ROYALE

Demitasse Coffee (page 16)
Small sugar cubes
Brandy

Fill demitasse cup with hot coffee. Place lump of sugar in a spoon balanced on cup. Fill spoon with brandy. Let stand over the hot coffee a few seconds, or until warm; then light with match. As flame begins to fade, pour contents of spoon into cup.

TINY CHEESE PINWHEELS

⅛ teaspoon cayenne
¼ teaspoon salt
½ teaspoon paprika
¼ cup butter
2 cups sifted all-purpose flour
2 teaspoons double-acting baking powder
¾ teaspoon salt
½ teaspoon cream of tartar
2 teaspoons sugar
¾ cup shortening
¾ cup grated Cheddar cheese
1 tablespoon chopped parsley
⅔ cup light cream

Cream together cayenne, ¼ teaspoon salt, paprika, and butter in a small bowl. Set aside. Sift together flour, baking powder, ¾ teaspoon salt, cream of tartar, and sugar. Cut in shortening until mixture resembles coarse crumbs. Add grated cheese and parsley. Then add light cream all at once, stirring until soft dough is formed.

Divide dough in half. Roll one piece ¼ inch thick into a 14- by 10-inch rectangle. Spread with half of butter mixture. Then roll dough as for jelly roll, starting from the 14-inch side. Slice into thin rounds, about 1/4 inch thick, and place on ungreased baking sheets. Repeat with other half of dough.

Bake in hot oven (425° F.) 18 to 20 minutes or until golden brown. Serve warm with cocktails. Makes about 5 dozen pinwheels.

GLAZED CAVIAR CANAPÉS

- 1/8 teaspoon sweet basil
- 1 cup water
- 1 package (3 ounces) lemon flavor gelatin
- 1/2 teaspoon salt
- 1 tablespoon lemon juice
- 1 cup sauterne wine
- 24 slices small party rye bread
- 1/4 cup butter, softened
- 2 packages (3 ounces each) cream cheese, whipped
- 1 jar (4 ounces) black caviar
- 1 can (4 ounces) pimiento, drained

Simmer the sweet basil in water about 3 minutes; strain. Then dissolve gelatin and salt in the hot liquid. Add lemon juice and wine. Chill until slightly thickened.

Meanwhile, place rye bread on a rack set on a tray. Spread bread with butter and whipped cream cheese. Cover cream cheese with caviar. Cut pimiento into small squares or diamond, heart, or bell shapes; place a piece in the center of each canapé.

Spoon slightly thickened gelatin mixture over canapés, allowing about 2 tablespoons mixture for each. Chill until firm. If necessary, cover each canapé with more gelatin mixture and chill again. (If gelatin mixture becomes too firm for glazing canapés, set bowl in a pan of hot water.) Makes 24 canapés.

ANTIPASTO

- 1 large head lettuce, cut into 8 wedges
- 2 stalks fennel, trimmed and cut into 8 pieces
- 1 can (6 ounces) ripe olives, drained
- 1 peeled cucumber, scored and sliced thin
- 1/4 pound thinly sliced Provolone cheese
- 1/4 pound thinly sliced salami
- 1 can (2 ounces) rolled anchovy fillets

Arrange ingredients attractively on a large platter or lazy susan. Serve with cruets of oil and wine vinegar. Makes 8 servings.

Nice to know: *Any of the following items may be substituted for those above, as desired: thinly sliced prosciutto ham or pepperoni, artichoke or celery hearts, ham slivers, sliced or quartered hard-cooked eggs, pickled mushrooms, peppers, or beets, pimiento strips, tomato sections, green pepper rings, green olives, scallions, or radishes. An antipasto usually contains at least 6 or 7 different items.*

CHEESE MAYONNAISE PUFFS

- 1 egg white
- ½ cup mayonnaise
- ¼ cup grated Parmesan cheese
- ¼ teaspoon onion salt
- 1 teaspoon dry mustard
- 20 Melba toast rounds

Beat egg white until stiff shiny peaks form. Fold in remaining ingredients except toast rounds. Spread on toast rounds and place under preheated broiler until puffy and golden brown. Serve immediately. Makes 20 small puffs.

CHICKEN LIVER PÂTÉ

- ½ cup butter
- 1 cup chopped onions
- 1 pound chicken livers
- 2 hard-cooked egg yolks
- 1½ teaspoons salt
- ⅛ teaspoon pepper
- ⅛ teaspoon ground nutmeg
- 1 teaspoon lemon juice
- 2 tablespoons chopped parsley

Melt ¼ cup of the butter in a skillet. Add onions and cook until transparent, stirring frequently. Remove onions and set aside. Melt remaining butter in skillet. Add the chicken livers and sauté, stirring frequently, until livers are tender—about 10 minutes. Cool slightly.

Press onions, livers, and egg yolks through a sieve or food grinder. Add the remaining ingredients and mix well. Spoon into a 2-cup greased bowl or mold. Cover tightly and chill.

When ready to serve, loosen mold from bowl with a spatula.

Invert on a platter. Surround with salty rye bread rounds, crackers, or Melba toast. Makes 1¼ cups.

Nice to know: *Recipe may be doubled, if desired. Spoon into two 2-cup bowls for chilling.*

CLAM DIP

- 1 package (3 ounces) cream cheese*
- ½ cup sour cream*
- 1 envelope onion salad dressing mix
- 1 can (10½ ounces) minced clams, drained
- 1 teaspoon lemon juice
- Assorted crackers or raw vegetables

*Or omit cream cheese and use 1 cup sour cream and 3 tablespoons mayonnaise.

Beat cream cheese until smooth. Add sour cream and salad dressing mix; blend well. Stir in drained clams and lemon juice. Chill thoroughly. Serve with crackers and assorted vegetable sticks. Makes about 1½ cups.

COCKTAIL MEAT BALLS

- 1 pound ground beef
- ½ pound ground pork or mild bulk sausage
- 1 egg
- 1 envelope old fashion French salad dressing mix
- 1 tablespoon chopped green pepper
- 1 tablespoon chopped parsley
- 2 tablespoons chopped onion
- ¼ cup dry bread crumbs
- 1 tablespoon butter or margarine
- 1 can (8 ounces) whole tomatoes, broken up

Combine meats, egg, 1 tablespoon of the salad dressing mix, the chopped vegetables, and bread crumbs; mix well. Shape into small balls, about 1 inch in diameter. Melt butter in large skillet. Sauté meat balls in butter until evenly browned. Drain off excess fat. Then add tomatoes and remaining salad dressing mix. Stir carefully to mix thoroughly. Cover and simmer 5 to 7 minutes. Spear each meat ball with a wooden pick or skewer. Serve hot. Makes about 4 dozen meat balls.

COCKTAIL PARTY MIX

- ½ cup butter or margarine
- 1 tablespoon Worcestershire sauce
- 1 envelope bleu cheese or garlic salad dressing mix
- 2 cups bite-size shredded wheat biscuits
- 2 cups bite-size shredded rice biscuits
- 2 cups ready-to-eat oat cereal
- 1 cup pretzel sticks
- 2 cups blanched unsalted almonds

Melt butter in shallow pan. Add Worcestershire sauce and salad dressing mix; blend well. Then add the remaining ingredients. Mix or shake until all ingredients are evenly coated. Toast in a slow oven (300° F.) for 30 minutes, stirring every 10 minutes. Makes 2½ quarts.

CREAMY CHEESE DIP

- 1 package (8 ounces) cream cheese
- ¼ cup milk
- 1 tablespoon onion salad dressing mix
- 1 tablespoon grated Parmesan cheese

Place cream cheese in small bowl and stir to soften. Add milk, salad dressing mix, and cheese; beat until smooth and blended. Serve with small crackers or crisp vegetable sticks. Makes 1¼ cups.

MARINATED ARTICHOKE HEARTS

- 1 package (9 ounces) frozen artichoke hearts
- 1 cup salted water
- ¼ cup vinegar
- 2 tablespoons sherry
- 1 envelope Parmesan salad dressing mix
- ¾ cup salad oil

Place artichokes and salted water in saucepan. Cover and bring quickly to a boil over high heat, separating artichokes with a fork to hasten thawing. Reduce heat and simmer until artichokes are tender but still crisp—about 6 minutes. Drain.

Meanwhile, combine vinegar and sherry in a cruet or a jar with tightly fitting cover. Add salad dressing mix and shake well. Add salad oil and shake again. Measure ¼ cup and pour over drained artichokes. Let stand in refrigerator at least 3 hours to marinate. Serve as an appetizer or salad. Makes 4 servings as salad.

MARINATED MUSHROOMS

1 cup button mushrooms, fresh or canned
½ cup prepared old fashion French salad dressing

Wash and trim fresh raw mushrooms, or drain a 6- or 8-ounce can of mushrooms. Cover with salad dressing. Cover and marinate overnight in refrigerator. Serve chilled as hors d'oeuvres.

ONION CONFETTI DIP

¼ cup finely chopped cucumber
Salt
1 envelope onion salad dressing mix
1 cup sour cream*
¼ cup finely chopped green pepper
¼ cup finely diced pimiento

***Or use ¾ cup sour cream and ¼ cup mayonnaise.**

Sprinkle cucumber with salt; set aside. Meanwhile, combine remaining ingredients. Then drain cucumber, discarding excess liquid. Add cucumber to sour cream mixture. Chill at least 1 hour to blend flavors. Serve as a dip with crackers. Makes about 1¾ cups.

Coffee Break: U.S.A.

Any day, any time, at home or at work, the coffee break is a signal for pleasant relaxation—and good coffee go-withs like these.

CHOCO-SPICE SQUARES

1½ cups water
1 cup raisins
1 cup sugar
2 squares semi-sweet chocolate*
1 tablespoon butter
½ teaspoon salt
1½ cups sifted all-purpose flour
1 teaspoon baking soda
½ teaspoon ground cinnamon
½ teaspoon ground nutmeg
¼ teaspoon ground cloves
½ cup coarsely chopped walnuts
2 packages (3 ounces each) cream cheese
Dash of salt
Orange Sauce (see below)

***Or use 1 square unsweetened chocolate.**

Combine water, raisins, sugar, chocolate, butter, and ½ teaspoon salt in heavy 3-[illegible] saucepan. Bring to a boil over high heat, stirring constantly. Then reduce heat and simmer uncovered 5 minutes without stirring. Remove from heat and let cool at least 15 minutes.

Meanwhile, sift together flour, soda, and spices. Add flour mixture and nuts to the cooled chocolate, stirring until all flour is moistened—*do not beat.* Pour into a greased 8-inch square pan. Bake in a moderate oven (350° F.) 30 to 35 minutes or until cake has pulled away from sides of pan slightly and springs back when lightly pressed in center.

Cream the cheese with a dash of salt until softened. Cut warm cake into squares; top with a dollop of cream cheese and some Orange Sauce. Makes 9 servings.

Orange Sauce: Combine ½ cup sugar, 2 tablespoons flour, and ⅛ teaspoon salt. Gradually add sugar mixture to 1 cup boiling water and cook 5 minutes, stirring constantly. Remove from heat. Stir in 2 tablespoons butter or margarine, 2 tablespoons orange juice, 1½ teaspoons lemon juice, and 1 teaspoon grated orange rind. Serve warm or cooled. Makes 1⅓ cups.

BROWNIE KISSES

- **2 packages (4 ounces each) sweet cooking chocolate**
- **1 tablespoon butter**
- **2 eggs**
- **¾ cup sugar**
- **¼ cup unsifted all-purpose flour**
- **¼ teaspoon double-acting baking powder**
- **⅛ teaspoon salt**
- **¼ teaspoon ground cinnamon**
- **¾ cup finely chopped pecans**
- **½ teaspoon vanilla**

Melt chocolate and butter in top of a double boiler over hot water, stirring occasionally. Remove from heat and cool slightly.

Beat eggs until foamy. Gradually add sugar, about 2 tablespoons at a time, beating constantly until thickened and light in color. (This takes 5 minutes in an electric mixer and longer with a rotary beater.) Blend in chocolate mixture. Then add flour, baking powder, salt, and cinnamon; blend well. Stir in pecans and vanilla.

Drop by teaspoonfuls onto gre[illegible]aking sheets. Bake in a moderate oven (350° F.) about 10 minutes or until cookies feel "set" when lightly touched. Store in tightly covered container. Makes about 3 dozen cookies.

CUT-UPS

- **½ cup maple-blended syrup**
- **¼ cup butter**
- **4 to 6 slices bread**
- **Confectioners' sugar**

Heat syrup and butter in a large skillet over medium heat. Meanwhile, trim crusts from bread. Cut the bread into squares, rectangles, or strips. Place all pieces in skillet at one time. Cook about 2 minutes. Turn and cook 5 minutes or until golden brown. Again turn and cook until golden brown. Remove from skillet and place on wax paper. Cool. Sprinkle with confectioners' sugar. Makes 16 to 24 Cut-Ups.

Fancy Cut-Ups: Prepare Cut-Ups, increasing bread to 8 slices and cutting it with 2-inch cookie cutters. Makes about 16 Fancy Cut-Ups.

CHEWY PEANUT BUTTER BARS

1 cup granulated sugar
¼ cup firmly packed brown sugar
½ cup peanut butter
⅓ cup shortening
2 eggs, unbeaten
1 teaspoon vanilla
1 cup unsifted all-purpose flour
1 teaspoon double-acting baking powder
¼ teaspoon salt
1⅓ cups (about) flaked coconut

Cream sugars, peanut butter, and shortening together until light and fluffy. Add eggs and vanilla; beat well. Add flour, baking powder, and salt; mix until thoroughly blended. Then stir in coconut. Spread dough evenly in a greased 13- by 9-inch pan. Bake in moderate oven (350° F.) until golden brown—about 25 minutes. Cool. Cut into bars. Makes about 3 dozen.

COCONUT OATMEAL COOKIES

1 cup sifted all-purpose flour
½ teaspoon double-acting baking powder
½ teaspoon salt
½ teaspoon baking soda
½ cup butter or other shortening
½ cup granulated sugar
½ cup firmly packed brown sugar
1 egg, unbeaten
1 teaspoon vanilla
½ cup rolled oats
1 cup flaked coconut

Sift together flour, baking powder, salt, and soda. Cream butter; gradually add sugars, creaming until light and fluffy. Add egg and vanilla; beat well. Add flour mixture about ¼ cup at a time, beating just until smooth after each addition. Mix in rolled oats and coconut. Drop by teaspoonfuls onto ungreased baking sheets. Bake in a moderate oven (375° F.) 10 to 12 minutes or until golden brown. Makes 2½ dozen cookies. Recipe may be doubled, if desired.

MELTING MOMENTS

½ cup cornstarch
½ cup confectioners' sugar
1 cup sifted all-purpose flour
1 cup butter, softened
1⅓ cups (about) flaked coconut*

*Or use about 1 cup packaged grated coconut.

Sift together cornstarch, confectioners' sugar, and flour. Blend butter into flour mixture until a soft dough is formed. Shape into small balls, ½ to 1 inch in diameter. Roll in coconut and place on ungreased baking sheets, about 1 to 1½ inches apart. (If dough is too soft to handle, cover and chill about 1 hour.) Flatten cookies with lightly floured fork. Bake in a slow oven (300° F.) 20 to 25 minutes or until lightly browned. Makes 3 to 3½ dozen.

COCONUT DAINTIES

1½-inch cubes (about 18) leftover cake or bread
½ cup maple-blended syrup or light corn syrup
½ cup flaked coconut or finely crushed corn flakes

Roll cake or bread cubes in syrup, coating all sides. Then roll in coconut. Place on greased baking sheet. Bake in moderate oven (375° F.) 8 to 10 minutes. Remove at once from baking sheet. Serve with coffee or as a dessert accompaniment. Makes about 18 Dainties.

LEMON MERINGUE PIE

1 package (3⅝ ounces) lemon pudding and pie filling mix
¾ cup sugar
2¼ cups water
2 eggs, separated
1 baked 8- or 9-inch pie shell, cooled

Combine pie filling mix, ½ cup of the sugar, and ¼ cup of the water in a saucepan. Blend in egg yolks. Add the remaining 2 cups water. Cook and stir over medium heat until mixture comes to a *full* boil and is thickened—about 5 minutes.

Cool only about 5 minutes, stirring once or twice. Then pour into the pie shell.

Beat egg whites until foamy throughout. Then add remaining ¼ cup sugar, 2 tablespoons at a time, beating after each addition until blended. Continue beating until meringue will form stiff, shiny peaks. Spread meringue over pie filling. Bake in hot oven (425° F.) 5 to 10 minutes or until meringue is delicately browned. Cool before serving.

Nice to know: *For a higher meringue on a 9-inch pie, use 3 egg whites and 6 tablespoons sugar.*

CHOCOLATE CHIP COOKIES

- ½ cup butter or other shortening
- ½ cup granulated sugar
- ¼ cup firmly packed brown sugar
- 1 egg
- 1 teaspoon vanilla
- 1 cup unsifted all-purpose flour
- ½ teaspoon baking soda
- ½ teaspoon salt
- 1 package (6 ounces) semi-sweet chocolate chips
- ½ cup chopped nuts

Beat butter, sugars, egg, and vanilla until light and fluffy. Blend in flour, soda, and salt. Then stir in chips and nuts. Drop by teaspoonfuls onto ungreased baking sheets, placing cookies about 2 inches apart. Bake in moderate oven (375° F.) 8 to 10 minutes or until lightly browned. Makes about 4 dozen.

Coconut Chocolate Chip Cookies: Prepare Chocolate Chip Cookies, substituting ¾ to 1 cup packaged grated coconut or 1⅓ cups flaked coconut for the nuts.

Fruited Chocolate Chip Cookies: Prepare Chocolate Chip Cookies, substituting ½ cup raisins or chopped dates for the nuts.

Oatmeal Chocolate Chip Cookies: Prepare Chocolate Chip Cookies, decreasing flour to ⅔ cup and substituting 1 cup quick-cooking rolled oats for the nuts.

ORANGE CEREAL MUFFINS

- 1⅔ cups unsifted all-purpose flour*
- 3 teaspoons double-acting baking powder*
- ½ cup sugar
- ¾ teaspoon salt*
- 1 cup Post Grape-Nuts Cereal
- 2 eggs, well beaten
- ¾ cup orange juice
- 1 tablespoon grated orange rind
- 2 tablespoons melted butter

*Or use 1⅔ cups unsifted self-rising all-purpose flour and omit baking powder and salt.

Mix flour, baking powder, sugar, and salt. Add cereal. Then combine eggs, orange juice and rind, and butter. Add to flour mixture and mix *only* enough to dampen flour. Bake in greased muffin pans in hot oven (425° F.) 15 to 20 minutes. Makes 12 large muffins.

Nice to know: *If desired, sprinkle top of each unbaked muffin with 1 teaspoon of a mixture of ¼ cup sugar and 1 teaspoon grated orange rind.*

BOSTON CREAM PIE

- 1 package (3¼ ounces) vanilla or coconut cream pudding and pie filling mix
- 1¾ cups milk
- 1 cooled baked 9-inch cake layer
- 1 square unsweetened chocolate
- 1 tablespoon butter
- 1½ tablespoons hot milk
- ¾ cup sifted confectioners' sugar
- Dash of salt

Combine pudding mix and 1¾ cups milk in saucepan. Cook and stir over medium heat until mixture comes to a *full* boil. Remove from heat. Cool, stirring occasionally. Then split cake horizontally into two layers. Spread pudding between layers.

Melt chocolate and butter together over hot water. Combine milk, sugar, and salt in small bowl. Gradually add chocolate mixture, blending well. Spread warm glaze over top of cake. Makes 6 to 8 servings.

Heart of the Meal, 1

Searching for recipes with delightful, brand-new flavor? Try these very special coffee-based main dishes and earn a reputation as a gourmet cook.

BARBECUED SPARERIBS

4 pounds spareribs
Barbecue Sauce (see below)

Place spareribs, curved side down, on rack in shallow pan. Bake in very hot oven (500° F.) 10 minutes. Then reduce oven heat to moderate (325° F.) and bake 1 to 1½ hours, or until spareribs are tender, brushing frequently on both sides with Barbecue Sauce. If desired, any remaining sauce may be served in a bowl or poured over spareribs. Makes 4 to 6 servings.

BARBECUE SAUCE

½ cup brewed quality coffee
½ cup catsup
½ teaspoon salt
Dash of pepper
2 tablespoons Worcestershire sauce
2 tablespoons vinegar
¼ cup sugar
1 tablespoon grated onion

Combine all ingredients and simmer 10 minutes. Use for barbecuing spareribs, chicken, and other meats, or as topping on meat loaf. If desired, sauce may be covered and stored in refrigerator until needed. Makes 1⅓ cups sauce.

BEEF STROGANOFF

- ¼ cup unsifted all-purpose flour
- 1 teaspoon salt
- 2 pounds round steak
- ½ cup butter or other shortening
- 1 cup minced onions
- 1 pound mushrooms, sliced
- 1½ tablespoons instant quality coffee
- ½ cup water
- ½ cup red wine
- 1 teaspoon salt
- ¼ cup water
- 1 cup sour cream
- 4 cups (about) hot cooked rice

Combine flour and 1 teaspoon salt. Pound flour mixture into steak; then cut steak into 2- by ¼- by ¼-inch strips. Brown in ¼ cup of the butter in heavy skillet. Then place meat in a 2-quart saucepan.

Melt remaining ¼ cup butter in the skillet, add onions and brown lightly. Then add mushrooms and cook until lightly browned.

Meanwhile, add instant coffee, ½ cup water, the wine, and 1 teaspoon salt to the meat; cover and simmer 30 minutes. Then stir in mushroom mixture and ¼ cup water; cover and simmer another 30 minutes, or until the meat is very tender. If desired, add salt to taste.

Just before serving, gradually add sour cream and heat gently—*do not boil.* Serve over rice. Makes about 5 cups stroganoff mixture, or 6 servings.

COFFEE-GLAZED HAM SLICE

- 1 slice (about 1½ inches thick) fully cooked ham
- 1 teaspoon instant quality coffee
- 2 tablespoons orange juice
- ¼ cup maple-blended syrup or corn syrup
- ¼ cup brown sugar
- 2 tablespoons butter

Place ham slice in a shallow baking dish. Cover. Bake in a slow oven (325° F.) 30 minutes. Meanwhile, combine instant coffee with orange juice in a small saucepan, stirring until blended. Add remaining ingredients; heat and stir until blended. Then uncover ham, spoon on glaze, and bake another 30 minutes, uncovered, basting occasionally with coffee mixture. Makes 4 servings.

Nice to know: *The glaze for the ham slice (page 44) may also be used on a small canned ham, ham loaf, pork roast, or canned luncheon meat. Makes about ½ cup glaze.*

FISH BRAZILIA

- 1 pound fresh flounder or sole fillets*
- 2 teaspoons instant quality coffee
- 1 tablespoon lemon juice
- 3 tablespoons salad oil
- ½ teaspoon onion salt
- Lemon slices (optional)
- Ripe or stuffed green olives (optional)

*Or use 1 package (12 ounces) frozen flounder or sole fillets, thawed.

Place fish fillets in a shallow baking dish. Dissolve instant coffee in lemon juice; combine with oil and salt, mixing thoroughly. Pour coffee mixture over fish and let stand 30 minutes, turning once after about 15 minutes. Broil 3 inches from heat 5 to 7 minutes, or until fish will flake easily with a fork. Garnish with lemon slices and olives. Makes 3 servings.

ROAST LAMB WITH COFFEE GRAVY

- 1 boned, rolled leg of lamb (about 5 pounds)
- Salt
- Pepper
- 2 cloves of garlic, peeled and cut in half
- 2 cans (4 ounces each) sliced mushrooms
- 1½ cups chopped onions (about 3 medium)
- 6 tablespoons all-purpose flour
- 1 cup brewed quality coffee (flavored with cream and sugar)
- 2 cups water

Place roast, fat side up, on rack in shallow baking pan. Sprinkle with salt and pepper. Rub with garlic and insert garlic cloves in small gashes in surface of lamb. Insert meat thermometer through fat side into center of roast.

Place in a slow oven (325° F.) and roast about 25 minutes per pound for rare meat or to a temperature of 165° F.; about 28 minutes per pound for medium or to a temperature of 175° F.; or to 180° F. for well done. About 45 minutes before roast is done, take from oven, remove rack, and set meat in pan.

Combine mushrooms including liquid with onions and add to drippings in pan. Continue roasting, basting with mushroom liquid and drippings several times. Plan to have roast done about 20 minutes before serving to allow for easier slicing. Place roast on serving platter, arrange mushrooms and onions around base, and keep warm until serving time.

Pour all except about 6 tablespoons drippings from roasting pan. Place over medium heat and stir in the flour. Then gradually add coffee and water, stirring until gravy is thickened and smooth. Season to taste with salt and pepper. Serve with the roast lamb. Makes 10 to 12 servings.

SWEDISH MEAT BALLS

1 teaspoon instant quality coffee
¾ cup hot milk
1½ cups soft bread crumbs
¼ cup finely chopped onion
¼ cup butter or other shortening
¼ teaspoon ground nutmeg
1½ teaspoons salt
⅛ teaspoon pepper
1 egg, slightly beaten
1 pound ground beef
¼ cup unsifted all-purpose flour
1 cup light cream
1 teaspoon instant quality coffee
1½ tablespoons all-purpose flour
2 tablespoons water
¼ to ½ cup hot water
Salt and pepper

Combine 1 teaspoon instant coffee and the hot milk, stirring until coffee is dissolved. Pour over bread crumbs; set aside. Sauté onion in butter in a large skillet until golden brown. Add onion to bread mixture, leaving any remaining butter in skillet. Add nutmeg, salt, pepper, and egg; mix well. Add ground beef and mix thoroughly. Shape into 1-inch balls and roll in the ¼ cup flour. Brown meat balls in the butter remaining in skillet. Then pour cream over meat balls, cover, and simmer 5 minutes. Remove from heat, arrange meat balls on serving platter, and keep hot.

Combine 1 teaspoon instant coffee, 1½ tablespoons flour, and the water, blending well. Stir into milk and drippings in skillet. Cook and stir until smooth and thickened. Then continue to cook and stir, gradually adding hot water until gravy is of desired consistency. Season to taste with salt and pepper.

Pour the gravy over the meat balls and serve at once. Makes 6 servings.

SHRIMP TEMPURA WITH COFFEE SWEET-SOUR SAUCE

- ¾ pound fresh shrimp (about 21 small shrimp)
- ¾ cup sifted all-purpose flour
- 1 teaspoon double-acting baking powder
- ½ teaspoon salt
- 1 egg
- ½ cup water
- Coffee Sweet-Sour Sauce (see below)

Shell and devein shrimp, leaving tail on. Rinse and thoroughly dry the shrimp. Sift flour with baking powder and salt. Beat egg slightly, add flour mixture, and stir until blended. Add water, one tablespoon at a time, stirring constantly until batter is smooth and the consistency of a custard sauce.

Dip the shrimp, one at a time, in batter and fry in hot fat (350° to 360° F.) until golden brown—about 3 minutes. Do not fry too many at one time. Remove shrimp from fat and drain on paper towels. Serve with Coffee Sweet-Sour Sauce. Makes 4 servings.

COFFEE SWEET-SOUR SAUCE

- 1 teaspoon instant quality coffee
- ½ cup water
- ½ cup firmly packed brown sugar
- 1 tablespoon cornstarch
- ½ cup vinegar
- ¼ teaspoon salt
- 2 tablespoons catsup
- Dash of pepper
- 1 can (8¾ ounces) pineapple tidbits
- 1 medium tomato, cut into small wedges
- 1 medium green pepper, cut in small squares
- 1 tablespoon salad oil

Dissolve instant coffee in water. Mix sugar and cornstarch. Stir in coffee; then add vinegar, salt, catsup, pepper, and pineapple. Stir over medium heat until sauce is thickened.

Sauté tomato and green pepper very slightly in oil. Add to the thickened sauce. Serve with or over fried shrimp, roast pork, spareribs, or ham. Makes 1½ cups sauce.

SPAGHETTI WITH QUICK ITALIAN MEAT SAUCE

- 1 clove garlic, minced
- 1 medium onion, chopped
- 2 tablespoons olive or salad oil
- 1 pound ground beef
- 1 can (10¾ ounces) condensed tomato soup
- 2 cans (6 ounces each) tomato paste
- ¾ cup brewed quality coffee or prepared instant quality coffee
- ½ teaspoon sugar
- 1 can (3 ounces) chopped broiled mushrooms
- ¼ teaspoon basil or oregano
- Salt and pepper
- 1 pound spaghetti, cooked
- Grated Parmesan cheese

Brown garlic and onion lightly in olive or salad oil. Add meat and brown, stirring frequently. Add soup, tomato paste, coffee, and sugar. Simmer 30 minutes. Then add mushrooms, basil, and salt and pepper to taste; simmer 5 minutes longer. Serve on spaghetti with grated Parmesan cheese. Makes 5½ cups sauce or 6 servings.

Heart of the Meal, 2

Good things to serve with those delicious coffee main dishes, plus ways to dress up your dinners for company. In Section 3 are recipes for some of the other dishes.

BARBECUED SPARERIBS (page 43)
TWICE-BAKED POTATOES
BUTTERED GREEN BEANS   CALICO COLESLAW (page 53)
EASY COFFEE SMOOTHIE (page 190) MELTING MOMENTS (page 40)

Nice to know: Scrub one potato per serving, but don't peel them. Try to choose them very much of a size, so they'll all be baked at the same time—this can be early in the day. Then slice tops from baked potatoes and scoop out the insides. Whip and season the scooped-out potatoes; then spoon back into shells and chill. Before serving, bake until lightly browned and thoroughly heated.

If company comes: *Start with a simple appetizer, such as frosty grapefruit juice with a sprig of mint. Add butter-browned almonds to the green beans, or use frozen French-style green beans with toasted almonds. Dress up each serving of the Easy Coffee Smoothie with chocolate sauce.*

BEEF STROGANOFF WITH RICE (page 44)
EASY CAESAR SALAD (page 53)
CAKE À LA MODE WITH COFFEE SAUCE (page 96)

Nice to know: You can make the stroganoff, except for adding the sour cream, in advance. In fact, it's a good recipe to double or triple, then divide into 2 or 3 containers and freeze until you need it.

If company comes: *Add an appetizer of fresh, crisp vegetables with a dip of mayonnaise, chili sauce, and seasonings. Almost any in-season vegetable can be used—such as cauliflower, celery, carrots, tiny tomatoes, green pepper strips. You may also wish to serve buttered broccoli and hot rolls with the stroganoff.*

COFFEE-GLAZED HAM SLICE (page 44)
MASHED SWEET POTATOES SPINACH RING (page 53)
SPICED CRAB APPLES
THREE-WAY COFFEE ANGEL CUPCAKES (page 70)

Nice to know: Like the thrifty French housewife, save leftover vegetables for a rainy day, use them in a sauce for the Spinach Ring. Any combination of what's left from yesterday and the day before will do: peas, carrots, green beans, lima beans, etc. Add chopped celery, grated onion to taste, and mix with cream sauce.

If company comes: *Start with a grapefruit-and-avocado appetizer. Add a little interest to the potatoes by sprinkling them with chopped nuts. And serve the cupcakes with ice cream.*

FISH BRAZILIA (page 45)
CONFETTI RICE (page 54) BUTTERED PEAS
MARINATED ARTICHOKE HEARTS (page 35)
BANANA COCONUT PIE

Nice to know: Artichokes, once a luxury item and a seasonal one, are everybody's dish now that they have been frozen and packaged. Served as above, they can be either salad or appetizer. A package, quickly cooked, can be used to extend and glamorize a tossed salad. As a vegetable, they can also be served hot with lemon butter or hollandaise sauce.

If company comes: *Serve the artichokes as an appetizer, and make a tossed salad. Add Quick Corn Crisps to the menu: use packaged corn muffins—the thin, flat kind that fit in an automatic toaster. Split them and place, cut side up, on a baking sheet. Sprinkle with celery salt or sesame seeds. Dry out—à la Melba toast—in a very slow oven for half an hour.*

ROAST LAMB WITH COFFEE GRAVY (page 45)
NEW POTATOES AND GREEN PEAS
BUTTERED CARROTS MINTED PEAR SALAD (page 54)
FRESH STRAWBERRY SHORTCAKE (page 129)

Nice to know: Scrub little new potatoes, but don't peel them. Choose them very much of a size so they'll all be cooked at same time. After cooking remove the "jackets" and combine with peas. On an especially busy day, use canned or frozen small potatoes.

If company comes: *Marinate some asparagus in salad dressing for an appetizer. With the salad, serve cream cheese balls rolled in chopped nuts. Pretty-up the shortcake with whipped cream, adding a teaspoonful of freshly grated orange or lemon rind for special zest.*

SHRIMP TEMPURA WITH COFFEE SWEET-SOUR SAUCE (page 47)
RICE CHINESE NOODLES
WILTED LETTUCE (page 55)
GINGERED FRUIT AND FORTUNE COOKIES

Nice to know: Although the Shrimp Tempura you make yourself is always best, you can substitute frozen French-fried shrimp to serve with the Coffee Sweet-Sour Sauce. Spicy, gingered fruit may be served hot or cold—depending on the season and your family's likes and dislikes.

If company comes: *Add an appetizer or egg drop soup to the menu. For the appetizer, skewer cooked chicken livers and water chestnuts, laced or wrapped with bacon slices, and broil until bacon is crisp. An extra-special dessert could be preserved kumquats—look for them in the gourmet foods section of your supermarket.*

SPAGHETTI WITH QUICK ITALIAN MEAT SAUCE (page 48)
TOSSED GREEN SALAD BREAD STICKS
FROZEN AMBROSIA (page 55)

Nice to know: Stores carry bread sticks in several varieties—

short and chunky (flavored or plain) or long, thin, and crisp. These thin, crisp sticks make fine dunkers to serve with dips—a nice change from chips or crackers. To serve with a sauce such as this one, choose a thin pasta—spaghettini, linguine, or fettucini.

If company comes: *Start the meal with Antipasto (page 32), and finish by complementing the delicate flavors of the Ambrosia with crisp chocolate wafers—the packaged kind, if you haven't time to make them. If you'd like to add a vegetable to the menu, try frozen Italian green beans—cook according to package directions and serve them, buttered, with a sprinkling of grated Romano or Parmesan cheese.*

SWEDISH MEAT BALLS (page 46)
DILL-BUTTERED POTATOES BUTTERED BEETS
HEARTS OF LETTUCE ROQUEFORT DRESSING (page 55)
MIXED FRUIT WITH SOUR CREAM

Nice to know: Serve fresh fruit if you like, when it's in season—but out of season, delicious frozen fruit is available. In any case, serve the fruit icy cold, with a dollop of sour cream. If desired, top the cream with a sprinkle of light brown sugar for sweet-dessert addicts or of fresh lemon rind for those who prefer tart zestiness.

If company comes: *Start with an egg-and-anchovy appetizer. Have thin-sliced rye bread—if you live near a Scandinavian bakery, get real Swedish* limpa. *With the fruit, serve unfrosted sponge, angel food, or pound cake.*

Heart of the Meal, 3

Here are recipes for some of the dishes in the menus on the preceding pages.

CALICO COLESLAW

- 2 cups shredded green cabbage
- 2 cups shredded red cabbage
- 1 cup grated carrots
- ½ cup minced green pepper
- Seasoned Sour Cream Dressing (see below)

Combine cabbage, carrots, and green pepper; mix thoroughly. Add salad dressing. Toss well. Makes 4 to 6 servings.

Seasoned Sour Cream Dressing: Blend 1 cup sour cream, 2 tablespoons milk, and 2 to 3 teaspoons onion salad dressing mix. Chill 2 to 3 hours to blend flavors.

EASY CAESAR SALAD

- 2 quarts bite-size pieces romaine or assorted salad greens
- ½ cup Parmesan salad dressing
- 1 egg, slightly beaten
- 6 anchovy fillets, chopped (optional)
- 1 cup bread croutons

Place romaine in salad bowl. Add salad dressing and toss together. Add egg and toss with greens until specks of egg disappear. Add anchovy fillets and croutons. Toss together lightly. Makes 8 to 10 servings.

SPINACH RING

- 2 packages (10 ounces each) frozen leaf spinach
- Salted water
- ¼ cup butter, melted
- 2 eggs, slightly beaten
- 1½ teaspoons minced onion
- Dash of pepper

Cook spinach in salted water as directed on the package; drain. Add remaining ingredients and mix very thoroughly. Spoon into a well-greased 3-cup ring mold. Place in pan of hot water. Bake in moderate oven (375° F.) 30 minutes or until firm. Unmold. Serve with a vegetable sauce, if desired. Makes 2½ cups or 4 or 5 servings.

Nice to know: *To serve Spinach Ring as an entree, fill center with scrambled eggs and bacon.*

CONFETTI RICE

- 1⅓ cups packaged pre-cooked rice
- ½ teaspoon salt
- 1⅓ cups boiling water
- 2 tablespoons chopped parsley
- 1 tablespoon diced pimiento
- 2 tablespoons butter

Add rice and salt to boiling water in saucepan, mixing just to moisten all rice. Cover, remove from heat, and let stand 5 minutes. Add parsley, pimiento, and butter to rice, mixing lightly with a fork. Makes about 2⅔ cups or 4 servings.

Nice to know: *If desired, sauté ¼ cup finely chopped onion in the butter and add with parsley and pimiento.*

MINTED PEAR SALAD

- 2 packages (3 ounces each) or 1 package (6 ounces) lime flavor gelatin
- ⅛ teaspoon salt
- 2 cups boiling water
- 1 can (1 pound) pear halves
- 8 drops mint extract

Dissolve gelatin and salt in boiling water. Drain pears, measuring syrup. Add water to syrup to equal 1¾ cups. Add to gelatin with mint extract. Chill until slightly thickened. Cut each pear half into 4 pieces; add to the thickened gelatin. Pour into an 8- by 4-inch loaf pan or 1½-quart mold. Chill until firm—at least 3 hours. Unmold on lettuce. Makes about 5 cups or 8 to 10 servings.

WILTED LETTUCE

- 2 medium heads leaf lettuce
- 4 bacon slices, diced
- ¼ cup old fashion French salad dressing
- ¼ teaspoon celery salt
- 2 tablespoons chopped chives
- 2 tablespoons vinegar
- 1 tablespoon sugar

Tear or cut lettuce into bite-size pieces and place in a bowl. Sauté bacon in skillet until brown and crisp. Add remaining ingredients; bring to a boil. Pour over the lettuce, cover with a plate, and allow to steam 5 or 6 minutes. Then toss lettuce and serve on warm plates. Makes 4 servings.

Nice to know: *If desired, fresh spinach (6 to 8 cups) may be substituted for the lettuce in recipe above.*

FROZEN AMBROSIA

- 2 oranges
- 1 package (3 ounces) lemon flavor gelatin
- ¼ cup sugar
- ¼ teaspoon salt
- 1 cup boiling water
- ½ cup heavy cream
- 1 cup flaked coconut

Grate rind from oranges to make 1 teaspoon grated rind. Peel and section oranges; set aside. Dissolve gelatin, sugar, and salt in boiling water. Then drain orange sections, measuring juice and adding water to make 1 cup; add juice mixture to gelatin mixture. Chill until slightly thickened. Whip the cream. Fold coconut, orange sections and rind, and whipped cream into the slightly thickened gelatin. Pour into freezing tray or shallow pan and freeze until firm—3 to 4 hours. Makes 6 to 8 servings.

ROQUEFORT DRESSING

- ¼ cup vinegar
- 2 tablespoons water
- 1 envelope Italian salad dressing mix
- ⅔ cup salad oil
- 3 tablespoons crumbled Roquefort or bleu cheese

Mix vinegar and water in a cruet or jar with tight-fitting cover. Add salad dressing mix. Cover and shake well. Add salad oil, cover, and shake again. Add cheese. Makes 1 cup salad dressing.

Nice to know: *If desired, instead of water, 2 tablespoons of any of the following may be used: vermouth, sherry, chili sauce, catsup, tomato juice, or mayonnaise.*

Cook's Pride Cakes

Some women buy new hats when they feel like celebrating—good cooks bake cakes! Please your family tonight with one of these. Choose a feather-light angel food or chiffon-type, a richly frosted layer cake, or one dotted with fruit, smelling sweetly of spice. Whichever you decide on, it will have a wonderful, what-is-it flavor . . . and the secret is coffee.

AUSTRIAN MOCHA TORTE

¼ cup water
1 tablespoon instant quality coffee
½ cup semi-sweet chocolate chips
6 egg yolks (at room temperature)
½ cup sugar
⅓ cup butter (at room temperature)
½ cup sifted all-purpose flour
6 egg whites
¼ teaspoon cream of tartar
Coffee Torte Filling (page 79)

Combine water and coffee in a small saucepan. Bring to a boil. Then reduce heat and add chocolate chips. Heat and stir until chips are melted and mixture is smooth. Cool. Beat egg yolks until foamy. Gradually add sugar, beating until thick and lemon-colored. Add butter and beat until smooth. Add slightly cooled chocolate mixture and beat until creamy. Fold in flour. Mix egg whites and cream of tartar; beat until mixture will hold stiff peaks. Carefully fold into the chocolate mixture.

Grease two 8-inch layer pans on bottoms, line with paper, and grease paper. Pour about ¼ of the batter (about 1 cup) into each pan. Bake in slow oven (325° F.) for 15 minutes. Cool in pans 5 minutes. Then remove from pans and invert onto rack. Remove paper carefully and cool layers completely. While first layers cool, bake 2 more layers, using remaining batter. Fill and frost layers with Coffee Torte Filling. Makes 12 to 18 servings.

COFFEE CRUMB CAKE

- 2 cups biscuit mix
- ½ cup granulated sugar
- 4 teaspoons instant quality coffee
- ¾ cup milk
- 1 egg, well beaten
- 1 tablespoon butter
- 1 tablespoon flour
- ⅓ cup firmly packed brown sugar
- ½ teaspoon ground cinnamon
- ¼ teaspoon ground nutmeg
- ½ cup finely chopped nuts

Combine biscuit mix and granulated sugar in bowl. Dissolve 2 teaspoons instant coffee in milk and mix with egg. Add to biscuit mix and stir until blended. Pour into greased 9-inch pie pan.

Melt butter in small saucepan. Add flour and stir until blended. Remove from heat. Add 2 teaspoons instant coffee, brown sugar, and spices and mix well. Stir in nuts. Sprinkle this topping over batter in pan. Bake in moderate oven (375° F.) 25 to 30 minutes. Serve hot. Makes about 9 servings.

PENNSYLVANIA DUTCH CAKE

FOR PASTRY:

- 1½ cups sifted all-purpose flour
- 1 teaspoon salt
- ½ cup shortening
- 2 to 3 tablespoons cold water

Combine flour and salt. Cut in shortening until mixture is consistency of corn meal. Stir in cold water. Put dough on wax paper. Press and knead gently into a ball and let stand for 15 to 20 minutes at room temperature while sauce is being made.

FOR SAUCE:

- ⅓ cup butter or margarine
- 1 cup firmly packed brown sugar
- 2 tablespoons light corn syrup
- 1 tablespoon instant quality coffee
- ½ cup hot water

Combine butter, brown sugar, light corn syrup, and instant coffee in saucepan. Place over low heat. Cook and stir until mixture comes to a boil. Remove from heat and slowly stir in hot water. Bring again to a boil. Boil 2 minutes. Remove from heat and set aside.

Roll pastry on lightly floured board to fit into a 9- or 10-inch pie plate. Line plate with pastry, letting it extend 1 inch beyond the edge of the plate. Turn edge of pastry under and make a high fluted rim.

FOR CAKE:

- 1¼ cups sifted cake flour
- 1½ teaspoons double-acting baking powder
- ½ teaspoon salt
- ¾ cup sugar
- ¼ cup shortening (at room temperature)
- ½ cup milk
- 1 teaspoon vanilla
- 1 egg, unbeaten
- ¼ cup chopped nuts or flaked coconut

Measure flour, baking powder, salt, and sugar into sifter. Place shortening in mixing bowl. Sift in dry ingredients. Add milk and vanilla and mix until all flour is dampened. Then beat 2 minutes with electric mixer, or 300 strokes by hand. Add egg and beat 1 minute longer, or 150 strokes.

Pour batter into pastry-lined pie plate. Pour lukewarm sauce gently over cake batter. (When cake is baked, sauce will form a layer between cake and pie shell.) Sprinkle with chopped nuts or coconut. Bake in moderate oven (350° F.) about 50 minutes. Cake is best served warm. If desired, top with whipped cream or ice cream.

MOCHA CHIFFON CAKE

- 1 package (4 ounces) sweet cooking chocolate
- ¾ cup boiling water
- 1⅔ cups sifted cake flour
- 1½ cups sugar
- 2 tablespoons instant quality coffee
- 2 teaspoons double-acting baking powder
- ¾ teaspoon salt
- 7 eggs, separated
- ½ cup salad oil
- ½ teaspoon cream of tartar
- Coffee Whipped Cream (page 82)

Combine chocolate and boiling water in small saucepan. Stir over very low heat until chocolate is completely melted. Remove from heat and set aside to cool.

Measure sifted flour, add 1¼ cups of sugar, the instant coffee, baking powder, and salt, and sift together into a large bowl. Make a well in the center of the dry ingredients. Add egg yolks, oil, and the cooled chocolate mixture. Beat at low speed of electric mixer or with a spoon until batter is smooth —about 2 minutes.

Combine egg whites and cream of tartar in large bowl. Beat at high speed of electric mixer or with hand beater until foamy—about 1 minute. Gradually add remaining ¼ cup sugar and continue beating until egg whites will hold very stiff peaks. Gradually pour the chocolate mixture over the egg whites and fold mixtures together until just blended, using a wire whip or rubber scraper. Pour batter into an ungreased 10-inch tube pan. Bake in moderate oven (350° F.) 60 to 65 minutes. Invert cake and cool completely.

Prepare 3 cup recipe of Coffee Whipped Cream. When cake is completely cool, loosen around tube and edges with a spatula. Remove cake from pan. Using a sharp knife, horizontally split cake into 3 layers. Invert top layer of cake onto serving plate, spread with 1 cup of the filling. Add the middle cake layer and spread with 1 cup of the filling. Repeat, using remaining cake layer and filling. Garnish top of cake with chocolate curls or slivered toasted almonds, if desired. Store cake in refrigerator.

MOCHA-FILLED ANGEL CAKE

- 1 package (6 ounces) chocolate pudding and pie filling mix
- 2 tablespoons instant quality coffee
- 2½ cups milk
- ¼ cup heavy cream
- 1 tablespoon sugar
- 1 baked 9-inch angel food cake
- ¼ cup crushed toffee candy or chopped nuts

Combine pudding mix, instant coffee, and milk in a medium saucepan. Cook and stir over medium heat until the mixture comes to a *full* boil. Remove from heat. Place wax paper directly on surface of pudding. Cool. Whip cream, adding sugar. Fold into the pudding mixture. Split the cake horizontally into 3 layers. Spread pudding mixture between layers and on top of cake. Garnish with candy or nuts. Store in refrigerator. Makes 8 to 10 servings.

MOCHA SPICE CAKE

- 2 cups sifted cake flour
- ½ teaspoon double-acting baking powder
- 1 teaspoon baking soda
- ½ teaspoon salt
- 1 teaspoon ground cinnamon
- ½ cup cocoa
- ½ cup butter or margarine
- 1½ cups sugar
- 2 eggs, unbeaten
- 1 cup minus 2 tablespoons buttermilk or sour milk
- ½ cup brewed quality coffee
- 1 teaspoon vanilla
- Mocha Cream Frosting (page 82)

Sift flour with baking powder, soda, salt, cinnamon, and cocoa.

Cream butter or margarine; add sugar gradually, creaming together until light and fluffy. Add eggs, one at a time, beating thoroughly after each. Combine buttermilk, coffee, and vanilla. Add flour mixture to egg mixture, alternately with liquid, beating after each addition until smooth.

Pour batter into two 9-inch layer pans that have been lined on bottoms with wax paper. Bake in moderate oven (350° F.) 35 minutes or until cake springs back when pressed lightly. Cool; then frost with Mocha Cream Frosting.

MOCHA POUND CAKE

- 1 package (4 ounces) sweet cooking chocolate
- 2¾ cups sifted cake flour
- 1¾ cups sugar
- 1½ tablespoons instant quality coffee
- 1 teaspoon salt
- ¾ teaspoon cream of tartar
- ½ teaspoon baking soda
- ¼ teaspoon ground cinnamon
- 1 cup butter or margarine (at room temperature)
- ¾ cup milk
- 1 teaspoon vanilla
- 3 eggs
- 1 egg yolk

Heat chocolate over hot water until partially melted. Remove from hot water and stir rapidly until entirely melted. Cool.

Sift flour with sugar, instant coffee, salt, cream of tartar, soda, and cinnamon.

Stir butter to soften. Add flour mixture, milk, and vanilla. Mix until all flour is dampened. Then *beat 2 minutes* at medium speed of electric mixer or 300 vigorous strokes by hand, scraping bowl occasionally. Add eggs, yolk, and melted chocolate. *Beat 1 minute* longer or 150 vigorous strokes by hand.

Pour batter into a 10-inch tube pan which has been greased and floured on sides and tube and lined on bottom with wax paper. Bake in moderate oven (350° F.) about 1 hour and 5 minutes or until cake tester inserted in center comes out clean and cake is free from sides of pan. Cool in pan 15 minutes; then loosen from tube and sides, remove from pan, and cool thoroughly on rack. Cover cake to store.

Nice to know: *If a shiny glaze is desired, spread it on cake while cake is still warm—try one of the coffee- or mocha-flavored glazes on pages 77 to 84.*

MOCHA SOUFFLÉ ROLL

- 2 tablespoons water
- 1 teaspoon instant quality coffee
- 1 package (4 ounces) sweet cooking chocolate, broken into squares
- 5 eggs, separated
- Dash of salt
- 1 cup sifted confectioners' sugar
- 1 teaspoon vanilla
- ¼ cup cocoa
- Coffee Whipped Cream (page 82)

Place water, instant coffee, and chocolate in saucepan. Place over very low heat and stir until chocolate is completely melted. Remove from heat and let stand in warm place.

Place egg yolks and salt in small mixing bowl. Beat until yolks are thickened and lemon-colored—at least 3 minutes. Add ¾ cup of the confectioners' sugar, 1 tablespoon at a time, beating constantly. Add vanilla; beat well. Slowly fold warm chocolate into egg yolk mixture. (Mixture will be thick.)

Beat egg whites until stiff but not dry. Fold chocolate mixture into egg whites until thoroughly blended. Pour into a 13- by 9-inch pan which has been greased on the bottom and sides, lined with wax paper, and greased again. Bake in a moderate oven (350° F.) 15 to 18 minutes or until cake tester inserted into center comes out clean and cake will spring back when lightly pressed in center.

Meanwhile, blend remaining ¼ cup confectioners' sugar and the cocoa. Sprinkle over a large towel. Cool cake on rack 3 minutes. Loosen around edges of pan and immediately invert onto cocoa-sprinkled towel. Roll up cake and towel very loosely. Cool rolled cake on rack 30 minutes.

Prepare Coffee Whipped Cream. Carefully unroll cooled cake. Spread cake with filling. Carefully reroll cake, eliminating towel, and reserving remaining cocoa mixture. Chill cake. Sprinkle cake with cocoa mixture just before serving. Makes 8 servings.

CHOCOLATE CHIP CAKE

- 1 package (6 ounces) semi-sweet chocolate chips
- 2 cups sifted all-purpose flour*
- 2½ teaspoons double-acting baking powder*
- 1 teaspoon salt
- ⅓ cup butter
- 1 package (3 ounces) cream cheese
- 1 cup sugar*
- 1½ tablespoons instant quality coffee
- 2 eggs, unbeaten
- ¼ teaspoon red food coloring (optional)
- 1 cup milk
- 1 teaspoon vanilla
- Mocha Butter Frosting (page 81)

*Or use 2¼ cups sifted cake flour, increasing baking powder to 3 teaspoons and decreasing sugar to ¾ cup.

Melt chocolate chips over hot water. Sift flour, baking powder, and salt together. Cream butter with cream cheese. Gradually add sugar and coffee, creaming thoroughly. Add eggs, one at a time, beating well after each. Stir in melted chocolate and the food coloring. Combine milk and vanilla. Alternately add flour mixture and milk to the butter mixture, beginning and ending with flour and blending after each addition. Pour batter into a well-greased and floured 13- by 9-inch pan. Bake in a moderate oven (350° F.) for 30 to 35 minutes. Cool. Spread top with Mocha Butter Frosting. Makes 12 to 15 servings.

MOCHA CUPCAKES

1⅓ cups sifted cake flour
½ teaspoon salt
½ teaspoon baking soda
½ teaspoon double-acting baking powder
¼ cup cocoa
1 tablespoon instant quality coffee
½ cup milk*
½ cup butter
¾ cup sugar
1 egg, unbeaten
1 teaspoon vanilla

***With vegetable shortening, increase milk to ⅔ cup.**

Sift flour with salt, baking soda, baking powder, and cocoa. Dissolve coffee in milk. Cream butter, gradually add sugar, and cream together until light and fluffy. Add egg and beat well. Add vanilla. Alternately add flour and coffee-flavored milk in small amounts, beginning and ending with flour and beating until smooth after each addition.

Spoon batter into paper baking cups set in muffin pans, filling each slightly less than half full. Bake in moderate oven (350° F.) about 25 minutes. Makes 20 to 22 cupcakes.

COFFEE ANGEL FOOD CAKE

1 cup sifted cake flour
1½ cups sifted sugar
1½ to 2 tablespoons instant quality coffee
1½ cups (about 12) egg whites (at room temperature)
¼ teaspoon salt
1¼ teaspoons cream of tartar
1 teaspoon vanilla

Sift flour with ½ cup of the sugar and the coffee. Combine egg whites, salt, cream of tartar, and vanilla in a large bowl. Beat at high speed of electric mixer until egg white mixture will form soft, rounded peaks. Gradually add 1 cup sugar, sprinkling ¼ cup at a time over egg whites and beating until sugar is blended after each addition. When beating by hand, beat 25 strokes or turns after each addition of sugar.

Sift flour mixture in four additions over egg white mixture; fold in with 15 complete fold-over strokes, turning bowl frequently. (To fold, use a flat wire whip, rubber scraper, or wooden spoon. Cut down through mixture, lift up, and fold over. *Do not stir or beat.)* After last addition, use 10 to 20 extra folding strokes.

Pour batter into ungreased 10-inch tube pan. Cut through batter with spatula to remove large air bubbles. Bake in moderate oven (375° F.) 30 to 35 minutes or until cake springs back when pressed lightly. Invert pan on rack, or invert and place tube over bottle; let stand 1 hour or until cake is thoroughly cooled. Then loosen from sides and center tube with knife and gently remove cake from pan.

Nice to know: *Remove eggs from refrigerator several hours before using. Egg whites beat up lighter and more readily when at room temperature and give increased fineness of grain and delicacy of texture to angel food cakes.*

TRIPLE FLAVOR CAKE

- 3 cups sifted cake flour
- 3 teaspoons double-acting baking powder
- ½ teaspoon salt
- 1 cup shortening*
- 2 cups sugar
- 4 eggs
- Milk*
- Flavorings (see below)

*With butter or margarine, use ¾ cup plus 2 tablespoons milk. With vegetable shortening, use 1 cup milk.

Sift flour with baking powder and salt. Cream shortening thoroughly. Gradually add sugar, beating until mixture is very fluffy and sugar is blended. Add eggs, one at a time, beating well after each. Then add flour mixture alternately with milk, beginning and ending with flour. Divide batter into thirds and add any one of the flavorings suggested below to each third. Pour each third into an 8-inch layer pan which has been lined on bottom with wax paper. Bake in moderate oven (350° F.) 25 to 30 minutes.

Suggested flavorings:

Coffee. Fold 1 tablespoon instant quality coffee into ⅓ of the batter.

Pistachio. Add ½ teaspoon almond extract and about 4 drops green food coloring to ⅓ of the batter.

Peppermint. Add ¼ teaspoon peppermint extract and about 4 drops red food coloring to ⅓ of the batter.

Spice. Combine ¼ teaspoon ground allspice, ¾ teaspoon ground nutmeg, and 2 teaspoons ground cinnamon; fold into ⅓ of the batter.

Chocolate. Melt 1½ squares unsweetened chocolate. Remove from heat. Add 2 tablespoons sugar and ¼ cup hot water. Stir until smooth. Set aside to cool. Stir in ⅛ teaspoon soda. Fold into ⅓ of the batter.

QUICK COFFEE LAYER CAKE

1¾ cups sifted cake flour
4 teaspoons instant quality coffee
2¼ teaspoons double-acting baking powder
½ teaspoon salt
½ cup shortening
1 cup plus 2 tablespoons sugar
2 eggs
¾ cup milk
½ teaspoon vanilla
Rich Coffee Frosting (page 83)

Sift flour with instant coffee, baking powder, and salt. Cream shortening, add sugar gradually, and cream together until light and fluffy. Add eggs, one at a time, beating well after each. Then add flour, alternately with milk, beating after each addition until smooth. Mix in vanilla.

Pour batter into two 8-inch layer pans, which have been lined on bottom with wax paper. Bake in moderate oven (375° F.) 25 to 30 minutes. Cool. Frost with Rich Coffee Frosting.

MOCHA DEVIL'S FOOD CAKE

1½ cups sifted cake flour
1¼ cups sugar
1 tablespoon instant quality coffee
¾ teaspoon salt
¾ teaspoon baking soda
½ cup shortening
⅔ cup water
2 squares unsweetened chocolate, melted
2 eggs
1 teaspoon vanilla

Measure sifted flour into sifter; add sugar, instant coffee, salt, and soda. Stir shortening just to soften. Sift in flour mixture. Add water and mix until all flour is dampened. Then *beat 2 minutes* at medium speed in electric mixer, or 300 vigorous strokes by hand.

Add chocolate, eggs, and vanilla and *beat 1 minute* longer in mixer, or 150 strokes by hand.

Pour batter into a 9-inch square pan or two 8-inch layer pans, lined on bottom with wax paper. Bake in moderate oven (350° F.) 40 to 45 minutes for square cake or 25 to 30 minutes for layers.

Mix-Made Cakes With Character

Today's well-stocked kitchen wouldn't be complete without a package or two of cake mix . . . and today's mix-made cakes are so good it takes an expert to tell them from homemade ones. The little touches you add yourself—flavor variations, special toppings, extra-good frostings—make all the difference. Here are coffee how-to secrets of those extra, added touches which turn a mix cake into one that's truly your own.

COFFEE MERINGUE-TOPPED CAKE

- 1 package yellow or butterscotch cake mix
- 1¼ cups water
- 2 eggs, unbeaten
- 2 egg whites
- Dash of salt
- 2 teaspoons instant quality coffee
- ½ cup sugar
- 1 teaspoon vanilla
- Dash of ground cinnamon

Prepare cake mix with water and eggs as directed on package. Pour batter into a greased and floured 13- by 9-inch pan.

Beat egg whites and salt until foamy. Gradually add instant coffee and then the sugar, 2 tablespoons at a time, beating after each addition until well blended. Continue beating until mixture will form stiff, shiny peaks. Blend in vanilla and cinnamon.

Drop spoonfuls of meringue on cake batter in pan and spread carefully. Bake in moderate oven (350° F.) 40 to 45 minutes. Cool in pan on rack. Makes about 15 servings.

QUICK MOCHA SPICE CAKE

- 1 package devil's food cake mix
- ½ teaspoon ground cinnamon
- ¼ teaspoon ground allspice
- ¼ teaspoon ground nutmeg
- 4 teaspoons instant quality coffee
- 1¼ cups water
- 2 eggs, unbeaten

Empty cake mix into bowl. Add remaining ingredients. Blend; then beat until smooth and creamy. Pour batter into two round 8-inch cake pans that have been greased and floured on bottoms and sides. Bake in moderate oven (350° F.) 40 to 45 minutes.

Nice to know: *This cake may also be baked in two 9-inch layer pans 35 to 40 minutes, or in one 9- by 9- by 2-inch pan 55 to 60 minutes, or in one 13- by 9-inch pan 40 to 45 minutes.*

COFFEE-MARBLED CAKE

- 1 package white cake mix
- 1¼ cups water
- 2 egg whites, unbeaten
- ½ teaspoon vanilla
- ½ teaspoon ground cinnamon
- ¼ teaspoon ground cloves
- 1 teaspoon instant quality coffee
- 1 tablespoon water
- Coffee Four Minute Frosting (page 80)

Prepare cake mix with 1¼ cups water and the egg whites as directed on package, adding vanilla.

Combine spices, instant coffee, and 1 tablespoon water; mix well. Place 1½ cups of the batter in a small bowl; add the coffee mixture and mix well.

Grease and flour bottoms and sides of two 8-inch layer pans. Spoon the batters into the pans, alternating mixtures. Cut through batter *once* with a knife in zigzag course to marble. Bake as directed on cake mix package. Frost with Coffee Four Minute Frosting, if desired.

COFFEE ANGEL FOOD

- 1 tablespoon instant quality coffee
- 1⅓ cups water
- 1 package angel food cake mix
- ½ teaspoon vanilla

Dissolve instant coffee in the water in a large mixing bowl. Then prepare cake mix with the coffee-flavored water and vanilla as directed on package.

Pour batter into an ungreased 10-inch tube pan. Cut through batter to remove large air bubbles. Bake on bottom rack in moderate oven (375° F.) until top springs back when pressed lightly with finger—about 40 minutes. Cool upside down in pan, placing tube over bottle so air will circulate under cake. Then remove from pan and glaze, if desired.

Coffee Angel Cupcakes: Prepare Coffee Angel Food, spooning batter into paper baking cups that have been placed in muffin pans or on ungreased baking sheets, filling each about ⅔ full. Bake in moderate oven (375° F.) 15 to 20 minutes. Makes about 4½ dozen.

Three-Way Coffee Angel Cupcakes: Prepare Coffee Angel Food, spooning about ⅔ of the batter into paper baking cups (about 3 dozen) that have been placed in muffin pans or on ungreased baking sheets, filling each about ⅔ full. Sprinkle half of the filled cups with ⅓ cup flaked coconut. Then fold ⅓ cup chopped pecans into remaining batter and spoon into paper cups. Bake in moderate oven (375° F.) 15 to 20 minutes. Makes about 4½ dozen, or 18 of each type.

COFFEE POUND CAKE

- 1 package yellow cake mix
- 1 package (3 ounces) orange or orange-pineapple flavor gelatin
- 4 teaspoons instant quality coffee
- ¾ cup water
- ½ cup salad oil
- 4 eggs, unbeaten

Empty cake mix into large bowl. Add remaining ingredients. Blend; then beat 3 minutes until smooth and creamy. Pour batter into a 10-inch tube pan which has been lined on bottom with wax paper. Bake in moderate oven (350° F.) 50 to 55 minutes. Cool in pan 15 minutes. Then loosen from sides and tube, turn out, and cool on cake rack.

Nice to know: *This cake may also be baked in the following pans which have been lined on bottom with wax paper: one 9-inch* *tube pan 60 to 65 minutes; two 9- by 5-inch loaf pans 40 to 45 minutes; one 13- by 9-inch pan 40 to 45 minutes; two 9-inch layer pans 30 to 35 minutes; or two 8-inch layer pans 35 to 40 minutes.*

COFFEE CAKE

- 1 package yellow cake mix
- 2 teaspoons instant quality coffee
- 1¼ cups water
- 2 eggs, unbeaten

Combine cake mix and coffee in bowl. Add water and eggs. Blend; then beat 3 minutes until smooth and creamy. Pour batter into 2 greased and floured 8- or 9-inch layer pans. Bake as directed on package. Cool; then frost with your favorite chocolate frosting.

QUICK COFFEE CAKE

- ½ package (2¼ cups unsifted) white cake mix
- ½ cup plus 2 tablespoons water
- 1 egg white
- 3 tablespoons butter, melted
- ¼ cup sugar
- 1½ teaspoons instant quality coffee
- ¼ cup chopped nuts (optional)

Empty cake mix into small mixing bowl. Add water and egg white. Blend; then beat 2 minutes until smooth and creamy. Pour into a greased and floured 8-inch square pan. Bake as directed on package.

Dribble melted butter over warm cake. Combine sugar and instant coffee; sprinkle over cake. If desired, sprinkle with the chopped nuts. Serve warm.

Quick Coffee-Spice Cake: Prepare Quick Coffee Cake, adding ¼ teaspoon ground cinnamon to the sugar-coffee mixture.

"Coffee and . . ." Special: Doughnuts

Dunking is an old, firmly entrenched American custom —here are recipes to provide hours of dunking delight for the whole family. Is dunking socially acceptable? No less an authority than Emily Post says yes—provided that you break the doughnut in half before its baptism!

RAISED POTATO DOUGHNUTS

- 2 cups milk
- 1 cup sugar
- ½ cup shortening
- 1½ teaspoons salt
- 1 cup freshly mashed potatoes*
- 1½ packages active dry yeast
- ¼ cup warm water
- 3 eggs, well beaten
- ½ teaspoon lemon extract
- ½ teaspoon ground cinnamon
- 8 cups unsifted all-purpose flour

*Cook and mash 2 medium (about 12 ounces) potatoes or prepare instant mashed potatoes.

Scald the milk. Add sugar, shortening, salt, and potatoes. Stir and cool to lukewarm. Meanwhile, dissolve yeast in warm water and let stand 5 minutes. Then add potato mixture and eggs to yeast. Stir in lemon extract and cinnamon. Gradually add flour, stirring until well blended after each addition.

Scrape into a greased bowl; cover. Let rise in a warm place, free from drafts, until it holds the impression of your finger when you touch it lightly. Then punch down to release air bubbles. Roll out on lightly floured board to ¼ inch thickness. Cut with 2¾-inch doughnut cutter, place on floured dish towel, and cover with another towel. Let rise in a warm place, free from drafts, until doubled in bulk. Fry in at least 1 inch of hot fat (375° F.) until golden on both sides, turning gently with a fork only once. Drain on absorbent paper. If desired, doughnuts may be glazed with a thin confectioners' sugar glaze (see Doughnut Glaze, page 74) or rolled in sugar. Makes 5 to 6 dozen.

Nice to know: *To make about 3 dozen doughnuts, halve all ingredients except use 1 package active dry yeast dissolved in ¼ cup warm water. (To halve eggs, use 1 egg plus 1½ tablespoons slightly beaten egg.)*

RAISED DOUGHNUTS

- **¾ cup milk**
- **⅓ cup sugar**
- **1 teaspoon salt**
- **¼ cup margarine**
- **¼ cup warm water**
- **1 package active dry yeast**
- **2 eggs, beaten**
- **¼ teaspoon ground nutmeg**
- **3¼ cups (about) unsifted all-purpose flour**

Scald milk; then stir in sugar, salt, and margarine. Cool to lukewarm. Measure warm water into large, warm mixing bowl. Sprinkle in yeast, stirring until dissolved. Add lukewarm milk mixture, eggs, nutmeg, and half of the flour. Beat until smooth. Stir in enough additional flour to make a soft dough. Turn dough out onto well-floured board. Knead until smooth and elastic—about 10 minutes. Place in greased bowl, turning to grease all sides. Cover; let rise in warm place, free from drafts, until doubled in bulk—about 1 hour.

Punch dough down. Roll out to about ½-inch thickness. Cut with 2¾-inch doughnut cutter and place on greased baking sheets. Cover and let rise in warm place, free from drafts, until doubled in bulk—about 1 hour. Fry in at least 1 inch hot fat (375° F.) until brown on both sides—about 2 minutes. Drain on absorbent paper. If desired, glaze doughnuts with a thin confectioners' sugar glaze (see Doughnut Glaze, page 74) or roll in granulated or confectioners' sugar or a mixture of granulated sugar and cinnamon. Makes about 2 dozen.

Filled Doughnuts: Prepare Raised Doughnuts, removing center from cutter before cutting. When doughnuts have been fried and cooled, puncture a small hole in the side of each and fill with tart jelly or preserves or vanilla pudding, using a pastry bag and tip. If desired, use 1 package (3¼ ounces) vanilla pudding and pie filling mix prepared as directed on package and chilled; then beaten until smooth and creamy. Filled doughnuts may be glazed or rolled in granulated or confectioners' sugar. Makes about 18.

FRENCH DOUGHNUTS OR CRULLERS

- ¼ cup butter
- ½ cup boiling water
- ⅔ cup unsifted all-purpose flour
- 1 tablespoon sugar
- ½ teaspoon salt
- 2 eggs
- Fat for frying
- Doughnut Glaze (see below)

Add butter to water and heat until butter melts. Add flour, sugar, and salt all at once and stir vigorously until a ball forms in the center of the pan. Remove from heat and let stand 5 minutes. Add eggs, one at a time, beating until thoroughly blended after each addition. (Mixture should be very stiff.)

Using cookie press or pastry bag with rosette tip, form mixture into 2½-inch rings on wax paper or aluminum foil. (Or if desired, mixture may be dropped by teaspoonfuls into hot fat.) Heat about 1½ inches of fat to 375° F. Dip a spatula or pancake turner into the hot fat; then use it to pick up formed doughnuts and gently lower them into the fat. Fry until brown on both sides—about 3 to 5 minutes. Drain on absorbent paper. When cooled, glaze tops with Doughnut Glaze. Makes about 12 doughnuts or about 18 dropped from spoon.

DOUGHNUT GLAZE

- 3 to 4 teaspoons water
- ¾ cup sifted confectioners' sugar
- ½ teaspoon vanilla

Gradually add water to sugar and vanilla until mixture is smooth and of desired consistency. Makes enough to glaze 12 to 18 doughnuts.

BISCUIT DOUGHNUTS

- 2 cups sifted all-purpose flour
- 2½ teaspoons double-acting baking powder
- ¾ teaspoon salt
- 5 tablespoons shortening
- ¾ cup (about) milk

Sift flour with baking powder and salt. Cut in shortening. Add milk and stir with fork until soft dough is formed (about 20 strokes). Knead on lightly floured board 20 turns. Pat or roll lightly 1/4 inch thick and cut with floured 2-inch biscuit cutter. Fry in 1 inch of hot fat (400° F.) about 2 1/2 minutes on each side or until browned. Drain on absorbent paper. If desired, roll in confectioners' or granulated sugar. Makes about 12 doughnuts.

DOUGHNUTS WITH HOT BUTTERED PINEAPPLE SAUCE

- 1/4 cup butter
- 2/3 cup firmly packed brown sugar
- 1 can (8 1/2 ounces) sliced pineapple
- 1/2 cup flaked coconut
- 4 doughnuts

Melt butter in small skillet. Add sugar and stir until dissolved. Drain pineapple, measuring 2/3 cup syrup. Then gradually add syrup to sugar mixture, stirring constantly. Bring to a full rolling boil. Add pineapple slices and coconut and bring again to a boil. Simmer gently 3 to 4 minutes. Split doughnuts and place a slice of pineapple between halves of each doughnut in dessert dishes. Pour hot sauce over doughnuts. Garnish with whipped cream, if desired. Makes 4 servings.

GRANDMA'S CAKE DOUGHNUTS

- 4 cups unsifted all-purpose flour
- 1 cup sugar
- 3 teaspoons double-acting baking powder
- 1 1/2 teaspoons ground nutmeg
- 1 teaspoon salt
- 2 eggs, well beaten
- 1 cup milk
- 1/4 cup heavy cream

Mix flour with sugar, baking powder, nutmeg, and salt in mixing bowl. Combine eggs, milk, and cream; add to flour mixture, mixing just enough to form a soft dough. Turn out on lightly floured board and knead gently 15 to 20 turns, or just until dough can be handled easily. (If dough is too soft to knead, cover and chill for 30 minutes.)

Roll out ⅜ inch thick and cut with floured 2¾-inch doughnut cutter. Fry in at least 1 inch of hot fat (375° F.) until golden brown, about 2 minutes on each side, turning only once. Drain on absorbent paper. If desired, doughnuts may be rolled in granulated or confectioners' sugar or a mixture of granulated sugar and ground cinnamon. Makes 2 to 2½ dozen doughnuts.

GRANDMA'S BUTTERMILK DOUGHNUTS

4 cups unsifted all-purpose flour
1 cup sugar
2 teaspoons double-acting baking powder
1½ teaspoons ground nutmeg
1 teaspoon baking soda
1 teaspoon salt
2 eggs, well beaten
1 cup buttermilk
2 tablespoons butter, melted
1 teaspoon vanilla

Mix flour with sugar, baking powder, nutmeg, baking soda, and salt in mixing bowl. Combine eggs, buttermilk, butter, and vanilla; add to flour mixture, mixing just enough to form a soft dough. Turn out on lightly floured board and knead gently 15 to 20 turns, or just until dough can be handled easily. (If dough is too soft to knead, cover and chill for 30 minutes.)

Roll out ⅜ inch thick and cut with floured 2¾-inch doughnut cutter. Fry in at least 1 inch of hot fat (375° F.) until golden brown, about 2 minutes on each side, turning only once. Drain on absorbent paper. If desired, doughnuts may be rolled in granulated or confectioners' sugar or a mixture of granulated sugar and ground cinnamon. Makes 2 to 2½ dozen doughnuts.

Finishing Touches

What makes a good cake better? A heavenly, high-piled frosting! Better still? A smoothly luscious filling to marry the layers in blissful richness! Try these, all delightfully coffee flavored.

Nice to know: *A cake should be thoroughly cooled, and all loose crumbs brushed away, before you frost it. Strips of wax paper placed around the edge of your cake plate will catch drips, can be whisked away to leave the plate clean when you've finished frosting. For a layer cake, start by putting one layer, top side down, on the plate. Spread frosting or filling to the edge. Then place the next layer, bottom side down, on the filling. Frost the sides of the cake next, using upward strokes; finally, frost the top, piling all the remaining frosting on and spreading it to the edges, swirling and rippling it as you go for eye-appeal.*

COCOA-COFFEE FROSTING

3 cups sifted confectioners' sugar
2 tablespoons cocoa
Dash of salt
⅓ cup shortening
¾ teaspoon instant quality coffee
¼ cup cold water
¼ teaspoon vanilla

Sift sugar, cocoa, and salt together. Cream shortening. Add about a cup of the sugar mixture gradually, blending after each addition until light and fluffy. Dissolve instant coffee in water and add alternately with remaining sugar, beating after each addition until smooth, until frosting is thick enough to spread. Blend in vanilla. Makes about 1½ cups frosting, or enough to frost an 8-inch square cake or the top of a 13- by 9-inch cake.

FLUFFY COFFEE FROSTING

½ cup butter, softened
2 tablespoons instant quality coffee
1 pound sifted confectioners' sugar
2 tablespoons milk
1 egg white
1 teaspoon vanilla

Cream together butter and instant coffee. Add about 1 cup of the sugar and blend well. Then add remaining sugar alternately with milk and egg white, beating after each addition until smooth and fluffy. Blend in vanilla. Makes about 2½ cups frosting, or enough to fill and frost a 9-inch square cake, which has been split into 2 layers, or two 8- or 9-inch layers.

EASY COFFEE FROSTING

1 package (3¼ ounces) vanilla pudding and pie filling mix
¼ cup sugar
1 tablespoon instant quality coffee
Dash of salt
1½ cups milk
2 tablespoons butter

Combine pudding mix, sugar, instant coffee, salt, and milk in saucepan. Add butter. Cook and stir over medium heat until mixture comes to a *full* boil. Cool 10 to 15 minutes, or until of spreading consistency, stirring occasionally. Makes about 2 cups frosting, or enough for tops and sides of two 8-inch layers, a 9-inch square cake, or a 13- by 9-inch cake.

Easy Mocha Frosting: Prepare as directed for Easy Coffee Frosting, substituting 1 package (4 ounces) chocolate pudding and pie filling mix for the vanilla pudding mix.

Nice to know: *If desired, 1 cup brewed quality coffee may be substituted for 1 cup of the milk and the 1 tablespoon instant coffee.*

THIN COFFEE GLAZE

1½ cups sifted confectioners' sugar
Dash of salt
1 tablespoon butter
2 teaspoons instant quality coffee
2 tablespoons milk

Combine sugar and salt in bowl. Place remaining ingredients in saucepan. Heat and stir until butter is melted and coffee is dissolved. Gradually beat into the sugar. Spoon over cake, or drizzle over white frosting on a cake. Makes about ½ cup, enough for glazing a 9- or 10-inch tube cake.

COFFEE TORTE FILLING

- 2 tablespoons instant quality coffee
- 2 tablespoons milk
- 1 pound sifted confectioners' sugar
- ⅔ cup butter, softened
- 1 egg white
- 1 teaspoon vanilla

Dissolve coffee in milk. Then add alternately with 2 cups of the sugar to the softened butter, beating well after each addition. Add remaining sugar, egg white, and vanilla. Beat well. Makes 2¾ cups, or enough to frost 4 thin 8-inch layers—see Austrian Mocha Torte (page 57).

CLEVER JUDY MOCHA FROSTING

- 2 cups sifted confectioners' sugar
- ½ cup cold brewed quality coffee
- 1 egg
- 1 teaspoon vanilla
- 4 squares unsweetened chocolate, melted
- 2 tablespoons softened butter

Place sugar in metal bowl or saucepan. Gradually add coffee to egg, blending thoroughly. Then stir into the sugar. Add remaining ingredients and beat with rotary beater until well blended. Place bowl in pan of ice and water and continue beating until of right consistency to spread—about 3 minutes. Makes 2¼ cups frosting, or enough to cover tops and sides of two 8-inch layers.

MOCHA FILLING

- 1 package (3¼ ounces) coconut cream pudding and pie filling mix
- 2 tablespoons cocoa
- 1½ teaspoons instant quality coffee
- 1½ cups milk
- ½ cup chopped pecans
- ½ cup heavy cream

Combine pudding mix, cocoa, coffee, and milk in a medium saucepan. Cook and stir over medium heat until mixture comes to a *full* boil. Remove from heat. Pour into a bowl, place wax paper directly on surface, and chill. Then beat until smooth and creamy. Stir in pecans. Whip the cream and fold into pudding mixture. Makes about 3 cups filling, or enough to spread between four 8- or 9-inch cake layers.

COFFEE FOUR MINUTE FROSTING

- 1 egg white
- ¾ cup sugar
- 2 teaspoons instant quality coffee
- Dash of salt
- 3 tablespoons water
- 1 teaspoon light corn syrup
- ¼ teaspoon vanilla

Combine egg white, sugar, instant coffee, salt, water, and corn syrup in top of double boiler. Beat with rotary beater or electric mixer 1 minute, or until thoroughly mixed. Then place over rapidly boiling water and beat with rotary beater or at high speed of electric mixer 4 minutes, or until frosting will stand in stiff peaks. (Stir frosting up from bottom and sides of pan occasionally.) Remove from boiling water. Add vanilla and beat 1 minute, or until thick enough to spread. Makes about 2 cups, or enough to frost top of a 9-inch square or a 13- by 9-inch cake.

CREOLE FROSTING

- ½ cup butter or other shortening
- 6 cups sifted confectioners' sugar
- ¾ teaspoon vanilla
- ¼ teaspoon salt
- 3 squares unsweetened chocolate, melted
- ½ cup (about) brewed quality coffee

Cream butter; add part of the sugar gradually, blending after each addition. Add vanilla, salt, and chocolate; mix well. Add remaining sugar, alternately with coffee, until of right consistency to spread, beating after each addition until smooth. Makes 3½ cups frosting, or enough to frost two 9-inch cake layers or a 9- or 10-inch tube cake.

MOCHA BUTTER FROSTING

- ¼ cup milk
- 1 tablespoon instant quality coffee
- 1½ squares unsweetened chocolate
- ⅓ cup butter
- Dash of salt
- 1 pound sifted confectioners' sugar
- ½ teaspoon vanilla
- 2 tablespoons (about) milk

Combine ¼ cup milk, the instant coffee, and chocolate in small saucepan. Place over low heat until chocolate melts and mixture thickens, stirring constantly. Cream butter; add salt and part of the sugar gradually, blending after each addition. Add remaining sugar, alternately with chocolate mixture, beating well after each addition. Add vanilla. Gradually add about 2 tablespoons milk until mixture is of right consistency to spread. Makes about 2 cups frosting, or enough to cover tops and sides of two 8-inch layers.

COFFEE-MINT TOPPING

- 1 envelope whipped topping mix
- 2 tablespoons sugar
- 2 tablespoons instant quality coffee
- ½ cup *cold* milk
- ⅛ teaspoon mint or peppermint extract

Blend all ingredients in a small bowl with narrow bottom. Whip as directed on whipped topping mix package. Serve on ice cream, cake, or pudding. Makes about 2 cups.

CHOCO-MOCHA ICING

- 3½ cups sifted confectioners' sugar
- ⅓ cup evaporated milk
- 1 tablespoon instant quality coffee
- 1 teaspoon vanilla
- 1 package (6 ounces) semi-sweet chocolate chips
- ¼ cup butter, softened

Combine confectioners' sugar, milk, instant coffee, and vanilla in a bowl; mix thoroughly. Melt chocolate chips in a saucepan over low heat, stirring constantly. Then stir into the sugar mixture, blending well. Add the butter and beat until smooth. Makes 2⅓ cups, or enough to frost two 8-inch cake layers.

COFFEE WHIPPED CREAM

½ cup heavy cream
1 tablespoon confectioners' sugar
½ teaspoon instant quality coffee
¼ teaspoon vanilla

Combine ingredients in small bowl; chill, if desired. Beat until mixture will hold soft peaks. Use as filling for cake roll, as frosting on cakes, or as topping for puddings and other desserts. Makes about 1 cup.

COFFEE GLAZE

1 teaspoon instant quality coffee
Dash of salt
3 tablespoons milk
2½ cups sifted confectioners' sugar
¼ teaspoon vanilla

Dissolve instant coffee and salt in milk. Add confectioners' sugar and vanilla; blend. Makes about ¾ cup glaze, or enough to glaze 3 dozen cookies.

Nice to know: *For a thinner glaze, add milk, a few drops at a time, until mixture has desired consistency.*

MOCHA CREAM FROSTING

1 pound sifted confectioners' sugar
¼ cup cocoa
⅛ teaspoon salt
¼ cup butter
¼ cup vegetable shortening
6 tablespoons (about) cold brewed quality coffee*
½ teaspoon vanilla

*Or use 1 teaspoon instant quality coffee dissolved in about 6 tablespoons cold water.

Sift sugar, cocoa, and salt together. Cream butter and shortening. Gradually add part of sugar mixture, blending after each addition until light and fluffy. Add remaining sugar alternately with coffee, until of right consistency to spread, beating after each addition until smooth. Blend in vanilla. Makes about 3 cups frosting, or enough to frost tops and sides of two 9-inch layers, three 8-inch layers, two 8-inch squares, or a 9- or 10-inch tube cake.

COFFEE PRUNE FROSTING

¾ cup butter or margarine
½ teaspoon salt
½ teaspoon ground cinnamon
1 teaspoon instant quality coffee
6 cups sifted confectioners' sugar
¼ cup (about) prune juice
1 teaspoon vanilla

Cream shortening until soft and fluffy. Add salt, cinnamon, and instant coffee; beat well. Gradually add part of sugar, beating after each addition until smooth. Alternately add remaining sugar and prune juice, beating after each addition, until of right consistency to spread. Add vanilla. Makes about 3¼ cups, or enough to cover the tops and sides of three 9-inch cake layers.

RICH COFFEE FROSTING

½ cup butter
¼ teaspoon vanilla
Dash of salt
5 cups (about) sifted confectioners' sugar
2 teaspoons instant quality coffee
¼ cup hot water

Cream butter; blend in vanilla and salt. Gradually add part of sugar, blending after each addition. Dissolve instant coffee in hot water. Then alternately add coffee and remaining sugar to creamed mixture, until of right consistency to spread, beating after each addition until smooth. Makes 2½ cups, or enough to frost tops and sides of two 8-inch layers or a 9-inch tube cake, or tops of 2 dozen cupcakes.

CINNAMON-COFFEE FROSTING

¾ cup butter or margarine
½ teaspoon ground cinnamon
Dash of salt
1 tablespoon instant quality coffee
2 teaspoons vanilla
6 cups sifted confectioners' sugar
5 tablespoons (about) milk

Cream butter; blend in cinnamon, salt, coffee, and vanilla. Then add sugar alternately with milk until of right consistency to spread, beating after each addition until smooth. Makes 3½ cups, or enough to frost three 9-inch layers, four 8-inch layers, or 3 dozen cupcakes.

COFFEE TOPPING

½ cup *cold* milk
½ teaspoon vanilla
1 tablespoon instant quality coffee
2 tablespoons sugar
1 envelope whipped topping mix

Combine ingredients in a deep narrow-bottom bowl. Whip with rotary beater or at high speed of electric mixer until topping peaks. Then continue beating until topping is light, fluffy, and fully whipped—about 2 minutes longer. Makes about 2 cups.

Nice to know: *Any leftover topping may be covered and stored in the refrigerator. If desired, whip before serving, adding a little cold milk if topping seems too thick.*

DE LUXE COFFEE GLAZE

3 cups unsifted confectioners' sugar
2 tablespoons butter, melted
¼ cup cold brewed quality coffee*
2 teaspoons vanilla

*Or use 1 teaspoon instant quality coffee dissolved in ¼ cup water.

Measure sugar into small bowl. Gradually add butter and coffee, beating until smooth. Blend in vanilla. Makes about 1⅓ cups glaze, or enough to frost top of 13- by 9-inch cake or two 13- by 9-inch pans of bar-type cookies.

Coffee Break: Vienna

These Continental delicacies are guaranteed to turn any coffee break into a long-remembered treat. Put a waltz on the record player—and bake up a memory of Old Vienna!

SPICED VIENNESE COFFEE

3 tablespoons instant quality coffee*
7 cloves
2½-inch stick of cinnamon
3½ cups boiling water*
¼ cup sugar
Whipped cream
Cinnamon

*Or use 3½ cups hot brewed quality coffee, omitting 3½ cups boiling water.

Place instant coffee in a saucepan. Put cloves and cinnamon stick in a cheesecloth bag and place in the saucepan. Pour boiling water over coffee and spices. Cover; bring almost to a boil. Remove from heat and let steep 5 to 8 minutes. Remove spice bag. Stir in sugar until dissolved. Garnish each serving with whipped cream. Sprinkle with cinnamon and serve at once. Makes 3½ cups, or 5 servings, about 6 ounces each.

VIENNESE CAFÉ AU LAIT

Prepare Café au Lait (page 224) or Quick Café au Lait (page 224). Then, in authentic Viennese style, top each serving with a dollop of unsweetened whipped cream.

LINZER COOKIES

- ½ cup butter
- ¼ cup granulated sugar
- 1 egg
- 1 teaspoon vanilla
- ¼ teaspoon almond extract
- ½ teaspoon salt
- 1¼ cups sifted cake flour
- ¾ cup dry bread crumbs
- 1 cup very finely ground blanched almonds*
- Confectioners' sugar
- ¾ cup red raspberry jam

*Sift ground almonds to remove any large pieces.

Cream butter until softened. Gradually add granulated sugar, creaming until light and fluffy. Add egg and beat well. Stir in flavorings and salt. Add flour, bread crumbs, and almonds; stir until well blended.

Roll out half of the dough 1/16 inch thick on a board which has been lightly dusted with flour and then sprinkled with granulated sugar. Cut into round cookies, using a 3½-inch scalloped cutter. Cut a hole in the center of half of the cookies, using a plain 1½-inch round cutter. Roll and cut remaining dough in same way.

Place cookies on lightly greased baking sheets. Bake in moderate oven (375° F.) about 7 minutes. Remove from sheet and cool on racks. Sift confectioners' sugar over cookies that have holes in the centers. Spread about 1 tablespoon jam over the bottom of the whole cookies and top with sugar-sprinkled cookies; press together. Makes 1 dozen double cookies.

COCONUT FILBERT COFFEE RING

- ¼ cup firmly packed brown sugar
- ¼ cup chopped filberts
- 1 cup packaged grated coconut
- 2 cups sifted all-purpose flour
- 2½ teaspoons double-acting baking powder
- 1 teaspoon salt
- ⅓ cup granulated sugar
- ⅓ cup shortening
- 1 egg, slightly beaten
- ⅓ cup milk
- 3 tablespoons butter, melted
- 1 cup sifted confectioners' sugar
- 1 tablespoon (about) hot milk

Combine brown sugar, nuts, and ¾ cup of the coconut, mixing thoroughly; set aside. Sift together flour, baking powder, salt, and granulated sugar. Cut in the shortening. Combine egg and milk. Add to flour mixture and stir until soft dough is formed.

Knead 30 seconds on lightly floured board. Roll into an 18- by 9-inch rectangle. Brush with part of the melted butter. Spread with coconut mixture. Roll as for jelly roll. Wet edge to seal. Bring the ends together to form a ring.

Place on ungreased baking sheet. With scissors, cut 1-inch slices almost through the ring. Turn each slice cut-side up, pointing the outer edges. Brush with remaining melted butter. Bake in hot oven (400° F.) for 20 to 25 minutes. Combine confectioners' sugar and hot milk. Place hot coffee ring on rack and drizzle with glaze. Sprinkle with remaining ¼ cup coconut. Makes 8 servings.

DOBOS TORTE

- ¾ cup sifted cake flour
- ¾ teaspoon double-acting baking powder
- ¼ teaspoon salt
- 4 eggs (at room temperature)
- ¾ cup sugar
- 1 teaspoon vanilla
- 6 eggs
- 1 cup sugar
- 3 squares unsweetened chocolate, melted
- ¾ cup butter
- ⅓ cup sugar

Sift together flour, baking powder, and salt. Beat 4 eggs at highest speed in electric mixer or with rotary beater until light and fluffy—about 3 minutes. Add ¾ cup sugar gradually and beat until mixture becomes fluffy, thick, and light in color. Gradually fold in flour mixture and vanilla.

Pour about 1⅔ cups batter into each of three 8-inch layer pans, which have been greased on bottoms and sides and lined on bottoms with wax paper. Bake in hot oven (400° F.) for 10 minutes. Loosen cakes around edges, turn out onto cake rack, and cool 10 minutes. Then cut warm layers horizontally to make 6 thin layers.

Beat 6 eggs with 1 cup sugar in the top of a double boiler. Then cook over gently boiling water, stirring constantly, until mixture is thickened—about 10 minutes. Pour into a mixing bowl and add the melted chocolate. Beat until cool; then beat in the butter. Chill slightly in the refrigerator until of spreading consistency. Spread a thin layer of frosting, about ⅓ cup, on top of 5 of the layers of cake. Then stack the 6 layers, leaving top unfrosted. Frost sides of the cake with remaining frosting.

Then place ⅓ cup sugar in a skillet; cook and stir over low heat until sugar melts and turns brown. Swirl the browned sugar over the top of the cake to glaze. Mark the cake into 12 portions while the glaze is still warm. Cover and store in refrigerator 4 to 6 hours or overnight. Makes 12 servings.

CHOCOLATE ALMOND TORTE

- 1 package (4 ounces) sweet cooking chocolate
- ⅓ cup water
- ¾ cup sugar
- ⅛ teaspoon salt
- 2 eggs, beaten
- 1 teaspoon vanilla
- 1 package (4 ounces) sweet cooking chocolate
- ¾ cup blanched almonds
- 1½ cups dry bread crumbs
- 1½ teaspoons double-acting baking powder
- 1 teaspoon ground cinnamon
- ¼ teaspoon salt
- ¾ cup butter
- 1½ cups sugar
- 5 eggs
- 2 cups heavy cream
- Sifted confectioners' sugar
- Toasted slivered almonds

First, prepare the filling. Melt 1 package chocolate in ⅓ cup water in a saucepan over low heat. Add ¾ cup sugar and ⅛ teaspoon salt and continue stirring over low heat until sugar is dissolved. Remove from heat. Slowly stir a small amount of chocolate mixture into the 2 eggs; then add eggs to chocolate mixture in pan. Cook over low heat until mixture begins to thicken slightly, about 2 minutes. Remove from heat and pour into large bowl. Chill. Then stir in vanilla.

Meanwhile, prepare the torte. Grind 1 package chocolate and the almonds together in a food grinder. Combine bread crumbs, baking powder, cinnamon, and salt. In a large bowl, cream butter until soft. Gradually add 1½ cups sugar, beating until light and fluffy. Add 5 eggs, one at a time, beating well after each addition. Stir in chocolate and almonds. Gradually add bread-crumb mixture, about ⅓ cup at a time, blending well after each addition.

Generously grease and flour bottoms and sides of four 9-inch layer pans. Line bottoms of pans with paper and grease the paper. Spread 1¼ cups batter in each pan. (If oven is small or only 2 pans are available, half the batter may be held and baked when the first two layers are out of the oven.) Bake in moderate oven (350° F.) 20 to 25 minutes, until layers spring back when lightly pressed with finger. Cool in pans 5 minutes; then loosen around edges with knife, invert on a rack, and tap bottom of pan to release. Finish cooling on a rack, about 20 minutes.

While layers are cooling, whip 2 cups heavy cream to soft peaks and fold into the chilled filling. Then place one layer right side up on a plate and spread with about 1⅓ cups filling. Repeat with remaining layers. Cover torte with cake cover and store overnight in the refrigerator. Just before serving, sprinkle top of cake with confectioners' sugar and toasted almonds. Makes about 16 servings.

COCONUT PUDDING TORTE

1 package (3¼ ounces) vanilla or coconut cream pudding and pie filling mix
1½ cups milk
⅔ cup butter, softened
2¼ cups sifted confectioners' sugar
⅛ teaspoon almond extract
½ cup very finely chopped pecans
2 cups packaged grated coconut, toasted
24 ladyfingers, split
¼ cup orange juice

Prepare pie filling according to package directions, using only 1½ cups milk. Cream butter until light and fluffy; alternately add sugar and pie filling. Blend in almond extract, pecans, and coconut.

Line an 8-inch square dish or pan with two layers of wax paper, allowing paper to extend 2 inches over rim of pan. Sprinkle ladyfingers with orange juice. Line sides and bottom of pan with some of the ladyfingers. Pour about a third of the pie filling mixture into pan. Make another layer of ladyfingers;

pour half of the remaining filling over them. Then add a final layer of ladyfingers and filling.

Chill thoroughly—at least 4 hours. To serve, carefully lift torte onto serving platter, using paper tabs. Then slide paper from underneath. Garnish with whipped cream, if desired. Makes 12 large or 18 small servings.

COCONUT PEACH KÜCHEN

1¼ cups sifted cake flour
¾ teaspoon double-acting baking powder
½ teaspoon salt
1 tablespoon granulated sugar
6 tablespoons cold shortening
2½ tablespoons (about) cold water
2⅓ cups sliced fresh peaches*
Lemon juice (optional)
¼ cup firmly packed brown sugar
2 tablespoons cake flour
¼ teaspoon ground cinnamon
2 tablespoons butter or margarine, softened
1⅓ cups (about) flaked coconut
¼ cup granulated sugar
Dash of salt
1 egg, well beaten
2 tablespoons light cream

*Or use 2 cups (1-pound 13-ounce can) drained sliced cling peaches.

Sift together 1¼ cups flour, baking powder, ½ teaspoon salt, and 1 tablespoon granulated sugar. Cut in shortening until pieces are about the size of small peas. Add water, a small amount at a time, mixing lightly with a fork after each addition. (Mix and handle pastry as little as possible.) Wrap in wax paper and chill thoroughly.

Then roll chilled pastry into a 9-inch square on a lightly floured board. Line an 8-inch square pan with pastry, allowing it to extend up sides of pan. Arrange peaches in rows on pastry. Sprinkle with lemon juice. Combine brown sugar, 2 tablespoons flour, and the cinnamon. Add softened butter and mix with a fork until mixture is of crumblike consistency. Sprinkle over peaches. Bake in a hot oven (400° F.) for 20 minutes.

Meanwhile, combine coconut, ¼ cup granulated sugar, a dash of salt, egg, and light cream. Remove pastry from oven and sprinkle with coconut mixture. Bake an additional 20 minutes. Serve warm with plain or whipped cream, if desired. Makes 9 servings.

CHOCOLATE DROPS

(German name: Schokoladeplatzchen)

- 3 egg whites
- ⅛ teaspoon salt
- ½ cup sugar
- ¾ cup (4 ounces) grated blanched almonds
- 1 package (4 ounces) sweet cooking chocolate, grated

Beat egg whites with salt until stiff, shiny peaks will form. Gradually add sugar, beating constantly. When all sugar is added, beat 2 minutes longer. Fold in grated almonds and chocolate. Drop by teaspoonfuls onto well-greased baking sheets. Bake in very slow oven (275° F.) 35 to 40 minutes or until dry. Remove from baking sheets at once. Makes 4 dozen cookies.

APRICOT SURPRISE COFFEE CAKE

- ½ cup chopped cooked dried apricots
- ½ cup drained canned crushed pineapple
- ¼ cup sugar
- ¼ teaspoon grated orange rind
- 1½ tablespoons orange juice
- ⅓ cup flaked coconut
- 1½ cups sifted all-purpose flour
- 2 teaspoons double-acting baking powder
- ¾ teaspoon salt
- ½ cup sugar
- ⅓ cup shortening
- 1 egg, well beaten
- ¾ cup milk

Combine apricots, pineapple, and ¼ cup sugar in saucepan. Cook and stir over low heat 3 minutes or until clear. Cool. Add rind, juice, and coconut.

Sift together flour, baking powder, salt, and ½ cup sugar. Cut in shortening. Combine egg and milk. Add to flour mixture and stir only until all flour is dampened.

Spread ⅔ of the batter in greased 9-inch pie pan. Alternate tablespoonfuls of fruit mixture and remaining batter on top. Run spatula in a wide zigzag through batter to marble slightly. Bake in hot oven (400° F.) about 30 minutes. Serve warm. Makes 8 servings.

Nice to know: *Other fruit fillings, puréed fruit, jam, or a cottage* *cheese filling may be substituted for the fruit mixture in the Surprise Coffee Cake.*

GUGELHÜPF

½ cup milk
½ cup sugar
½ teaspoon salt
¼ cup margarine
1 package active dry yeast
¼ cup warm water
2 eggs, beaten
3 cups unsifted all-purpose flour
½ teaspoon grated lemon rind
½ teaspoon almond extract
2 tablespoons dry bread crumbs
14 to 16 whole blanched almonds
½ cup raisins
2 tablespoons chopped almonds
2 to 4 tablespoons chopped candied fruit

Scald milk; then combine with sugar, salt, and margarine in a mixing bowl. Cool to lukewarm.

Sprinkle yeast over warm water; stir until dissolved. Then add yeast mixture, eggs, flour, lemon rind, and almond extract to milk mixture. Beat at low speed in electric mixer until ingredients are moistened. Then beat at medium speed for 2 minutes, or until mixture is well blended. Cover; let rise in warm place, free from drafts, until doubled in bulk—about 1 hour.

Sprinkle bread crumbs over sides and bottom of well-greased 2-quart gugelhüpf pan, 9-inch tube pan, or fancy mold with tube. Arrange whole almonds on bottom.

Stir batter down. Add raisins, chopped almonds, and candied fruit. Beat thoroughly. Carefully spoon into pan. Cover; let rise in warm place, free from drafts, until doubled in bulk—about 1 hour. Bake in moderate oven (375° F.) 35 minutes. Remove from pan immediately. Serve warm or cooled.

"Coffee and . . ."
Special: Bakers' Dozens

Danish pastry, coffee cakes, sweet breads, rolls, fruit-and-nut treats, sticky buns, küchen . . . just reciting the names is enough to make your mouth water. Do better than recite them—browse through these recipes, make a choice (if you can!) and make a batch of goodies this very day. You'll be amply rewarded by the look your family wears when they sniff those heavenly, hot-from-the-oven baking smells.

CARAMEL CRUMB CAKE

- 1/3 cup firmly packed brown sugar
- 2 tablespoons biscuit mix
- 2 teaspoons instant quality coffee
- 1 teaspoon ground cinnamon
- 2 tablespoons butter
- 1/4 cup chopped walnuts
- 1 1/3 cups biscuit mix
- 1/2 cup granulated sugar
- 3 tablespoons vegetable shortening
- 1 egg
- 2 teaspoons instant quality coffee
- 3/4 cup milk
- 1 teaspoon vanilla

Combine brown sugar, 2 tablespoons biscuit mix, 2 teaspoons instant coffee, and cinnamon. Cut in butter with pastry blender or two knives. Stir in walnuts. Set aside to use as topping.

Combine 1 1/3 cups biscuit mix, granulated sugar, vegetable shortening, egg, 2 teaspoons instant coffee, and 1/4 cup of the milk. Beat 1 minute, or until batter is smooth. Stir in 1/2 cup milk and vanilla; beat 1/2 minute longer. Pour into a greased and floured 8-inch square pan or 9-inch layer pan. Sprinkle topping evenly on batter. Bake in moderate oven (350° F.) 35 to 40 minutes. Serve warm. Makes 9 servings.

SPICY RAISIN BISCUITS

- ⅓ cup raisins
- 1½ cups biscuit mix
- ¼ teaspoon ground cinnamon
- ¼ teaspoon ground nutmeg
- 2 tablespoons sugar
- 1 egg, beaten
- ⅓ cup cooled brewed quality coffee
- 2 tablespoons heavy cream
- 2 tablespoons sugar

Cover raisins with boiling water and let stand 5 minutes; drain and cool. Combine biscuit mix, spices, and 2 tablespoons sugar. Combine egg and coffee; add to dry ingredients. Stir in raisins. Pat out ½ inch thick on lightly floured board. Cut with small biscuit cutter. Bake on ungreased baking sheet in hot oven (450° F.) 10 to 12 minutes. Whip cream with fork and add 2 tablespoons sugar. Brush over biscuits. Place under broiler just until browned and glazed. Makes about 18 small biscuits.

CHOCOLATE PECAN MUFFINS

- 1¾ cups sifted cake flour
- 2 teaspoons double-acting baking powder
- ½ teaspoon salt
- ½ cup sugar
- 3 tablespoons cocoa
- ⅓ cup butter or other shortening
- ½ cup chopped pecans
- 1 egg, beaten
- ⅔ cup milk

Sift together flour, baking powder, salt, sugar, and cocoa. Cut in shortening until very fine. Mix in pecans. Combine the egg and milk; add all at once to flour mixture, stirring just to moisten flour.

Spoon batter into small greased muffin pans, filling each ⅔ full. Bake in hot oven (400° F.) 20 minutes. Makes about 2 dozen small muffins.

COCONUT MUFFINS

- 2 cups sifted all-purpose flour
- 2 teaspoons double-acting baking powder
- ½ cup sugar
- 1 teaspoon salt
- 1 cup flaked or packaged grated coconut
- 1 egg, well beaten
- 1 cup milk
- ¼ cup butter or other shortening, melted

Sift together flour, baking powder, sugar, and salt. Add coconut. Combine egg and milk; add to flour mixture. Then add butter and mix only enough to dampen flour. Spoon into greased muffin pans, filling each about ⅔ full. Bake in hot oven (425° F.) 20 to 25 minutes. Makes 12 muffins.

MINCEMEAT BRAN MUFFINS

- ¾ cup sifted all-purpose flour
- 2½ teaspoons double-acting baking powder
- ¼ teaspoon salt
- 2 tablespoons sugar
- 1 egg, beaten
- ½ cup milk
- 3 tablespoons shortening, melted
- ¾ cup moist mincemeat*
- 1½ cups 40% bran flakes

*If condensed mincemeat is used, cook as directed on package. If no directions are given on package, place mincemeat in saucepan, add 1½ cups water for each 9-ounce package, and cook over medium heat for 1 minute; then measure ¾ cup.

Sift together flour, baking powder, salt, and sugar. Combine egg and milk; add to flour mixture. Then add shortening and mix only enough to dampen flour. Fold in mincemeat and cereal. Fill greased muffin pans ⅔ full. Bake in hot oven (425° F.) 15 to 20 minutes. Makes 12 medium muffins.

Nice to know: *These muffins may be prepared at night and baked the next morning. Prepare muffin batter as directed and pour into greased muffin pans. Wrap pans in dampened cheesecloth and then in wax paper; store overnight in refrigerator. Remove pans from refrigerator about 15 minutes before baking, or while oven is heating. Bake as directed.*

APRICOT BREAD

- ⅔ cup dried apricots
- Hot water
- 1⅓ cups milk, scalded
- ⅔ cup Post Grape-Nuts Cereal
- 1 egg, well beaten
- 3 tablespoons shortening, melted and cooled
- 2 cups sifted all-purpose flour
- 2½ teaspoons double-acting baking powder
- 1 teaspoon salt
- ⅔ cup firmly packed light brown sugar

Cover apricots with hot water, bring to a boil, and cook 7 to

8 minutes, or about half as long as directed on package. (This will prevent apricots from being too soft in bread.) Drain and cool. Then cut into pieces.

Pour scalded milk over cereal in mixing bowl; stir in apricots. Let stand to cool. Then add egg and shortening; mix well. Mix flour, baking powder, salt, and sugar. Add to cereal mixture and mix only enough to dampen all flour. Pour into a greased 8- by 4-inch loaf pan. Bake in moderate oven (350° F.) 1 hour or until cake tester comes out clean. Cool about 10 minutes. Remove from pan; finish cooling on rack. When bread is cool, wrap in wax paper, transparent Saran, or aluminum foil. For best slicing and mellowing of flavors, chill bread overnight. Makes 1 loaf.

Nice to know: *If desired, 1 cup chopped raisins or currants may be substituted for the cooked apricots. Or fruit may be omitted from bread entirely.*

BUTTERSCOTCH NUT PINWHEELS

- 2 cups sifted all-purpose flour
- 2½ teaspoons double-acting baking powder
- ¾ teaspoon salt
- 5 tablespoons shortening
- ¾ cup (about) milk
- 2 tablespoons butter or margarine
- ⅓ cup firmly packed brown sugar
- 1 tablespoon butter or margarine
- 1 tablespoon water
- 2 tablespoons brown sugar
- ½ cup broken nuts

Sift flour, baking powder, and salt into mixing bowl. Cut in shortening; add milk and stir with fork until soft dough is formed. Knead 30 seconds on lightly floured board. Roll into 12- by 10-inch rectangle, ¼ inch thick. Cream together butter and sugar; spread on dough. Roll as for jelly roll and cut in 1-inch slices.

Melt butter in 8-inch square pan; add water and sugar. Cook over low heat until mixture bubbles, stirring constantly. Remove from heat and sprinkle nuts over mixture. Place rolls in pan, cut-side down. Bake in hot oven (400° F.) 40 minutes or until golden brown. Remove from pan at once. Makes 10 to 12 pinwheels.

CHERRY-ALMOND RING

2½ cups sifted cake flour
3 teaspoons double-acting baking powder
1 teaspoon salt
½ cup shortening
1 egg, slightly beaten
⅓ cup milk
¼ cup butter, melted
⅓ cup sugar
1 teaspoon ground cinnamon
½ cup chopped blanched almonds
¼ cup coarsely chopped maraschino cherries
1 cup sifted confectioners' sugar
2 tablespoons (about) milk

Sift together flour, baking powder, and salt. Cut in shortening. Combine egg and ⅓ cup milk, add to flour mixture, and stir until a soft dough is formed.

Turn out on well-floured board and knead 20 turns. Roll into a 12- by 7-inch rectangle. Brush with part of the melted butter. Add rest of melted butter to sugar, cinnamon, and almonds; sprinkle over dough. Then sprinkle with the cherries. Roll from wide side, wetting edges to seal. Cut in 12 slices. Pinch each slice at sealed edge to form a slight point.

Arrange slices in circle on greased baking sheet with sides of points touching, leaving about a 4-inch circle in center. Pat lightly to shape sides. Bake in hot oven (400° F.) 20 to 25 minutes. Remove to plate and let cool 5 minutes. Make glaze by combining sifted confectioners' sugar and about 2 tablespoons milk; spread on the ring. Serve warm.

Pecan-Spice Ring: Prepare Cherry-Almond Ring, sifting ¼ teaspoon ground nutmeg with flour mixture, substituting ½ cup coarsely chopped pecans for the almonds, and using 1 to 2 tablespoons maraschino cherry juice instead of milk in the glaze, if desired. Garnish with pecan halves and maraschino cherries, if desired.

COCONUT CURLICUES

2 tablespoons butter, softened
¼ cup firmly packed brown sugar
2 cups sifted all-purpose flour
2½ teaspoons double-acting baking powder
¾ teaspoon salt
5 tablespoons shortening
¾ cup (about) milk
2 tablespoons butter, softened
2 tablespoons brown sugar
½ cup packaged grated coconut*

*Or use ¾ cup flaked coconut.

Prepare muffin pans by placing ½ teaspoon butter and 1 teaspoon brown sugar in each of 12 sections of pans.

Sift together flour, baking powder, and salt. Cut in shortening. Add milk and stir with fork until soft dough is formed (about 20 strokes). Knead on lightly floured board 30 seconds. Pat or roll lightly into 12- by 9-inch rectangle about ⅛ inch thick. Spread with 2 tablespoons butter; sprinkle with 2 tablespoons brown sugar and the coconut. Roll from wide side, wetting edges to seal. Cut in 12 slices and place in prepared muffin pans. Bake in hot oven (450° F.) 12 to 15 minutes. Remove from pans immediately. Makes 12 curlicues.

DATE NUT LOAF

- 1 cup hot water
- ½ teaspoon baking soda
- 1½ cups finely cut dates
- 2¼ cups sifted all-purpose flour
- 2 teaspoons double-acting baking powder
- ¾ teaspoon salt
- ¾ cup firmly packed brown sugar
- ½ cup chopped walnuts
- 1 egg, well beaten
- 2 tablespoons shortening, melted

Add hot water and baking soda to dates; let stand while mixing other ingredients. Sift together flour, baking powder, salt, and sugar. Add nuts. Add egg and shortening to date mixture; then add to flour mixture. Mix until all flour is dampened. Pour into greased 9- by 5-inch loaf pan. Bake in moderate oven (350° F.) about 1 hour or until cake tester inserted near center comes out clean. Cool 10 minutes. Remove from pan and finish cooling on rack. Store overnight before slicing. Makes 1 loaf.

BANANA BREAD

- 1½ cups sifted all-purpose flour
- 2½ teaspoons double-acting baking powder
- ¼ teaspoon salt
- ⅔ cup firmly packed light brown sugar
- 2 cups crisp oat flakes
- 1 cup mashed ripe banana
- ⅓ cup orange juice
- 1 egg, slightly beaten
- ⅓ cup shortening, melted and slightly cooled
- ¼ cup coarsely chopped nuts

Sift flour, baking powder, salt, and sugar together into bowl. Add cereal, banana, orange juice, egg, and shortening. Blend just until flour is dampened. Stir in nuts. Pour into a well-greased 9- by 5-inch loaf pan. Bake in a moderate oven (350° F.) 60 to 65 minutes. Cool in pan about 10 minutes; then turn out onto rack to finish cooling. When bread is cool, wrap in wax paper, transparent Saran, or aluminum foil. For best slicing and for mellowing of flavor, chill bread 12 hours or overnight. Makes 1 loaf.

Nice to know: *Bread may be frozen, if desired.*

CRUMB-TOP COFFEE CAKE

- 1¼ cups sifted cake flour
- 2 teaspoons double-acting baking powder
- ½ teaspoon salt
- ¼ cup butter
- 1 cup sugar
- 2 egg yolks, well beaten
- ½ cup milk
- 2 egg whites, stiffly beaten
- ¼ teaspoon vanilla
- Crumb Topping (see below)

Sift together flour, baking powder, and salt. Cream butter until soft, add sugar, and cream until light and fluffy. Add egg yolks and beat thoroughly. Then add flour mixture alternately with milk, beating after each addition until smooth. Fold in stiffly beaten egg whites; then mix in vanilla.

Pour batter into well-greased 9-inch square pan. Bake in moderate oven (350° F.) about 30 minutes or until top is lightly browned and cake is just firm in center. Gently remove cake from oven, quickly sprinkle with Crumb Topping, and return to oven. Bake about 15 minutes longer or until cake tester comes out clean. Serve warm.

Crumb Topping: Sift together ½ cup sifted all-purpose flour, ½ cup granulated sugar, 1½ teaspoons ground cinnamon, and ¼ teaspoon salt. Add ½ cup firmly packed brown sugar. Cut in ¼ cup butter with a pastry blender or two knives until mixture forms crumbs.

ALMOND-FILLED GEMS

1 cup ground almonds*
2 tablespoons maple-blended syrup
1 tablespoon butter, melted
Sliced bread or brown-and-serve rolls

*Grate almonds with a hand grater or place a few at a time in a blender and blend at high speed until finely ground.

Combine almonds, syrup, and butter; blend. Use as a filling to spread between sectioned brown-and-serve rolls, for turnovers of bread slices, or for pinwheel rolls made of bread slices; then bake as directed on package or heat thoroughly.

BROWN 'N' SERVE STICKIES

8 brown-and-serve clover-leaf rolls
⅓ cup maple-blended syrup
1 teaspoon orange rind
2 tablespoons orange juice
3 tablespoons butter, melted
¼ cup chopped nuts
¼ cup maple-blended syrup

Place rolls in shallow pan. Combine ⅓ cup syrup, orange rind and juice, butter, and nuts; mix well. Pour over the rolls. Bake in a hot oven (400° F.) 15 minutes; then baste with ¼ cup syrup and continue to bake until golden brown, about 5 more minutes. Makes 8 Stickies.

MAPLE-GLAZED COCONUT BUNS

¾ cup maple-blended syrup
⅓ cup butter, melted
⅔ cup flaked coconut
½ cup chopped pecans
1 package (1 dozen) brown-and-serve clover-leaf rolls

Combine ½ cup of the syrup and 2 tablespoons melted butter and pour into an 8-inch square pan. Place in hot oven (400° F.) for 5 to 8 minutes or until bubbly. Sprinkle coconut and pecans over the syrup mixture. Meanwhile, combine remaining syrup and butter; dip rolls into mixture, coating all sides. Arrange rolls on coconut mixture. Return to oven and bake 20 to 25 minutes, or until browned. Makes 1 dozen.

CHOCOLATE-FLECK NUT BREAD

- 3 cups biscuit mix
- ¾ cup sugar
- 1 egg, beaten
- ¾ cup milk
- ½ cup orange juice
- ¾ cup chopped walnuts
- 1 package (4 ounces) sweet cooking chocolate, chopped (about 1 cup)
- 2 teaspoons grated orange rind (optional)

Combine biscuit mix and sugar in large bowl. Then combine beaten egg, milk, and orange juice. Add to biscuit mix. Beat vigorously about 30 seconds. Stir in nuts, chocolate, and orange rind. Spoon into a well-greased 9- by 5-inch loaf pan. Bake in moderate oven (350° F.) 55 to 60 minutes. Let stand in pan about 15 minutes. Then turn out on rack to cool thoroughly. Wrap in aluminum foil or transparent Saran and allow to mellow for a day before slicing. Makes 1 loaf.

CHOCOLATE PUFFS

- 9 refrigerator biscuits
- 1 package (4 ounces) sweet cooking chocolate
- Fat for frying
- Confectioners' sugar (optional)

Cut each biscuit in half. Place 1 square of chocolate in the center of each half. Bring edges of dough over chocolate and pinch together tightly. Fry in hot fat (375° F.) until golden brown—about 2 minutes. If desired, roll in confectioners' sugar. Makes 18 puffs.

MOLASSES CORN STICKS

- 1 package corn muffin mix
- Molasses
- Water

Prepare corn muffin mix according to package directions, using half molasses and half water for the water specified on package. Fill well-greased corn stick or muffin pans ⅔ full. Bake in a hot oven (400° F.) 8 to 10 minutes for sticks or 20 minutes for muffins. Makes about 12 sticks or 16 muffins.

COFFEE CRUNCH KÜCHEN

2¼ cups unsifted all-purpose flour
2 cups firmly packed brown sugar
1 cup 40% bran flakes
3 teaspoons double-acting baking powder
Dash of salt
½ cup vegetable shortening
½ cup butter
½ cup brewed quality coffee
½ cup evaporated milk
⅛ teaspoon baking soda
2 eggs, beaten
1 teaspoon ground cinnamon
½ cup chopped pecans

Mix flour, brown sugar, cereal, baking powder, and salt. Cut in shortening and butter with pastry blender or two knives. Measure 1 cup of the mixture; set aside to use as topping.

Combine coffee, milk, and baking soda and add to remaining flour mixture; blend thoroughly. Stir in eggs. Pour into greased and floured 13- by 9-inch pan.

Add cinnamon to mixture reserved for topping. Sprinkle on batter; then sprinkle with pecans. Bake in moderate oven (375° F.) 30 to 35 minutes. Serve warm. Makes 15 or 16 servings.

Nice to know: *Baked küchen may be cooled, wrapped in aluminum foil, and frozen. Before serving, thaw and reheat in moderate oven.*

Party-Pretty Pies

Love your husband? Think those kids of yours are pretty wonderful? Tell them so—bake a pie for dinner tonight. And as long as you're at it, why not splurge and invite a guest or two? These pies are pretty enough to make any meal a party, delicious enough to serve to your very favorite people. The flavor secret is coffee, the loving homemade touch is yours!

Bear in mind: Pies with cream fillings, or topped with whipped cream, must be stored in the refrigerator. This applies to left-overs—if you manage to have any!—as well as to freshly made pie. It's safe, though, to take the pie from the refrigerator half an hour ahead of time, so it won't be too icy cold, and thus give flavors a chance to deepen and mellow before the pie comes to the table.

FROSTY COFFEE PIE

- **1 package (3 ounces) orange flavor gelatin**
- **½ cup sugar**
- **2 tablespoons instant quality coffee**
- **1¼ cups boiling water**
- **1 pint vanilla or coffee ice cream**
- **1 baked 8-inch pie shell, cooled**

Dissolve gelatin, sugar, and instant coffee in boiling water. Add ice cream by spoonfuls, stirring until melted. Then chill until thickened—15 to 25 minutes. Pour into pie shell. Chill until firm—20 to 30 minutes. Garnish with whipped cream, if desired.

Frosty Mocha Pie: Prepare Frosty Coffee Pie, substituting chocolate ice cream for the vanilla ice cream.

CHOCOLATE COFFEE PIE

1 package (4 ounces) chocolate pudding and pie filling mix
1½ to 2 tablespoons instant quality coffee
2 tablespoons sugar
1½ cups milk
½ cup heavy cream
1 baked 8-inch pastry shell or graham cracker crust
Chopped nuts (optional)

Combine pie filling mix, instant coffee, sugar, and milk in saucepan. Cook and stir over medium heat until mixture comes to a *full* boil. Remove from heat. Cover surface with wax paper and cool about 1 hour. Whip cream; fold into pie filling. Pour into cooled pie shell. Chill thoroughly. Sprinkle with chopped nuts, if desired.

CHOCOLATE ANGEL PIE AU CAFÉ

2 egg whites
⅛ teaspoon salt
⅛ teaspoon cream of tartar
½ cup sugar
½ cup finely chopped walnuts or pecans
½ teaspoon vanilla
1 package (4 ounces) sweet cooking chocolate
3 tablespoons water
1 teaspoon instant quality coffee
1 teaspoon vanilla
1 cup heavy cream

Combine egg whites, salt, and cream of tartar in mixing bowl. Beat until foamy throughout. Add sugar, 2 tablespoons at a time, beating after each addition until sugar is blended. Then continue beating until mixture will stand in stiff, shiny peaks. Fold in nuts and ½ teaspoon vanilla and blend. Spoon into lightly greased 8-inch pie pan and make a nestlike shell, building sides up ½ inch above edge of pan. Bake in slow oven (300° F.) 50 to 55 minutes. Cool.

Place chocolate and water in saucepan over low heat. Stir until chocolate is melted. Cool until thickened. Then add instant coffee and 1 teaspoon vanilla. Whip cream. Fold chocolate mixture into whipped cream. Pile into meringue shell. Chill about 2 hours before serving. Makes 6 to 8 servings.

For a refrigerator cake, substitute the following for the meringue shell. Line an 8- by 4-inch loaf pan or an ice cube tray with wax paper. Line bottom and sides with 12 ladyfinger halves or strips of sponge cake. Pile chocolate mixture into pan. Garnish with additional ladyfinger halves, if desired. Chill about 2 hours before serving.

FROSTY COFFEE PUDDING PIE

- 1 package (3¼ ounces) vanilla pudding and pie filling mix
- 1 envelope (1 tablespoon) unflavored gelatin
- 2 teaspoons instant quality coffee
- 1½ cups cold water
- 1 pint vanilla or coffee ice cream
- 1 baked 9-inch pie shell, cooled

Combine pie filling mix, gelatin, and coffee in 2-quart saucepan. Add water, mixing well. Cook and stir over medium heat until mixture comes to a *full* boil. Remove from heat and let stand 5 minutes, stirring once or twice. Then add ice cream by spoonfuls, stirring until melted. Spoon into pie shell. Chill until firm—20 to 25 minutes. Garnish with whipped cream and chopped nuts or coconut, if desired.

DE LUXE MOCHA PIE

- 1¼ cups chocolate cookie crumbs
- ¼ cup sugar
- ⅓ cup softened butter
- ⅔ cup sugar
- 4 teaspoons unflavored gelatin
- ¼ teaspoon salt
- 1 tablespoon instant quality coffee
- 1 package (4 ounces) sweet cooking chocolate, cut into pieces
- 2¼ cups milk
- 1 egg yolk, slightly beaten
- 1 teaspoon vanilla
- 1 egg white
- ½ cup heavy cream

Mix crumbs, ¼ cup sugar, and butter well. Press firmly into bottom and sides of a 9-inch pie pan. Chill at least 1 hour.

Set aside 2 tablespoons sugar. Mix remaining sugar, gelatin, salt, instant coffee, and chocolate. Add milk and bring to a boil over medium heat, stirring constantly. (Beat with a rotary beater to blend well, if necessary.) Gradually stir a small amount of hot mixture into egg yolk; then stir egg mixture into hot mixture. Cook and stir over medium heat until slightly thickened, about 2 minutes. Remove from heat. Add vanilla. Chill until thickened.

Beat egg white until foamy. Gradually add reserved 2 tablespoons sugar, beating until meringue stands in peaks. Whip the cream. Beat chocolate mixture until just smooth, about 2 minutes; fold in egg white mixture and whipped cream. Spoon into crumb crust. Chill 4 hours or until firm. To serve, garnish with additional whipped cream and chocolate curls, if desired.

MARVEL COFFEE PIE

- 1 envelope unflavored gelatin
- ⅓ cup sugar
- ¼ teaspoon salt
- 1¾ cups milk
- 2 egg yolks, beaten
- 3 tablespoons instant quality coffee
- ¼ cup water
- ½ teaspoon vanilla
- 2 egg whites
- ¼ cup sugar
- 1 baked 9-inch pie shell, cooled

Mix gelatin, ⅓ cup sugar, and salt in saucepan. Stir in milk and egg yolks. Stir over medium heat until gelatin is dissolved and mixture is slightly thickened. Add instant coffee, water, and vanilla; beat until smooth. Chill until slightly thickened.

Beat egg whites until foamy throughout. Add ¼ cup sugar, 2 tablespoons at a time, beating after each addition until sugar is blended. Continue beating until mixture will form stiff, shiny peaks. Then place coffee mixture in bowl of ice and water and beat until fluffy and thick. Fold egg white mixture into coffee mixture. Spoon into pie shell. Chill until firm. Garnish with whipped cream, if desired.

COFFEE CHIFFON PIE

- 1 teaspoon unflavored gelatin
- 1 tablespoon cold water
- 1½ tablespoons instant quality coffee
- ⅔ cup hot water
- 16 marshmallows
- 1 cup heavy cream
- ½ teaspoon almond extract
- 1 baked 9-inch pie shell

Add gelatin to cold water and let stand 5 minutes. Meanwhile, combine instant coffee, hot water, and marshmallows in a saucepan. Place over low heat and stir until marshmallows are melted. Add gelatin and stir until dissolved. Chill until slightly thickened. Whip cream; fold into coffee mixture with almond extract. Pour into pie shell and chill until firm. Garnish with additional whipped cream, if desired.

COFFEE VELVET PIE

- 1 envelope unflavored gelatin
- 3 tablespoons instant quality coffee
- ⅓ cup sugar
- 2 egg yolks, beaten
- 1¾ cups milk
- 1 teaspoon vanilla
- 2 egg whites
- ¼ teaspoon salt
- ¼ cup sugar
- ½ cup heavy cream
- 1 baked 9-inch pie shell

Combine gelatin, instant coffee, and ⅓ cup sugar in saucepan. Stir in egg yolks and milk. Cook and stir over medium heat until gelatin dissolves and mixture coats a metal spoon. Remove from heat and add vanilla. Chill until slightly thickened.

Then beat egg whites with salt until foamy throughout. Add ¼ cup sugar, 2 tablespoons at a time, beating after each addition until blended. Then continue beating until mixture will stand in stiff, shiny peaks. Whip the cream. Stir gelatin mixture slightly; fold in egg white mixture and then whipped cream. Pour into pie shell. Chill until firm. Garnish with additional whipped cream, if desired.

COFFEE COCONUT MERINGUE PIE

- ½ cup sugar
- ⅓ cup unsifted all-purpose flour
- 2 tablespoons instant quality coffee
- ⅛ teaspoon salt
- 1⅓ cups water
- ⅔ cup (1 small can) evaporated milk
- 3 egg yolks, beaten
- 1 cup flaked coconut
- 2 tablespoons butter
- 1 teaspoon vanilla
- 1 baked 9-inch pie shell
- 3 egg whites
- ⅓ cup sugar
- ⅓ cup (about) flaked coconut

Combine ½ cup sugar, flour, instant coffee, and salt in saucepan. Gradually stir in water and milk. Cook gently over medium heat, stirring constantly, until thickened. Blend a little hot mixture into egg yolks; then add egg yolks to mixture in pan. Cook over low heat, stirring constantly, 2 minutes. Remove from heat and add 1 cup coconut, butter, and vanilla. Cool thoroughly; then pour into pie shell.

Beat egg whites until foamy throughout. Gradually add ⅓ cup sugar, beating until sugar is blended after each addition. Then continue beating until stiff, shiny peaks will form. Fold in remaining coconut. Spread over pie filling. Bake in hot oven (425° F.) 5 to 10 minutes or until meringue is delicately browned.

COFFEE MACAROON PIE

3 egg yolks
¼ teaspoon salt
¼ cup water
1½ cups sugar
2 teaspoons instant quality coffee
2 tablespoons butter, melted
1 teaspoon lemon juice
¼ teaspoon almond extract
1⅓ cups (about) flaked coconut
3 egg whites
1 unbaked 9-inch pie shell

Beat egg yolks and salt until thick and lemon-colored. Blend in water. Then gradually beat in sugar. Add coffee, butter, lemon juice, and almond extract. Fold in coconut. Beat egg whites until stiff, shiny peaks will form; fold into coffee mixture. Pour into pie shell. Bake in moderate oven (375° F.) 40 to 45 minutes or until knife inserted near center comes out clean. Cool before serving.

PECAN PETAL TARTS

1 package (9½ or 10 ounces) pie crust mix*
1 egg
¾ cup firmly packed brown sugar
1 tablespoon instant quality coffee
Dash of salt
1 tablespoon butter or margarine, melted
½ teaspoon vanilla
⅓ cup coarsely broken pecans

*Or prepare enough pastry for 2-crust pie.

Prepare pie crust according to package directions. Roll very thin and cut with 2-inch cookie cutter into about 42 rounds.

Place pastry rounds in bottoms of 12 muffin cups. Cut remaining rounds in half; arrange 5 halves, cut-side down, overlapping around sides in each muffin cup. Press securely to seal edges. Prick with fork. Bake in hot oven (400° F.) about 15 minutes or until lightly browned.

Meanwhile, beat egg until foamy. Thoroughly beat in sugar, coffee, salt, butter, and vanilla. Then stir in nuts.

When lightly browned, remove tart shells from oven and reduce oven temperature to moderate (350° F.). Spoon filling into hot tart shells. Then bake in moderate oven 20 minutes. Cool slightly in pan before removing. Garnish with whipped cream, if desired. Makes 1 dozen tarts.

Coffee Party: "Come for Brunch!"

"Brunch" isn't a particularly pretty word, but it conjures up all sorts of pictures: an ample meal, more interesting than either the breakfast or lunch it combines and replaces, with time to savor its pleasures. A weekend or holiday meal, prepared at leisure and served when appetites demand—it's a fine time to invite guests. Fruit, eggs, crispy bacon or sausages or ham are always welcome. And, for the crowning, festive touch, one of the delicious sweet breads or coffee cakes that follow!

COFFEE NUT BLINTZES

2 eggs
2 tablespoons salad oil
1 cup milk
⅔ cup unsifted all-purpose flour
½ teaspoon salt
4 tablespoons (about) butter or margarine
1 cup (8 ounces) cottage cheese
1 tablespoon sugar
Dash of ground cinnamon
1 egg, slightly beaten
¼ cup currants
¼ cup finely chopped almonds
1 teaspoon instant quality coffee
½ cup sour cream
2 teaspoons instant quality coffee
2 tablespoons sugar
Additional sugar

Beat eggs, oil, and milk together. Add flour and salt and beat until smooth. In a 7-inch skillet, melt about ½ teaspoon butter, or just enough to cover bottom. Add 1 tablespoon batter, turning pan quickly so batter will spread over bottom of skillet. Cook until lightly browned on one side only. Place on a platter or plate, browned side up. Continue with remaining batter, using butter as required and stacking pancakes, browned side up.

Combine cottage cheese, 1 tablespoon sugar, cinnamon, egg, currants, almonds, and 1 teaspoon instant coffee. Place

1 tablespoon of the mixture in center of browned side of each blintz. Fold two opposite sides in a little; then roll carefully from an unfolded side.

Combine sour cream, 2 teaspoons coffee, and 2 tablespoons sugar, mixing well. Set aside. Melt just enough butter in a large skillet to cover bottom. Fry blintzes until lightly browned on both sides. Sprinkle with sugar. Serve immediately, topped with sour cream mixture. Makes about 24 blintzes, enough for 8 servings, 3 blintzes each.

Nice to know: *Extra-fine granulated sugar is best for sprinkling on fried blintzes.*

BISCUIT CRULLERS

- 3 cups sifted all-purpose flour
- 4 teaspoons double-acting baking powder
- ¾ teaspoon salt
- 1 tablespoon sugar
- ⅛ teaspoon ground nutmeg
- ½ cup shortening
- ¾ cup milk
- Cinnamon and sugar, confectioners' sugar, or granulated sugar

Sift flour, baking powder, salt, sugar, and nutmeg into mixing bowl. Cut in shortening. Add milk and stir with fork until blended. Turn dough out on floured board and knead for 2 minutes. Roll out dough ½ inch thick. Cut with floured 2½-inch doughnut cutter. Pull rings to elongate slightly and twist to form figure 8's. Fry in 1 inch of hot fat (375° F.) about 5 minutes, turning to brown both sides. Drain on absorbent paper. Then roll in sugar. Makes 15 crullers.

CHEESE BISCUIT FOLD-UPS

- 2 cups sifted all-purpose flour
- 4 teaspoons double-acting baking powder
- 1 teaspoon salt
- ½ teaspoon cream of tartar
- 2 teaspoons sugar
- ½ cup shortening
- 1 cup grated sharp Cheddar cheese
- ⅔ cup milk

Sift flour, baking powder, salt, cream of tartar, and sugar into mixing bowl. Cut in shortening. Stir in ¾ cup cheese. Add milk and stir with fork until soft dough is formed. Turn out on lightly floured board. Divide dough in half. Roll half of dough ⅛ inch thick, forming a 12- by 9-inch rectangle. Cut in 3-inch squares. Place about ½ teaspoon of the remaining cheese in center of each square. Moisten two opposite corners of each square and bring together in center, overlapping slightly, and press to seal. Place on ungreased baking sheet. Repeat with remaining dough. Bake in hot oven (450° F.) 10 to 12 minutes or until golden brown. Makes 2 dozen.

BAKING POWDER BISCUITS

- 2 cups sifted all-purpose flour
- 2½ teaspoons double-acting baking powder
- ¾ teaspoon salt
- 5 tablespoons shortening
- ¾ cup (about) milk

Sift flour, baking powder, and salt into mixing bowl. Cut in shortening. Add milk and stir with fork until soft dough is formed (about 20 strokes). Turn out on lightly floured board and knead 20 turns. Pat or roll out dough ½ inch thick. Cut with floured 2-inch biscuit cutter. Place on ungreased baking sheets. Bake in a hot oven (450° F.) 12 to 15 minutes or until golden brown. Makes 14 biscuits.

Date Biscuits: Use recipe for Baking Powder Biscuits, increasing salt to 1 teaspoon and adding ¾ cup finely chopped dates after cutting in the shortening. Mix in dates thoroughly.

Marmalade Biscuits: Use recipe for Baking Powder Biscuits, increasing shortening to 6 tablespoons. Make a small indentation in top of each biscuit and fill with ½ teaspoon marmalade. Bake as directed.

Nice to know: *For more crusty biscuits, roll out dough ¼ inch thick; cut with a 2¼-inch cutter.*

RICH BISCUITS

- 2 cups sifted all-purpose flour
- 4 teaspoons double-acting baking powder
- ½ teaspoon salt
- ½ teaspoon cream of tartar
- 2 teaspoons sugar
- ½ cup shortening
- ⅔ cup milk

Sift flour, baking powder, salt, cream of tartar, and sugar into mixing bowl. Cut in shortening until mixture resembles coarse crumbs. Add milk and stir with fork until soft dough is formed. Turn out on lightly floured board and pat or roll lightly ½ inch thick. Cut with floured 2-inch biscuit cutter. Bake on ungreased baking sheet in hot oven (450° F.) 10 to 12 minutes or until golden brown. Makes 16 biscuits.

BLUEBERRY MUFFINS

1½ cups sifted cake flour
2 to 3 tablespoons sugar
1½ teaspoons double-acting baking powder
½ teaspoon salt
1 egg, well beaten
½ cup milk
¼ cup butter or shortening
¾ cup fresh or thawed, drained frozen blueberries

Sift together flour, sugar, baking powder, and salt. Combine egg and milk. Add to flour mixture along with butter. Mix *only* enough to dampen flour. Fold in blueberries. Spoon into muffin pans. Bake in hot oven (425° F.) 20 to 25 minutes or until muffins are browned. Makes 10 to 12 medium or 6 to 8 large muffins.

BRAN FLAKES MUFFIN MIX

3 cups sifted all-purpose flour
3 tablespoons plus 1 teaspoon double-acting baking powder
1 teaspoon salt
½ cup sugar
¾ cup shortening
6 cups 40% bran flakes

Sift flour with baking powder, salt, and sugar into a large bowl. Cut in shortening until mixture resembles coarse meal. Add cereal and mix well. Makes about 9 cups mix.

Place in jar or bowl; cover lightly with cloth or plate to allow circulation of air. Store in refrigerator or other very cool, dry place. Keeps well for 3 weeks.

To make 9 medium muffins: Measure 2 cups Bran Flakes Muffin Mix into bowl. Add 1 well-beaten egg and ⅔ cup milk; then mix to dampen dry ingredients. Fill greased muffin pans, each ⅔ full. Bake in hot oven (425° F.) 15 to 20 minutes.

CORN BACON MUFFINS

- 1 cup sifted all-purpose flour
- ¾ cup corn meal
- 2 teaspoons double-acting baking powder
- ¾ teaspoon salt
- 2 tablespoons sugar
- 1 egg
- ¾ cup milk
- 5 slices bacon, cut in halves

Sift together flour, corn meal, baking powder, salt, and sugar into mixing bowl. Add egg and milk. Stir until blended. (Do not overmix.) Fill greased muffin pans ⅔ full. Place a half slice bacon across top of each muffin. Bake in a hot oven (425° F.) 25 minutes or until lightly browned. Makes 10 muffins.

For corn sticks, heat greased corn stick pans; pour in batter. Bake in hot oven (450° F.) 20 minutes or until golden brown. Makes 8 large corn sticks.

FRUITED CHRISTMAS BREAD

- ½ cup chopped raisins
- ¼ cup chopped candied cherries
- ¼ cup chopped citron
- ⅓ cup sugar
- 2 tablespoons water
- 1 tablespoon lemon juice
- 4 cups sifted all-purpose flour
- 5 teaspoons double-acting baking powder
- 1½ teaspoons salt
- ¼ cup sugar
- ⅔ cup shortening
- 1½ cups (about) milk

Combine raisins, cherries, citron, ⅓ cup sugar, water, and lemon juice. Cook and stir over low heat until mixture is well blended and slightly thickened, about 5 to 8 minutes. Cool.

Sift together flour, baking powder, salt, and ¼ cup sugar into mixing bowl. Cut in shortening. Add milk and stir with a fork until a soft dough is formed. Turn out on a lightly floured board and knead 20 turns.

Divide dough in half and roll or pat each half into a triangular-shaped piece, ¼ inch thick. Trim a narrow strip from the base of each triangle. Cut each strip in half.

Place one of the triangles on a lightly greased baking sheet. Fasten 2 of the strips on the base of the triangle to form the tree trunk. Spread cooled filling evenly over entire triangle, almost to the edges; moisten edges. Place second triangle and remaining 2 strips on top and press moistened edges together.

To form the tree branches, use a sharp knife to cut 4 to 6 angular slits on each side of tree; carefully twist so that filling shows.

Bake in a hot oven (425° F.) for 20 to 25 minutes. If desired, drizzle with a confectioners' sugar glaze while bread is still warm. Makes 10 to 12 servings.

JAM WHIRL COFFEE CAKE

- 2 cups sifted all-purpose flour
- ¼ cup sugar
- 2½ teaspoons double-acting baking powder
- ¾ teaspoon salt
- ½ cup shortening
- 1 egg, well beaten
- ½ cup light cream
- ½ cup red jam

Sift together flour, sugar, baking powder, and salt into mixing bowl. Cut in shortening. Blend together egg and cream. Add to flour mixture and stir until soft dough is formed. Turn out on lightly floured board and knead ½ minute.

Spread dough evenly in a greased round 9-inch layer pan. With a floured spoon, make a pinwheel design on top of dough. Fill grooves with jam. Bake in hot oven (400° F.) 25 minutes. Serve warm. Makes 8 to 10 servings.

NOVELTY COFFEE CAKE

- 1½ cups sifted cake flour
- 1¾ teaspoons double-acting baking powder
- ½ teaspoon salt
- ¼ cup shortening
- 3 tablespoons sugar
- 1 egg
- ½ cup milk
- ½ cup sugar
- 1 teaspoon ground cinnamon
- 2 tablespoons milk
- 2 tablespoons butter, melted

Sift together flour, baking powder, and salt. Cream shortening, add 3 tablespoons sugar and cream well. Add egg and beat thoroughly. Add flour mixture, alternately with milk, beating well after each addition. Turn into greased 9-inch layer pan or 9-inch square pan and form deep ridges in batter with knife.

Sprinkle with mixture of ½ cup sugar and cinnamon. Bake in moderate oven (375° F.) 20 minutes; then pour mixture of milk and butter over top and bake 15 minutes longer. Cut in wedge-shaped pieces. Serve warm. Makes 9 servings.

Blueberry Coffee Cake: Prepare Novelty Coffee Cake, folding ⅔ cup blueberries into batter before spreading in pan.

BREAD 'N' BUTTER WAFFLES

8 to 10 bread slices
Butter
1 egg
¾ cup of milk
Dash of salt
Maple-blended syrup

Spread bread slices lightly but evenly on both sides with butter. Beat egg slightly. Add milk and salt; blend well. Dip slices of bread in egg-milk mixture quickly. Drain. Bake in moderately hot waffle iron 5 minutes or until golden brown. Serve hot with syrup. Makes 8 to 10 waffles.

Cinnamon-Nut Waffles: Use recipe for Bread 'n' Butter Waffles. Just before baking, sprinkle ground cinnamon, sugar, and chopped nuts over dipped bread slice on waffle iron.

Nice to know: *For serving a large group, stack baked waffles on cake racks and reheat in moderate oven (350° F.) 3 to 5 minutes.*

PAN-SANS

Prepare pancake batter, using a mix or recipe. Bake on hot griddle, allowing about ⅓ cup batter for each pancake. To make a Pan-San, spread one pancake with any filling given below and cover with a second pancake, in the form of a sandwich. Serve hot with butter and maple-blended syrup.

Colorado Pan-Sans: Spread with currant or other tart jelly and cover with a layer of cooked bulk sausage meat.

Apple-Nut Pan-Sans: Spread with hot spiced applesauce and sprinkle with toasted chopped pecans.

Scrambled Egg Pan-Sans: Spread with scrambled eggs and sprinkle with minced cooked bacon, chopped ham, or frizzled fried beef.

Deviled Ham 'n' Egg Pan-Sans: Spread with deviled ham and cover with scrambled eggs.

Cheese 'n' Egg Pan-Sans: Spread with scrambled eggs and sprinkle with grated sharp Cheddar cheese.

Canadian Bacon Pan-Sans: Use a slice of Canadian bacon and cover with warm canned crushed pineapple.

COFFEE BREAKERS

- 1/4 cup warm water
- 2 packages active dry yeast
- 1 cup lukewarm milk
- 1 cup margarine, melted and cooled
- 2 eggs, beaten
- 1/4 cup granulated sugar
- 1 teaspoon salt
- 4 1/2 cups (about) sifted all-purpose flour
- 1 teaspoon grated lemon rind
- 1/2 cup margarine or butter
- 2/3 cup firmly packed brown sugar
- 2 teaspoons corn syrup
- 3/4 cup chopped pecans
- 1/4 cup margarine or butter, melted
- 1/2 cup firmly packed brown sugar
- 2 teaspoons ground cinnamon

Measure warm water into a small bowl. Sprinkle yeast over water; stir until dissolved. Combine milk, 1 cup margarine, eggs, 1/4 cup sugar, salt, dissolved yeast, flour, and lemon rind in a large mixing bowl. Beat until smooth, about 1 minute—dough will be very soft. Cover with a damp cloth. Place in refrigerator for 2 hours or more, or refrigerate overnight.

Meanwhile, melt 1/2 cup margarine in saucepan; add 2/3 cup brown sugar and the corn syrup and bring to a rolling boil. Pour immediately into two 15- by 10- by 1 1/2-inch jelly-roll pans or other large oblong pans. Sprinkle with pecans.

Divide dough in half. Roll out each half into a 12-inch square. Brush each half with 2 tablespoons melted margarine. Combine 1/2 cup brown sugar and the cinnamon and sprinkle center third of each square with 2 tablespoons of the mixture. Fold one-third over the center third. Sprinkle with 2 tablespoons of cinnamon mixture. Fold remaining third over the two layers. Cut with sharp knife crosswise into strips ½ to 1 inch wide. Take hold of each end of strip and twist in opposite directions. Seal ends firmly.

Place in prepared pans about 1½ inches apart. Cover. Let rise in warm place, free from drafts, until doubled in bulk—about 1 hour. Bake in hot oven (400° F.) about 20 minutes. Invert and serve warm. Makes 48 small or 24 large rolls.

DAINTY PANCAKE ROLL-UPS

- 2 eggs
- 1 teaspoon salt
- 1 tablespoon sugar
- 1 cup cold water
- ½ cup light cream
- ¾ cup sifted all-purpose flour
- Coffee Butter (page 229)

Beat eggs until very light and frothy. Then beat in salt and sugar. Add water and cream alternately with the flour, a *small* amount at a time, beating well after each addition. Pour batter onto a hot well-buttered griddle, making 3½-inch circles. Bake until golden brown on both sides. Place about 1 tablespoon Coffee Butter on rough side of each pancake and roll up. Serve with crisp bacon strips, if desired. Makes 4 luncheon servings, 5 pancakes each, or 6 dessert servings, 3 pancakes each.

Nice to know: *Leftover batter may be stored in the refrigerator. Beat thoroughly before using.*

Coffee Break: Sweden

No Scandinavian cook worth her salt would be caught without coffee ready to serve—and hospitality dictates having a little something sweet on hand to pass around with the coffee!

SWEDISH COFFEE

1 tablespoon water
1 egg
¾ cup regular grind quality coffee
4½ cups boiling water

Add 1 tablespoon water to egg and stir to blend. Measure coffee into pot. Add egg mixture and mix well. Pour boiling water over the coffee mixture, cover tightly, and bring to a full boil. Remove from heat, and let stand in a warm place 3 minutes. Strain into cups or mugs. Serve with sugar and cream, as desired. Makes 4 cups, or 5 servings, 6 ounces each.

LEMON CHOCOLATE TARTS

TART SHELLS:

⅔ cup butter
⅓ cup sugar
1 egg yolk
½ cup finely ground blanched almonds
½ teaspoon almond extract
1¾ cups unsifted all-purpose flour
2 packages (4 ounces each) sweet cooking chocolate
3 tablespoons water

FILLING:

1 envelope unflavored gelatin
¼ cup cold water
½ cup sugar
2 egg yolks
1¼ cups milk
½ cup thawed frozen concentrate for lemonade
½ cup heavy cream
2 egg whites
¼ teaspoon salt
¼ cup sugar

Cream butter and ⅓ cup sugar. Add 1 egg yolk, ground almonds, and almond extract; mix well. Gradually stir in flour. Roll about ¼ inch thick on lightly floured board. Cut into 3¾-inch rounds and gently fit into ungreased 3-inch tart pans. Bake in moderate oven (375° F.) 12 to 15 minutes or until lightly browned. Cool and carefully remove from pans.

Grate ½ package of the chocolate; set aside. Melt remaining 1½ packages chocolate with 3 tablespoons water over very low heat. Brush melted chocolate generously over inside of tart shells; set aside.

Combine gelatin and ¼ cup cold water; mix well. Mix ½ cup sugar and 2 egg yolks in saucepan. Gradually stir in milk. Cook and stir over medium heat until mixture coats a metal spoon. (Do not boil.) Pour over gelatin and stir until gelatin is dissolved. Then add concentrate for lemonade. Chill until thickened.

Whip the cream; fold into gelatin mixture. Beat egg whites with salt until foamy throughout. Add ¼ cup sugar, 2 tablespoons at a time, beating well after each addition. Then continue beating until soft, rounded peaks will form. Fold into gelatin mixture. Spoon into tart shells, using about ¼ cup filling in each. Chill until firm. Before serving, sprinkle top of tarts with the grated chocolate. Makes about 16 tarts.

DOUBLE CHOCOLATE ROUNDS

- ¾ cup butter
- ¾ cup sugar
- 1 egg
- ⅓ cup ground blanched almonds
- ¼ teaspoon almond extract
- 2½ cups sifted all-purpose flour
- 1 package (4 ounces) sweet cooking chocolate
- 2 tablespoons water
- 2 teaspoons unflavored gelatin
- ¼ cup cold water
- 1 cup heavy cream
- ½ teaspoon vanilla
- 1½ tablespoons cocoa
- 2 egg whites
- 6 tablespoons sugar

Cream butter and ¾ cup sugar. Add 1 egg, ground almonds, and almond extract; blend well. Gradually stir in flour. Roll out ¼ inch thick on a floured board. Cut into 2¾-inch rounds. Bake on an ungreased baking sheet in moderate oven (375° F.)

12 to 15 minutes or until lightly browned. Melt the chocolate with 2 tablespoons water. Brush a thin layer of chocolate over top of each round; allow to harden.

Meanwhile, add gelatin to ¼ cup cold water. Dissolve over hot water; then cool. Combine cream, vanilla, cocoa, and the cooled gelatin. Whip until mixture holds its shape. Beat egg whites until foamy throughout. Gradually add 6 tablespoons sugar, a tablespoon at a time, beating well after each addition. Continue beating until stiff peaks will form; fold into the gelatin mixture.

Spoon about ¼ cup filling mixture onto half of the cookie rounds. Top with remaining rounds, chocolate side up. Garnish with toasted almonds and a sprinkling of confectioners' sugar, if desired. Makes about 12 to 14 servings.

COCONUT SPRITZ COOKIES

- ½ cup butter or margarine
- ⅓ cup firmly packed light brown sugar
- 1 egg yolk
- 1 teaspoon vanilla
- 1 cup sifted all-purpose flour
- ⅛ teaspoon salt
- 1 egg white, slightly beaten
- 1 teaspoon water
- Flaked coconut, tinted green
- Red and green candied cherries (optional)

Cream butter and sugar together until light and fluffy. Mix in egg yolk and vanilla. Add flour and salt; mix well. Using a cookie press, form into wreaths on an ungreased baking sheet. Bake in a hot oven (400° F.) 8 to 10 minutes. Cool.

Combine the egg white with water and brush over the cookies. Sprinkle with coconut. If desired, decorate with red and green cherries. Makes 1½ dozen wreaths.

SCANDINAVIAN RICE DESSERT

- ⅔ cup packaged pre-cooked rice
- 1½ cups milk
- ¼ cup sugar
- ½ teaspoon salt
- ¼ cup chopped blanched or sautéed almonds
- 1 teaspoon vanilla
- ½ cup heavy cream
- Bing Cherry Sauce (page 122)

Combine rice, milk, sugar, and salt in a saucepan. Mix just to moisten all rice. Bring to a boil, uncovered, and boil gently 8 minutes, fluffing rice occasionally with a fork. Then remove from heat and cover tightly. Let stand 10 minutes. Add almonds and vanilla. Cover and chill. (If mixture seems dry after chilling, add a small amount of milk.) Just before serving, whip cream. Fold into rice mixture. Serve with Bing Cherry Sauce. Makes 6 servings.

BING CHERRY SAUCE

- 1 can (1 pound 1 ounce) pitted Bing cherries
- 2 tablespoons cornstarch
- Dash of salt
- 1 teaspoon lemon juice
- ½ teaspoon almond extract

Drain cherries, measuring syrup. Add water to cherry syrup to make 1½ cups liquid. Combine cornstarch and salt; stir in liquid. Cook until thickened and clear, stirring constantly. Remove from heat. Add cherries, lemon juice, and almond extract. Serve warm or cooled. Makes about 2⅓ cups.

CHOCOLATE FRUIT SQUARES

- ¾ cup butter
- ¾ cup sugar
- 1 egg
- ½ teaspoon vanilla
- ⅓ cup packaged grated coconut
- 2½ cups unsifted all-purpose flour
- 1 can (1 pound) apricot halves
- 1 can (1 pound) stewed prunes, drained, pitted
- 2 tablespoons cornstarch
- 1 tablespoon sugar
- ½ teaspoon almond extract
- 1 package (4 ounces) sweet cooking chocolate
- 2 tablespoons water

Cream butter and ¾ cup sugar. Add egg, vanilla, and coconut; mix well. Then add flour, stirring to form a dough. Roll on a lightly floured board into a large rectangle, about 18 by 12 by 8 inches. Cut into 18 small rectangles, each about 4 by 3 inches. Bake on an ungreased baking sheet in moderate oven (375° F.) 12 to 15 minutes or until lightly browned. Cool thoroughly.

Drain apricots, measuring syrup. Add enough water to syrup to make 2 cups liquid. Combine cornstarch and 1 tablespoon sugar, add liquid, and cook until thickened, stirring constantly. Stir in almond extract and cool.

Melt chocolate in 2 tablespoons water over low heat. Brush a thin layer of melted chocolate over top of each rectangle. Arrange some of each fruit on chocolate-glazed rectangles; spoon cooled cornstarch glaze over fruit. Makes 18 servings.

SWEDISH TEA ROLLS

2 cups sifted cake flour
3 teaspoons double-acting baking powder
¾ teaspoon salt
¼ cup sugar
½ cup shortening
1 egg, slightly beaten
¼ cup milk
Melted butter
Sugar and ground cinnamon mixture

Sift flour with baking powder, salt, and ¼ cup sugar into mixing bowl. Cut in shortening. Blend egg and milk; add to flour mixture and stir with fork until soft dough is formed. Knead on a lightly floured board about 20 turns.

Roll or pat out dough ¼ inch thick on lightly floured board. Cut in 2½-inch squares. Fold each square diagonally. Dip cut edges in melted butter and then in sugar-cinnamon mixture. Bake on ungreased baking sheet in hot oven (425° F.) 12 to 15 minutes or until golden brown. Makes 10 to 12 rolls.

Coffee Party: "Come for Dessert and Coffee!"

Get out your nicest dishes, polish the best silver—company's coming! One of the pleasantest ways to entertain is to invite guests to share dessert with you, along with a cup—or two or three—of fragrant coffee and a lot of good, stimulating conversation. So make a special pie or cake, a luscious mousse, a towering torte . . . and have a wonderful time!

EASY CHOCOLATE PANCAKES

- 1 cup pancake mix
- Milk, egg, and shortening
- ½ package sweet cooking chocolate, finely chopped (½ cup)
- Maple-blended syrup

Prepare pancake mix with milk, egg, and shortening as directed on package, adding chopped chocolate with the pancake mix. Bake on lightly greased griddle. Serve with syrup. Makes 2 cups batter, enough for 8 pancakes.

Easy Coconut Pancakes: Prepare as directed for Easy Chocolate Pancakes, substituting ⅔ cup packaged moist toasted coconut or ½ cup packaged grated coconut for the chocolate.

STRAWBERRY-FILLED DANISH FOLDS

- 2 tablespoons sugar
- ½ teaspoon ground cardamom seeds or ¼ teaspoon ground nutmeg
- 1½ cups pancake mix
- 4 eggs, well beaten
- 1⅔ cups milk
- ½ cup butter, melted
- 2 cups whole strawberries*
- Maple-blended syrup

*Or use 2 packages (1 pound each) frozen whole strawberries, thawed and drained.

Mix sugar, spice, and pancake mix lightly. Combine eggs, milk, and butter. Gradually add the pancake mix, beating until smooth. Spoon onto a hot ungreased griddle, spreading quickly to form thin 6-inch pancakes. Bake until bubbles form across top surface; then turn and bake on other side.

As pancakes are removed from the griddle, fold in half; then fold in half again to form triangular-shaped pancakes. Place on wire cake rack. Fill top and bottom folds with strawberries. Place in slow oven (300° F.) to keep hot until ready to serve. Serve with syrup. Makes about 2 dozen 6-inch pancakes or 6 to 8 servings.

CHOCOLATE ALMOND MOUSSE

- 2 squares unsweetened chocolate
- 6 tablespoons water
- ½ cup sugar
- Dash of salt
- 3 tablespoons butter
- ¾ teaspoon vanilla
- ⅔ cup sweetened condensed milk
- 2 cups heavy cream
- ½ cup slivered toasted blanched almonds

Place chocolate and water in saucepan over low heat, stirring until chocolate is melted and blended. Add sugar and salt. Cook and stir until sugar is dissolved and mixture thickens very slightly. Add butter and vanilla. Cool.

Combine the cooled chocolate sauce, condensed milk, and cream in the large bowl of electric mixer. Chill. Then whip until soft peaks form. Fold in almonds. Spoon into refrigerator tray and freeze until firm. Serve with additional toasted almonds, if desired. Makes 8 to 10 servings.

DE LUXE CHOCOLATE DESSERT

- 2 egg whites
- ⅛ teaspoon salt
- ⅛ teaspoon cream of tartar
- ½ cup granulated sugar
- ½ cup finely chopped pecans
- ½ teaspoon vanilla
- 1 package (4 ounces) sweet cooking chocolate
- 3 tablespoons water
- 2 egg yolks, beaten
- 1 cup heavy cream
- 1 tablespoon confectioners' sugar
- ⅛ teaspoon ground cinnamon

Combine egg whites, salt, and cream of tartar in mixing bowl. Beat until foamy throughout. Add granulated sugar, 2 tablespoons at a time, beating after each addition until sugar is blended. Then continue beating until mixture will stand in very stiff peaks. Fold in pecans and vanilla. Spoon into lightly greased 9-inch pie pan, building sides up ½ inch above edge of pan. Bake in a very slow oven (275° F.) 50 to 55 minutes. Cool.

Place chocolate and water in saucepan over low heat. Stir until chocolate is melted. Remove from heat. Gradually stir egg yolks into chocolate mixture. Return saucepan to low heat and cook for one minute, stirring constantly. Cool.

Whip heavy cream with confectioners' sugar and cinnamon in a chilled bowl. Spread about one cup of the whipped cream in the bottom of the meringue shell. Fold the remaining whipped cream into the chocolate mixture and spoon into shell. Chill several hours or overnight. Garnish with more whipped cream and pecans, if desired. Makes 8 servings.

SWEET CHOCOLATE CAKE

- 1 package (4 ounces) sweet cooking chocolate
- ½ cup boiling water
- 1 cup butter or margarine
- 2 cups sugar
- 4 egg yolks
- 1 teaspoon vanilla
- 2½ cups sifted cake flour
- 1 teaspoon baking soda
- ½ teaspoon salt
- 1 cup buttermilk
- 4 egg whites, stiffly beaten
- Coconut-Pecan Filling and Frosting (page 127)

Melt chocolate in boiling water; cool. Cream butter and sugar until light and fluffy. Add egg yolks, one at a time, beating after each addition. Add vanilla and melted chocolate and mix until blended. Sift flour with baking soda and salt. Add flour mixture alternately with buttermilk, beating after each addition until batter is smooth. Fold in stiffly beaten egg whites. Pour batter into three 8- or 9-inch layer pans, lined on bottoms with wax paper. Bake in moderate oven (350° F.) 35 to 40 minutes for 8-inch layers or 30 to 35 minutes for 9-inch layers, or until top springs back when lightly pressed. Cool.

(This delicate cake will have a flat contour and a slightly sugary top crust which tends to crack.) Frost layers and top with Coconut-Pecan Filling and Frosting.

Coconut-Pecan Filling and Frosting: Combine 1 cup evaporated milk, 1 cup sugar, 3 egg yolks, ½ cup butter or margarine, and 1 teaspoon vanilla in a saucepan. Cook over medium heat, stirring constantly, until thickened—about 12 minutes. Remove from heat. Add 1⅓ cups (about) flaked coconut and 1 cup chopped pecans. Beat until cool and of spreading consistency. Makes 2⅔ cups.

MINTED CHOCOLATE BAVARIAN

- 1 teaspoon unflavored gelatin
- 6 tablespoons sugar
- 3 egg yolks
- 1 cup milk
- 1 package (4 ounces) sweet cooking chocolate, broken in squares
- 3 egg whites
- 1 teaspoon vanilla
- ¼ teaspoon peppermint extract
- ¼ teaspoon brandy extract (optional)
- Whipped cream
- Slivered almonds

Mix gelatin and sugar. Combine egg yolks and milk in top of a double boiler and beat. Add gelatin mixture and cook over hot water until gelatin dissolves and mixture thickens, stirring constantly. Add chocolate and stir until melted. Combine egg whites, vanilla, and extracts and beat until mixture holds soft peaks. Fold into chocolate mixture. Chill in sherbet glasses. To serve, garnish with whipped cream and slivered almonds. Makes 6 to 8 servings.

SWEET CHOCOLATE-APRICOT TORTE

- ¼ cup water
- 1 package (4 ounces) sweet cooking chocolate
- 6 egg yolks
- ½ cup sugar
- ¼ cup butter or margarine (at room temperature)
- 6 egg whites
- ½ cup sifted all-purpose flour
- 1 cup heavy cream
- ¾ cup apricot jam

Combine water and chocolate in a small saucepan. Place over low heat and stir until chocolate is melted and mixture is smooth. Cool. Beat egg yolks until foamy. Gradually add sugar, beating until lemon-colored and thick. Add butter and beat until smooth. Then add cooled chocolate mixture and beat until smooth and creamy. Beat egg whites until stiff peaks will form. Gradually fold in the flour; then fold into the chocolate mixture.

Grease two 8-inch layer pans on bottoms, line with wax paper, and grease again. Pour about ¼ of batter (about 1 cup) into each pan. Bake in a slow oven (325° F.) for 15 minutes. Cool 5 minutes and then turn out onto rack. Remove paper carefully and continue to cool on rack. Repeat with remaining batter. Then whip the cream. Carefully fold in jam. Fill and frost layers with the apricot whipped cream. Makes 12 servings.

BAKED ALASKA

- **2 quarts ice cream (any flavor)**
- **6 egg whites**
- **¾ cup sugar**
- **1 baked 9-inch cake layer**

To make ice cream mold: Pack ice cream into a 1½-quart bowl that is not more than 8 inches in diameter. Freeze 2 to 3 hours, or until firm.

To prepare meringue: Beat egg whites until foamy throughout. Add sugar, 2 tablespoons at a time, beating after each addition until blended. Then continue beating until meringue will stand in stiff, shiny peaks.

To prepare Baked Alaska: Place cake layer on oven-proof plate, tray, or board. Loosen ice cream from bowl with a spatula. Invert over cake and remove bowl. Cover cake and ice cream completely with meringue, sealing meringue to cake. Place in very hot oven (500° F.) 3 to 5 minutes or just until meringue is lightly browned. Serve at once, or store in freezer (see page 129). Makes 12 to 16 servings.

Nice to know: To store, place Baked Alaska in freezer until meringue is firm; then wrap and return to freezer. Baked Alaska can be stored for a week, if desired.

PEARS BELLE HÉLÈNE

6 fresh or canned pear halves
1 quart vanilla or coffee ice cream
Regal Chocolate Sauce (page 193)

Place pear halves in 6 small shallow dessert dishes, cut-side up. Fill each pear half with a scoop of vanilla ice cream. Place two scoops of ice cream on each side of each pear half. Top with Regal Chocolate Sauce. Serve immediately. Makes 6 servings.

QUICK PEACH MELBA

1 quart vanilla ice cream
6 fresh peaches, peeled and cut in half, or 12 canned peach halves
Raspberry Sauce (see below)

Half-fill 6 stemmed sherbet glasses with vanilla ice cream. Top with 6 peach halves, cut-side up. Fill center of each peach with ice cream. Cut remaining peach halves into quarters and arrange around top layer of ice cream. Top with Raspberry Sauce. Serve immediately. Makes 6 servings.

Raspberry Sauce: Thaw slightly 1 package (10 ounces) frozen red raspberries; then blend until smooth in an electric blender. Or thaw raspberries thoroughly; then force through sieve or potato ricer.

FRESH STRAWBERRY SHORTCAKE

2¼ cups sifted cake flour
2 teaspoons double-acting baking powder
½ teaspoon salt
4 eggs (at room temperature)
1⅓ cups sugar
¼ cup shortening
1 cup milk
1 teaspoon grated lemon rind
1½ cups heavy cream
1½ quarts fresh strawberries, sliced and sweetened

Sift together flour, baking powder, and salt. Beat eggs until foamy; gradually add sugar, beating until very thick and light in color. Combine shortening and milk and heat until shortening melts. Then add to egg mixture, mixing very quickly. Add flour mixture and lemon rind; beat with rotary beater only until smooth.

Pour batter into three 9-inch layer pans which have been lined on bottoms with wax paper. Bake in moderate oven (375° F.) 15 minutes or until top springs back when touched lightly. Cool cakes right side up in pans; then remove from pans.

Whip cream; sweeten, if desired. Spread some of the whipped cream and some of the sliced berries between layers. Spread remaining whipped cream over top of cake; spoon on remaining berries. Chill until served. Makes 12 servings.

HOT MILK SPONGE CAKE

2 cups sifted cake flour
2 teaspoons double-acting baking powder
½ teaspoon salt
4 eggs
2 cups sugar
2 teaspoons vanilla*
1 cup milk
2 tablespoons butter
Broiled Coconut Topping (see below)

***Or use 1 tablespoon grated orange rind.**

Sift flour, baking powder, and salt together. Beat eggs in large deep bowl until very thick and light—about 5 minutes. Gradually beat in sugar. Add vanilla. Then add flour mixture a small amount at a time, blending by hand or at low speed in electric mixer. Bring milk and butter just to a boil. *Very quickly* stir into the flour mixture, blending thoroughly. (Batter will be thin.) Pour quickly into a 13- by 9-inch pan which has been greased and floured on bottom only. Bake at once in a moderate oven (350° F.) for 30 to 35 minutes. Cool. Then spread with Coconut Topping and broil as directed.

Broiled Coconut Topping: Cream ¼ cup butter and ¾ cup firmly packed brown sugar together. Add 1½ tablespoons milk and beat until smooth. Then mix in ¾ cup flaked coconut. Spread on cake in pan and broil about 3 minutes or until coconut is lightly toasted.

Nice to know: *Batter may also be baked in the following pans which have been greased and floured on bottoms only: two 8- or 9-inch square pans for 25 to 30 minutes or two 9- by 5-inch loaf pans for 40 to 45 minutes.*

CROWN JEWEL CAKE

- 1 package (3 ounces) orange flavor gelatin
- 1 package (3 ounces) cherry flavor gelatin
- 1 package (3 ounces) lime flavor gelatin
- 3 cups boiling water
- 2 cups cold water
- 1 cup pineapple juice
- ¼ cup sugar
- 1 package (3 ounces) lemon flavor gelatin
- 1½ cups graham cracker crumbs
- ⅓ cup butter or margarine, melted
- 2 envelopes whipped topping mix*

*Or use 2 cups heavy cream.

Prepare the orange, cherry, and lime flavors of gelatin separately, dissolving each in 1 cup boiling water; then add ½ cup cold water to each. Pour each flavor into separate 8-inch square pans and chill until firm, at least 4 hours, or overnight.

Combine pineapple juice and sugar in a saucepan; bring to a boil. Add to the lemon flavor gelatin and stir until dissolved. Add remaining ½ cup cold water. Chill until slightly thickened.

Meanwhile, mix graham cracker crumbs with melted butter. If desired, set aside about ¼ cup for a garnish. Press crumb mixture smoothly over bottom and sides to 1 inch from top of a 9-inch spring-form pan.

Prepare whipped topping mix as directed on package, or whip the cream. Blend the prepared whipped topping into the slightly thickened lemon gelatin. Then cut the three pans of firm gelatin into cubes about ½ inch square. Fold all the cubes into the lemon mixture. Spoon into spring-form pan. Chill until firm, at least 5 hours, or overnight. Just before serving, run a spatula around sides of pan, then gently remove sides. Garnish top with the ¼ cup crumbs. If desired, frost sides with additional prepared whipped topping or whipped cream. Makes 16 servings.

PUDDING CHEESE PIE

- 1 package (8 ounces) cream cheese, softened
- 2 cups cold milk
- 1 package (3¾ ounces) lemon instant pudding mix
- 1 baked 9-inch graham cracker crumb crust, cooled

Stir cream cheese until very soft. Gradually blend in ½ cup of the milk until smooth. Add remaining cold milk and pudding mix. Slowly mix with rotary beater until just blended, about 1 minute. Immediately pour into crust. Chill 1 hour—or until firm.

Electric Mixer Directions: Beat cream cheese until fluffy. Gradually blend in milk. Then add instant pudding mix and blend at a low speed 1 minute. Pour into crust. Chill.

QUICK PECAN PIE

- 1 package (3¾- or 4-ounce size) butterscotch or vanilla instant pudding mix
- 1 cup corn syrup
- ¾ cup evaporated milk
- 1 egg, slightly beaten
- 1 cup chopped pecans
- 1 unbaked 8-inch pie shell

Blend pudding mix with corn syrup. Gradually add evaporated milk and egg, stirring to blend. Then add pecans. Pour into pie shell. Bake in moderate oven (375° F.) until set—about 45 minutes. Cool at least 2 hours.

LEMON DELIGHT PIE

- 1 package (3⅝ ounces) lemon pudding and pie filling mix
- ½ cup sugar
- 2¼ cups water
- 1 egg
- 1 baked 8-inch pie shell
- 1 envelope whipped topping mix
- ½ cup *cold* milk
- 2 tablespoons sugar
- ½ teaspoon vanilla

Combine pie filling mix, ½ cup sugar, and ¼ cup of the water in saucepan. Add egg and blend well. Then add remaining 2 cups water. Cook and stir over medium heat until mixture comes to a *full* boil and is thickened—about 5 minutes. Remove from heat. Cool about 5 minutes, stirring once or twice. Measure 1 cup filling, place a piece of wax paper directly on surface of filling, and chill thoroughly—at least 2 hours. Pour remaining filling into pie shell.

Combine whipped topping mix, cold milk, 2 tablespoons sugar, and the vanilla in a deep bowl with narrow bottom. Whip as directed on whipped topping mix package. Stir chilled filling until smooth; blend in 1⅓ cups prepared whipped topping. Spoon over filling in pie shell. Chill thoroughly—about 3 hours. Garnish with remaining prepared whipped topping.

CHOCOLATE PASTRY CAKE

- **2 packages (4 ounces each) sweet cooking chocolate**
- **½ cup sugar**
- **½ cup water**
- **¼ teaspoon ground cinnamon**
- **2 teaspoons vanilla**
- **1 package (10 ounces) pie crust mix or Homemade Pie Crust Mix (about 2 cups or use recipe on page 134)**
- **2 cups heavy cream or 2 envelopes whipped topping mix**

Remove wrapper from one end of a package of chocolate. Dip vegetable peeler in hot water; shave 3 squares of chocolate into curls or shavings. Set aside.

Break remaining chocolate and combine with sugar, water, and cinnamon in a small saucepan. Cook and stir over low heat until sauce is smooth. Remove from heat; add vanilla. Cool to room temperature.

Then mix ¾ cup sauce into dry pie crust mix; divide into 4 portions. Press each part over bottom of inverted 8- or 9-inch round or square pan to within ¼ inch or more from edge. If you do not have 4 pans, remaining pastry may stand at room temperature while first layers bake. Bake in hot oven (425° F.) 6 to 8 minutes or until almost firm. If pastry has spread over edge of pan, trim with a sharp knife. Cool until firm—about 5 minutes. Carefully run knife under layers to loosen from pans. Place on racks to cool thoroughly.

Whip the cream just to soft peaks, or prepare whipped topping mix as directed on package. Fold in remaining sauce. Spread between and over top of pastry layers. Sprinkle with chocolate curls or shavings. Cover and chill at least 8 hours, or store in freezer. Makes 12 to 16 servings.

Homemade Pie Crust Mix: Mix 2 cups unsifted all-purpose flour and 1 teaspoon salt. Cut in ½ cup shortening until mixture resembles coarse meal; then cut in ¼ cup shortening until particles are size of peas.

MIRACLE CHERRY PIE

1 package (3¼ ounces) vanilla pudding and pie filling mix
¼ cup sugar
¼ teaspoon salt
2 teaspoons lemon juice
½ cup water
1 can (1 pound) pitted unsweetened red cherries
1 tablespoon butter
Few drops red food coloring
1 baked 8-inch pie shell, cooled

Combine pudding mix, sugar, salt, lemon juice, and water in a saucepan. Stir until smooth. Add cherries and juice; stir to blend. Cook and stir over medium heat until mixture comes to a *full* boil. Remove from heat. Add butter and food coloring. Cool 5 minutes. Pour into pie shell. Let stand about 3 hours, or until firm. Serve with whipped cream, if desired.

Miracle Fresh Cherry Pie: Prepare Miracle Cherry Pie, substituting 2 cups pitted fresh cherries for the canned cherries, increasing the water to 1 cup, and adding ⅛ teaspoon almond extract with the butter.

CHOCOLATE PARTY MERINGUE PIE

1 package (4 ounces) chocolate or chocolate fudge pudding and pie filling mix
2 tablespoons brown sugar
½ square unsweetened chocolate
2 cups milk
2 egg yolks
2 tablespoons butter
1 baked 8- or 9-inch pie shell
2 egg whites
4 tablespoons granulated sugar

Combine pie filling mix, brown sugar, chocolate, milk, and egg yolks. Blend well. Cook and stir over medium heat until mixture comes to a *full* boil. Remove from heat. Add butter and blend. Cool about 5 minutes, stirring once or twice. Pour into pie shell.

Beat egg whites until foamy throughout. Gradually add granulated sugar, 2 tablespoons at a time, beating after each addition until sugar is blended. Then continue beating until meringue will stand in stiff, shiny peaks. Pile lightly onto pie filling. Bake in hot oven (425° F.) 5 to 10 minutes or until meringue is delicately browned.

Coffee Cookie Jar

One of Mom's most important titles, as far as the kids are concerned, is Chief Cookie Maker. And Dad isn't above being caught with his hand in the cookie jar, either. To keep everybody happy, you need variety in cookie recipes. Here are new flavors, new combinations, new bars, drops, roll-outs—a whole new world of cookies that will surely win you a medal to go along with your title!

MOCHA BROWNIES

- ⅔ cup sifted all-purpose flour
- ½ teaspoon double-acting baking powder
- ¼ teaspoon salt
- ⅓ cup butter or other shortening
- 2 squares unsweetened chocolate
- 2 teaspoons instant quality coffee
- 1 cup sugar
- 2 eggs, well beaten
- ½ cup broken walnuts
- 1 teaspoon vanilla

Sift flour, baking powder, and salt together. Melt shortening and chocolate over hot water. Add coffee and sugar gradually to eggs, beating thoroughly. Add chocolate mixture and blend. Add flour mixture and mix well; then add nuts and vanilla. Spread in greased 8-inch square pan. Bake in moderate oven (350° F.) 25 minutes. Cool in pan; then cut into squares or rectangles. Makes about 20 brownies.

CHOCOLATE COFFEE BARS

- 2 cups sifted all-purpose flour
- 2 teaspoons instant quality coffee
- ½ teaspoon salt
- 1 cup shortening
- 1 cup firmly packed brown sugar
- 1 egg
- 1 teaspoon vanilla
- 1 package (6 ounces) semi-sweet chocolate chips
- ½ cup chopped nuts

Sift flour, instant coffee, and salt together. Cream shortening and brown sugar together until fluffy. Add egg and vanilla; blend thoroughly. Add the flour mixture and mix well. Spread evenly in a 15- by 10-inch pan. Sprinkle chips and nuts over the top. Bake in a slow oven (325° F.) 20 minutes. Cool. Cut into bars. Makes about 3 dozen.

MOCHA RUM CRISPIES

- 3½ cups sifted cake flour
- 2 teaspoons double-acting baking powder
- ½ teaspoon salt
- 2 teaspoons instant quality coffee
- 1 tablespoon water*
- ¾ cup butter or margarine*
- 1 cup sugar
- 1 egg
- 1½ teaspoons rum extract
- ½ cup finely chopped blanched almonds

***To use vegetable shortening, increase water to 2 tablespoons.**

Sift flour, baking powder, and salt together. Dissolve instant coffee in the water.

Cream butter until soft. Gradually add sugar, creaming until light and fluffy. Then add egg and beat well. Add flour mixture, coffee, rum extract, and almonds; mix thoroughly.

Chill dough until firm enough to roll. Then roll ⅛ inch thick on lightly floured board. Cut with floured cookie cutter. Place on ungreased baking sheets. Decorate with almond halves or candied fruit, if desired. Bake in moderate oven (375° F.) 6 to 8 minutes. Makes 10 dozen cookies.

MOCHA SQUARES

- 3 cups sugar coated crisp rice cereal or honey-flavored puffed wheat
- 1 cup chopped nuts
- ¾ cup sugar
- ¼ cup light corn syrup
- ½ cup brewed quality coffee*
- ½ teaspoon salt
- 1 square unsweetened chocolate
- 1 tablespoon butter or margarine

***Or use ½ teaspoon instant quality coffee dissolved in ½ cup water.**

Mix cereal and nuts in large greased bowl. Combine sugar, corn syrup, coffee, and salt in saucepan. Bring to a boil over medium heat, stirring to dissolve sugar. Add chocolate and stir until melted. Continue cooking, without stirring, until a small amount of mixture forms a soft ball in cold water (or to a temperature of 234° F.). Blend in butter.

Pour over cereal and nuts, mixing quickly. Press into a buttered 9-inch square pan or 13- by 9-inch pan, or two 9- by 5-inch loaf pans. Chill until firm. Cut in small squares. Makes 6 to 8 dozen pieces.

MOCHA RAISIN-NUT BARS

1 package butterscotch or white cake mix
1 cup cold brewed quality coffee*
2 eggs, unbeaten
1 cup raisins, chopped
1 cup chopped nuts
De Luxe Coffee Glaze (page 84)

***Or use 2 teaspoons instant quality coffee dissolved in 1 cup water.**

Empty cake mix into bowl. Add coffee and eggs. Blend; then beat 3 minutes until smooth and creamy. Mix in raisins and nuts. Pour batter into 2 greased 13- by 9-inch pans. Bake in moderate oven (350° F.) about 25 minutes or until cake tester inserted in center comes out clean.

While cakes are still warm, spread De Luxe Coffee Glaze over tops. When cool, cut each cake into 30 bars. Store in pans covered with aluminum foil. Makes 60 bars.

For cake-type squares, batter may be baked in one 13- by 9-inch pan 35 to 40 minutes or two 9-inch square pans about 30 minutes. Cut glaze recipe in half. Makes 15 to 18 squares.

COFFEE CASHEW KISSES

2 egg whites
1⅓ cups sugar
2 tablespoons instant quality coffee
¼ teaspoon salt
⅔ cup chopped cashew nuts
1 teaspoon vanilla

Beat egg whites until foamy throughout. Combine sugar, instant coffee, and salt; gradually add to egg whites, beating well after each addition. Then continue beating until mixture will form stiff, shiny peaks. Fold in cashew nuts and vanilla. Drop by teaspoonfuls onto greased baking sheets. Bake in moderate oven (325° F.) about 15 minutes or until golden brown. Makes 3 dozen.

COFFEE BUTTER BITS

- 1 cup sifted all-purpose flour
- ½ cup cornstarch
- ½ cup confectioners' sugar
- 1 tablespoon instant quality coffee
- 1 cup softened butter or margarine

Sift flour, cornstarch, confectioners' sugar, and instant coffee into mixing bowl. Blend in butter until a soft dough is formed. Chill about 1 hour.

Then shape into balls about 1 inch in diameter. Place on ungreased baking sheets, about 1½ inches apart. Flatten with lightly floured fork. Bake in slow oven (300° F.) 20 to 25 minutes or until lightly browned. Makes about 3 dozen cookies.

COFFEE LACE WAFERS

- 1 cup sifted cake flour
- ⅔ cup sugar
- 2 teaspoons instant quality coffee
- ⅛ teaspoon salt
- ½ cup molasses
- ½ cup shortening

Sift together flour, sugar, instant coffee, and salt. Bring molasses to a boil; add shortening and stir until melted. Gradually add flour mixture, blending thoroughly after each addition. Drop by teaspoonfuls 3 to 4 inches apart on a greased baking sheet. (Bake only a few at a time for ease in handling.)

Bake in moderate oven (350° F.) 8 to 10 minutes. Let cool on baking sheet about 1 minute; then remove each wafer with a wide spatula and roll quickly around handle of wooden spoon. Slide off quickly, seam side down, onto a rack to cool. If wafers cool too much to roll, return to oven for about a minute to soften. Makes about 4 dozen.

COFFEE COCONUT TREASURES

1½ cups sifted all-purpose flour
1 cup sugar
1 tablespoon instant quality coffee
1½ teaspoons double-acting baking powder
¼ teaspoon salt
½ cup butter or other shortening*
2 eggs*
¼ cup milk*
1 teaspoon vanilla
1 cup packaged grated coconut

*Have butter, eggs, and milk at room temperature.

Sift flour, sugar, instant coffee, baking powder, and salt into mixing bowl. Add butter, eggs, 2 tablespoons of the milk, and vanilla; beat 2 minutes. Then add remaining milk and coconut and beat ½ minute longer. (Beat vigorously by hand or at a low speed in electric mixer.) Chill 2 hours.

Spread chilled mixture in 2 greased 8-inch square pans. Bake in moderate oven (375° F.) 20 to 25 minutes. Cool. Sprinkle with confectioners' sugar or drizzle with a Coffee Glaze, if desired. Cut in squares or bars. Makes 3 to 4 dozen.

Nice to know: *To keep cookies soft, store in tightly covered container with a slice of fresh bread.*

MOCHA JUMBOS

¼ cup soft shortening
1 cup sugar
1 egg
2 tablespoons water
1 square unsweetened chocolate, melted
½ teaspoon vanilla
1½ cups unsifted all-purpose flour
2 tablespoons instant quality coffee
2 teaspoons double-acting baking powder
⅛ teaspoon salt
Additional sugar

Combine shortening, sugar, egg, and water; beat at medium speed in electric mixer or by hand until light and fluffy. Blend in chocolate and vanilla.

Mix flour, instant coffee, baking powder, and salt; blend into chocolate mixture. Wrap dough in wax paper; chill until firm or place in freezer for 1 hour.

Roll out dough about ⅜ inch thick for thicker cookies, or ⅛ inch thick for thinner cookies. Cut with doughnut cutter or

2-inch cookie cutter. Place on greased baking sheets and sprinkle with sugar. Bake in moderate oven (350° F.) 8 to 10 minutes for thick cookies or about 8 minutes for thin cookies. Cool on racks. Store in loosely covered containers. Makes about 3 dozen thick cookies or 4 dozen thin cookies.

Spicy Mocha Jumbos: Prepare Mocha Jumbos, increasing chocolate to 2 squares, omitting vanilla, increasing instant coffee to 3 tablespoons, and adding ½ teaspoon ground cinnamon to flour mixture.

HERMITS

- 1¼ cups unsifted all-purpose flour
- ½ teaspoon baking soda
- ½ teaspoon salt
- ½ teaspoon ground nutmeg
- ½ teaspoon ground cinnamon
- ½ cup butter
- 1 cup firmly packed brown sugar
- 1 egg
- ¼ cup cold brewed quality coffee or prepared instant quality coffee
- ½ cup raisins
- ½ cup chopped dates

Mix flour, soda, salt, and spices; set aside. Cream butter with sugar until light and fluffy. Add egg; beat until well blended. Gradually blend in the coffee. Then gradually beat in flour mixture, adding a third at a time. Stir in raisins and dates, mixing well. Drop by heaping teaspoonfuls onto lightly greased baking sheets. Bake in moderate oven (350° F.) about 10 minutes or until evenly browned. Cool slightly. Then remove and cool thoroughly on rack. Store in tightly covered containers—cookies soften during storage. Makes 2 dozen large cookies.

MOCHA NUT BUTTERBALLS

- 1 cup butter
- ½ cup sugar
- 2 teaspoons vanilla
- 1½ cups unsifted all-purpose flour
- ¼ cup cocoa
- 2 tablespoons instant quality coffee
- ½ teaspoon salt
- 2 cups finely chopped pecans
- Confectioners' sugar

Cream butter until soft; add sugar and vanilla, creaming until light and fluffy. Add flour, cocoa, instant coffee, and salt; mix well. Stir in pecans. Shape into 1-inch balls and place on ungreased baking sheets. Bake in slow oven (325° F.) 15 to 17 minutes. Carefully remove from baking sheets and place on racks until cooled. Then roll in confectioners' sugar. Makes about 5 dozen.

CHEWY MOCHA KISSES

1 package (6 ounces) semi-sweet chocolate chips
2 egg whites
⅛ teaspoon salt
½ cup sugar
½ teaspoon vinegar
2 teaspoons instant quality coffee
½ cup flaked coconut
¼ cup chopped walnuts

Melt chocolate chips over hot water; cool. Beat egg whites and salt until foamy throughout. Add sugar very gradually, beating after each addition until sugar is well blended. Then continue beating until mixture will stand in stiff peaks. Add vinegar and instant coffee and beat well. (Entire beating process takes about 10 minutes.) Fold in coconut, nuts, and melted chips.

Drop from teaspoon onto greased baking sheets. Bake in moderate oven (350° F.) 10 minutes. Makes 2½ to 3 dozen.

Nice to know: *If desired, recipe may be doubled.*

Coffee Break: Brazil

Brazil, says the song, has an awful lot of coffee—and Brazilians love it! Here are South American ways with the beverage and with sweets to accompany their all-day, everyday drink.

LIGHT COCONUT FRUIT CAKE

2⅔ cups (about) flaked coconut*
2 pounds (about 5 cups) mixed candied fruit
1 pound (2½ cups) pitted dates, cut in small pieces
1 pound (about 3 cups) white raisins, washed and dried
½ pound (1 cup) candied cherries, chopped
½ pound (2 cups) walnuts, chopped
2½ cups sifted all-purpose flour
½ pound butter or margarine
1¼ cups sugar
6 eggs
½ teaspoon double-acting baking powder
Dash of salt
1 teaspoon vanilla

***Or use 2 cups packaged grated coconut.**

Combine coconut, fruits, and nuts with ½ cup of the flour. Mix well. Cream butter, gradually add sugar, and cream together thoroughly. Add eggs, one at a time, beating well after each addition. Sift remaining flour with the baking powder and salt. Add to egg mixture, blending thoroughly. Add vanilla; then blend in fruit mixture.

Line bottom of one 10-inch tube pan and one 9- by 5-inch loaf pan or three 9- by 5-inch loaf pans with heavy brown paper. Spoon batter into pans up to 1 inch from top. For tube pan bake in very slow oven (275° F.) 1½ hours; then increase heat to 300° F. and bake 1 hour longer. (Total baking time 2½ hours.) For loaf pans, bake at 275 ° F. for 1 hour; then at

300° F. for ½ to 1 hour longer. (If tube pan cake and one loaf are being baked together, loaf pan should be put in oven ½ hour after tube pan.) Makes 7 pounds of cake.

Nice to know: *Cake may be served the day it's baked, or stored in tightly covered container for later use. For longer storage, wrap slightly warm cakes in pieces of cheesecloth dampened in brandy or wine and store in tightly covered containers.*

BRAZILIAN COFFEE

2 cups water*
¼ cup instant quality coffee*
1 square unsweetened chocolate
¼ cup sugar
Dash of salt
2 cups milk
Whipped cream

***Or use 2 cups brewed quality coffee.**

Place water, instant coffee, and chocolate in saucepan over very low heat, stirring constantly until chocolate is melted and blended. Add sugar and salt and bring to a boil. Then simmer 4 minutes, stirring constantly. Gradually stir in milk. Continue to heat and stir until hot. Beat with rotary beater until light and frothy. Serve hot in demitasse cups, or pour over cracked ice in tall glasses. Top with whipped cream. Makes about 1 quart, or 12 servings, about 3 ounces each, or 6 servings, about 5 ounces each.

Spiced Brazilian Coffee: Prepare Brazilian Coffee, increasing sugar to ½ cup and adding 1 teaspoon ground cinnamon and a dash of ground allspice with the sugar.

PINEAPPLE-COCONUT DROPS

2 cups sifted all-purpose flour
1 teaspoon double-acting baking powder
1 teaspoon salt
⅓ cup butter
⅔ cup firmly packed brown sugar
⅓ cup granulated sugar
1 egg
1 can (9 ounces) crushed pineapple, drained
½ teaspoon baking soda
⅓ cup chopped walnuts
1⅓ cups (about) flaked coconut

Sift flour with baking powder and salt. Cream butter; gradually add sugars, creaming until light and fluffy. Add egg and beat well. Combine pineapple and soda; add to egg mixture. (There may be curdling at this point, but this disappears when flour is added.) Stir in walnuts and coconut. Then add flour mixture, blending well. Drop by teaspoonfuls onto greased baking sheets. Bake in a moderate oven (350° F.) 20 minutes. Cool; then store in tightly covered containers. Makes about 5 dozen.

BANANAS BRAZILIAN STYLE

6 medium ripe bananas
½ cup orange juice
1 tablespoon lemon juice
¼ cup firmly packed brown sugar
⅛ teaspoon salt
2 tablespoons butter
1 cup flaked coconut

Peel bananas; cut in half lengthwise. Place in a buttered shallow casserole. Combine the orange and lemon juices, sugar, and salt. Pour over bananas. Dot with butter. Bake in a hot oven (400° F.) 10 to 15 minutes. Remove from oven and sprinkle with coconut. Makes 6 servings.

ORANGE COCONUT CAKE

2½ cups sifted cake flour
2½ teaspoons double-acting baking powder
¾ teaspoon salt
1½ cups sugar
¾ cup butter or margarine (at room temperature)
1 tablespoon grated orange rind
¾ cup milk
3 eggs
1 cup flaked coconut*

*Or use ½ cup packaged grated coconut.

Measure sifted flour into sifter; add baking powder, salt, and sugar. Stir butter and orange rind until butter is softened. Sift in flour mixture. Add milk and mix until all flour is dampened. Then *beat 2 minutes* at a medium speed in electric mixer or 300 vigorous strokes by hand. Add eggs and *beat 1 minute* longer in mixer or 150 strokes by hand. Stir in coconut.

Pour batter into two 9-inch layer pans which have been lined on bottoms with wax paper. Bake in moderate oven

(350° F.) 30 to 35 minutes, or until cake springs back when lightly pressed. Cool; then frost with a fluffy white frosting.

CARAMEL-TOP PUDDING

- 1 package (4 ounces) butterscotch or (3¼ ounces) vanilla pudding and pie filling mix
- 2 cups milk
- ¼ cup firmly packed brown sugar

Combine pudding mix and milk in saucepan. Cook and stir over medium heat until mixture comes to a *full* boil. Remove from heat. Pour into greased 1-quart baking dish or individual custard cups. Chill.

Sprinkle sugar over top and let stand at room temperature 10 to 15 minutes. Then place under broiler until sugar is melted and bubbly. Serve warm or cold. Makes 4 servings.

Spiced Caramel-Top Pudding: Prepare Caramel-Top Pudding, mixing ¼ teaspoon ground cinnamon and ⅛ teaspoon ground nutmeg with the sugar.

FILBERT CAKE

- 1 package (4 ounces) sweet cooking chocolate
- 2¾ cups sifted cake flour
- 2 teaspoons double-acting baking powder
- ½ teaspoon salt
- 1 cup butter or margarine
- 1⅔ cups sugar
- 4 egg yolks, unbeaten
- 1 teaspoon vanilla
- 1 cup milk
- 1 cup finely chopped filberts or walnuts
- 4 egg whites
- Coconut Topping (page 147)

Melt chocolate over hot water; then cool. Sift flour with baking powder and salt. Cream butter and sugar until light and fluffy. Add egg yolks, one at a time, beating well after each addition. Blend in melted chocolate and vanilla. Add flour mixture alternately with milk, beginning and ending with flour mixture. Fold in nuts. Beat egg whites until stiff, shiny peaks will form; fold into batter.

Pour into a well-greased and floured 10-inch tube pan or a 13- by 9-inch pan. Bake in moderate oven (350° F.) 1 hour and 10 to 15 minutes for 10-inch tube pan, or 50 to 55 minutes for 13- by 9-inch pan. Cool 15 minutes; then remove from pan onto rack. Cover with Coconut Topping and place under broiler until lightly browned and bubbly.

Coconut Topping: Melt ½ cup butter. Add 1 cup firmly packed brown sugar, 1⅓ cups (about) flaked coconut, and ⅓ cup light cream. Mix well. Let stand about 5 minutes before spreading on cake.

CHOCOLATE-APRICOT FLAKIES

- 1 package (6 ounces) semi-sweet chocolate chips
- ½ cup apricot jam
- ½ cup milk
- 1 package active dry yeast
- 3 cups unsifted all-purpose flour
- 1 tablespoon sugar
- ½ teaspoon salt
- 1 cup shortening
- 1 egg, slightly beaten
- 1 teaspoon lemon rind
- 2 cups unsifted confectioners' sugar

Combine chocolate chips and jam in a saucepan. Melt over very low heat, stirring constantly. Set filling aside to cool.

Scald milk and cool to lukewarm. Add yeast, stirring to dissolve. Mix flour, sugar, and salt together. Cut in shortening. Then combine egg and yeast mixture; add the flour mixture and lemon rind, mixing well.

Divide dough into four equal parts and dust each generously with confectioners' sugar. Then roll each part into a 10-inch square on a board dusted with confectioners' sugar. Cut and fill as directed below and on page 148. Bake on ungreased baking sheets in moderate oven (350° F.) 12 to 15 minutes. Remove immediately from baking sheets and roll in remaining confectioners' sugar. Cool. Makes about 4 dozen cookies.

Triangles: Cut each 10-inch square of dough into 2½-inch squares. Place about ½ teaspoon of the chocolate mixture in each square. Fold dough over filling to form a triangle; seal edges well.

Turnovers: Cut each 10-inch square into rounds with a 2½-inch cookie cutter. Place about ½ teaspoon of the chocolate mixture on half of each cookie. Turn other half of cookie over the filling and seal edges well.

Envelopes: Cut each 10-inch square into 2½-inch squares. Place about ½ teaspoon filling in center of each square. Fold opposite corners to center; seal edges well.

Bowknots: Cut each 10-inch square into 2½-inch squares. Place two ¼-teaspoon dabs of filling 1 inch apart on half of each cookie. Fold other half of cookie over filling. Press to seal edges. Twist cookies in center to form bowknots.

Sandwiches: Cut each 10-inch square into rounds with a 2½-inch cookie cutter. Place about ½ teaspoon of filling in the center of half of the cookies. Cut a small hole in the center of the remaining cookies and place them on filled cookies; seal edges.

Crescents: Cut each 10-inch square into rounds with a 2½-inch cookie cutter. Pull cookies slightly to make ovals. Place about ½ teaspoon filling on half of each cookie. Fold other half of cookie over filling. Press edges together to seal. Form into a crescent shape on baking sheet.

Coffee Salad Dressings

Work wonders with these brand-new salad dress-ups.

COFFEE-CREAM SALAD DRESSING

- 2 tablespoons butter
- ½ cup orange juice
- 2 teaspoons instant quality coffee
- 2 eggs, beaten
- ½ cup sugar
- 1 teaspoon salt
- 2 tablespoons lemon juice
- ½ cup sour cream

In top of double boiler over direct low heat, melt butter in orange juice. Then dissolve instant coffee in the hot mixture. Cool. Then beat in eggs. Add sugar and salt, mixing well. Place over hot water and cook until thickened, stirring constantly. Gradually add lemon juice. Chill thoroughly. Before serving, blend in sour cream. Serve on salads of mixed fresh fruits or of sliced oranges garnished with walnuts or chopped mint. Makes about 1 cup salad dressing.

COFFEE-LEMON SALAD DRESSING

- 1 cup sour cream*
- ¼ cup confectioners' sugar
- ¼ cup salad oil
- 1 tablespoon lemon juice
- 2 teaspoons instant quality coffee

*Or use ½ cup heavy cream and whip the cream before blending with other ingredients.

Blend ingredients together. Chill thoroughly. Stir and serve with salads of chilled canned or fresh fruit. Makes 1 cup.

Creamy Coffee-Lemon Salad Dressing: Prepare Coffee-Lemon Salad Dressing, substituting ½ cup mayonnaise for the salad oil and increasing lemon juice to 2 tablespoons.

COFFEE-ORANGE TOPPING

1 cup sour cream*
⅓ cup confectioners' sugar
1 tablespoon orange juice
2 teaspoons instant quality coffee
1 teaspoon grated orange rind

***Or use ½ cup heavy cream and whip the cream before blending with other ingredients.**

Blend ingredients together. Chill thoroughly. Stir and serve on fruit salads or desserts, cakes, or puddings. Makes 1 cup.

Happy Endings

Here's a mixed bag of desserts, all with the delicious flavor of coffee to make them very special indeed. Soufflés and custards, creams and cheesecakes, puddings and charlottes, and tortes—doesn't just reading the list make you want to go on a dessert-making spree? Guarantee: your family will be delighted, your guests enchanted, and you'll have a wonderful time—and add a whole new batch of answers to the everyday question, "What shall we have for dessert tonight?"

COFFEE TAPIOCA CREAM

- 1 egg white
- 2 tablespoons sugar
- 1 egg yolk
- 2 cups milk
- 3 tablespoons quick-cooking tapioca
- ⅛ teaspoon salt
- 2 tablespoons sugar
- 1½ tablespoons instant quality coffee
- ½ teaspoon vanilla

Beat the egg white until foamy. Add 2 tablespoons sugar, a tablespoon at a time, beating after each addition until blended. Continue beating until soft peaks will form.

Mix egg yolk, milk, tapioca, salt, 2 tablespoons sugar, and coffee in saucepan. Let stand 5 minutes. Then cook and stir over medium heat until mixture comes to a full boil—about 5 to 8 minutes. Pour a small amount of hot mixture gradually into egg white mixture, blending well. Quickly stir in remaining tapioca mixture. Add vanilla. Let stand 15 to 20 minutes; stir. Serve warm or cooled. Makes 4 or 5 servings.

Coconut-Coffee Tapioca Cream: Prepare Coffee Tapioca Cream, adding ¾ cup flaked coconut with vanilla.

Coffee-Nut Tapioca Cream: Prepare Coffee Tapioca Cream, adding ¼ cup pecan halves.

Raisin-Coffee Tapioca: Prepare Coffee Tapioca Cream, cooking ⅓ cup raisins with the tapioca mixture.

Fruited Coffee Tapioca: Prepare Coffee Tapioca Cream; chill. Then fold in 1 sliced banana or 1 cup drained sliced peaches.

COLD SOUFFLÉ ÉLÉGANTE

- 1 envelope unflavored gelatin
- ¼ cup cold water
- 1 package (4 ounces) sweet cooking chocolate
- 1 teaspoon instant quality coffee
- ¼ cup water
- 6 egg yolks
- ¼ cup sugar
- 6 egg whites
- 1 cup heavy cream

First, butter a 1-quart soufflé dish or casserole with straight sides. Then cut a strip of wax or brown paper about 4 inches deep and long enough to encircle the dish with a slight overlap. Tape the strip securely around outside rim of dish—paper should stand about 2 inches above the rim to form a collar. Brush inside of strip with oil or melted butter.

Add gelatin to ¼ cup cold water to soften. Melt chocolate with coffee and ¼ cup water over low heat, stirring constantly. Then add gelatin, stirring until dissolved. Remove from heat.

Combine egg yolks and sugar in top of double boiler. Place over hot water and beat with an electric mixer or a rotary beater until mixture is very thick and light-colored. Blend in chocolate mixture; then pour into a bowl. Beat egg whites until stiff, shiny peaks will form; fold into chocolate mixture. Cool about 10 minutes. Then whip the cream and fold into chocolate mixture.

Pour into prepared soufflé dish. Chill until firm—about 3 hours. Loosen paper collar and peel away from soufflé gently. Garnish with additional whipped cream, if desired. Makes 6 to 8 servings.

Nice to know: *A 1½-quart soufflé dish or casserole, without paper collar, may be used instead of 1-quart dish.*

MOCHA CHEESECAKE

- 1¼ cups fine zwieback crumbs
- 1 tablespoon sugar
- ¼ cup butter, melted
- 2 packages (4 ounces each) sweet cooking chocolate
- 1 tablespoon instant quality coffee
- 3 eggs
- ¾ cup sugar
- 3 packages (3 ounces each) cream cheese
- 1¼ cups heavy cream
- ⅓ cup sifted all-purpose flour
- Pinch of baking soda
- ¼ teaspoon salt
- 1 teaspoon vanilla

Combine crumbs and 1 tablespoon sugar. Add melted butter and mix thoroughly. Grease sides of a 9-inch spring-form pan. Sprinkle about ¼ cup of the crumb mixture around sides. Press remaining crumb mixture onto bottom of pan.

Melt chocolate with coffee in double boiler over hot water. Remove from heat and cool slightly. Beat eggs until thick and fluffy. Add ¾ cup sugar, a tablespoon at a time, beating after each addition until blended. Beat cheese until soft and fluffy. Add the cream and beat until smooth and of the consistency of whipped cream. Add chocolate mixture and stir until blended. Fold egg mixture into cheese mixture.

Sift together flour, soda, and salt. Fold into the cheese mixture. Add vanilla; blend. Pour into crumb-lined pan. Bake in slow oven (325° F.) I hour and 5 minutes or until cake tester inserted halfway between center and edge comes out clean. Cool; then spread whipped cream or prepared whipped topping over top of cake, if desired. Chill. Before serving, let cake warm to room temperature. Makes about 16 servings.

SOFT COFFEE CUSTARD

- 2 egg yolks, slightly beaten
- 1 whole egg, slightly beaten
- ⅓ cup sugar
- ⅛ teaspoon salt
- 1⅔ cups (1 tall can) evaporated milk
- 4 teaspoons instant quality coffee
- 1 cup boiling water
- ¼ teaspoon vanilla
- Floating Meringues (see below)

Combine eggs, sugar, and salt in top of double boiler. Add milk gradually, stirring until blended. Dissolve coffee in boiling water; add to egg mixture. Place over boiling water; cook and stir until mixture thickens slightly and coats a metal spoon. Cool. Add vanilla. Chill. To serve, spoon custard into individual serving dishes; top each with a Floating Meringue. Makes 6 servings.

Floating Meringues: Beat 2 egg whites until foamy throughout. Add 4 tablespoons sugar, 2 tablespoons at a time, beating after each addition until sugar is blended. Then continue beating until mixture will stand in stiff peaks. Drop meringue by spoonfuls onto a baking sheet covered with brown paper. Bake in a slow oven (275° F.) 35 minutes, or until delicately browned. Cool before serving. Makes 6 meringues.

MOCHA SKILLET SOUFFLÉ

- 1 package (4 ounces) sweet cooking chocolate
- 2 tablespoons water
- 4 egg yolks
- ⅓ cup sugar
- ⅛ teaspoon salt
- 1 teaspoon instant quality coffee
- 1 teaspoon vanilla
- 6 egg whites
- 1 tablespoon butter
- Additional sugar
- Packaged grated coconut

Melt chocolate with water in a small pan over low heat. Cool. Then beat egg yolks until light and lemon-colored. Gradually beat in ⅓ cup sugar. Add cooled chocolate, salt, coffee, and vanilla; blend well. Beat egg whites until stiff, shiny peaks will form. Fold about a third of the egg whites into the chocolate mixture, blending well. Then fold in remaining egg whites.

Place butter in an 8-inch oven-proof skillet or casserole Heat in a moderate oven (375° F.). Spread melted butter around sides of skillet; then sprinkle with sugar. Pour in the soufflé mixture. Bake at 375° F. about 15 minutes or until a cake tester inserted about 1 inch from center comes out clean. Remove from oven and sprinkle with coconut. Serve at once, with a custard sauce, if desired. Makes 6 to 8 servings.

Nice to know: *Soufflé may be baked in an 8-inch electric skillet at 375° F. for 15 minutes or until cake tester inserted about 1 inch from center comes out clean.*

COFFEE CREAM

- 2 tablespoons instant quality coffee
- ½ cup unsifted all-purpose flour
- ⅔ sup sugar
- ¼ teaspoon salt
- 3¼ cups milk
- 2 egg yolks, slightly beaten
- 1 teaspoon vanilla
- ½ cup heavy cream

Combine instant coffee, flour, sugar, and salt in top of double boiler. Add milk gradually, stirring constantly. Cook and stir over direct heat until mixture comes to a boil and is thickened. Pour small amount of hot mixture gradually on egg yolks, blending well. Then add remaining hot mixture, stirring constantly. Return to top of double boiler. Place over hot water; cook 3 minutes longer, stirring constantly. Remove from heat. Add vanilla. Cool for 15 to 20 minutes; chill. Just before serving, whip the cream and fold into pudding. Spoon into serving dishes. Makes 6 to 8 servings.

Coffee Cream Tarts: Prepare Coffee Cream, chill, and pour into 10 baked 4-inch tart shells. If desired, top with additional whipped cream.

COFFEE BOTTOM PUDDING

- 1 cup sifted all-purpose flour
- ½ cup sugar
- 2 teaspoons double-acting baking powder
- 1 teaspoon salt
- ½ cup milk
- 2 tablespoons butter, melted
- ½ teaspoon vanilla
- ½ cup chopped nuts
- 1 cup boiling water
- ½ cup corn syrup
- 2 tablespoons instant quality coffee
- 2 tablespoons sugar

Sift flour, ½ cup sugar, baking powder, and salt together. Add milk, butter, and vanilla; mix only until smooth. Add nuts. Spoon into greased custard cups, filling each about half full.

Combine water, syrup, instant coffee, and 2 tablespoons sugar in saucepan; mix well. Simmer 2 minutes. Pour boiling mixture over the batter in the cups, allowing about 3 tablespoonfuls to each cup. (This makes a coffee sauce in the bottom of the cup, when pudding is baked.) Bake in moderate oven (350° F.) 25 to 30 minutes or until tops are firm. Cool 2 or 3 minutes. Loosen around edges with knife. Turn pudding into serving dishes. Serve warm with plain or whipped cream. Makes 6 to 8 servings.

CHOCOLATE CAFÉ CRÈME

- 4 squares unsweetened chocolate
- ½ cup brewed quality coffee*
- 1 cup sugar
- ½ cup milk
- 3 egg yolks, slightly beaten
- 1 teaspoon vanilla
- 3 egg whites, stiffly beaten
- ½ cup heavy cream
- 1 tablespoon sugar
- ½ teaspoon aromatic bitters

*Or use 1 teaspoon instant quality coffee dissolved in ½ cup water.

Place chocolate and coffee in saucepan over low heat until smooth and thick, stirring constantly. Stir in ¾ cup of the sugar. Combine milk and beaten egg yolks; gradually stir into hot mixture. Continue stirring over low heat until sugar is dissolved. Fold remaining ¼ cup sugar and the vanilla into beaten egg whites. Then fold in hot mixture. Cool. Pour into serving dish; chill. Just before serving, whip cream, adding 1 tablespoon sugar and the bitters. Serve with the crème. Makes 8 to 10 servings.

COFFEE-RAISIN RICE PUDDING

- 1 tablespoon instant quality coffee
- ½ teaspoon salt
- 1⅓ cups water
- 1⅓ cups packaged pre-cooked rice
- ½ cup firmly packed brown sugar
- ⅛ teaspoon ground nutmeg
- ½ cup raisins
- ½ cup chopped walnuts
- 1 cup heavy cream*

*Or use 1 envelope whipped topping mix prepared according to package directions.

Combine instant coffee, salt, and water in saucepan. Bring to a boil. Add rice and mix just to moisten rice. Cover, remove from heat, and let stand 5 minutes. Then stir in brown sugar, nutmeg, raisins, and walnuts. Allow to cool to room temperature. Whip cream and fold into rice mixture. Chill. Serve with additional whipped cream, if desired. Makes about 6 servings.

BAKED COFFEE SOUFFLÉ

- 3 tablespoons butter
- 3 tablespoons flour
- ¼ teaspoon salt
- 2½ tablespoons instant quality coffee
- ¾ cup water
- 3 egg yolks
- ½ cup sugar
- ½ teaspoon vanilla
- 3 egg whites
- Custard sauce or cream

Melt butter in saucepan. Add flour, salt, instant coffee, and water and stir until smooth. Cook until thickened, stirring constantly. Remove from heat.

Beat egg yolks until thick and light; gradually add sugar, beating well after each addition. Add hot coffee mixture and vanilla.

Beat egg whites until stiff, shiny peaks will form. Fold in coffee-egg mixture. Pour into greased 1-quart soufflé or baking dish. Place in pan of hot water and bake in moderate oven (350° F.) 45 minutes or until cake tester inserted near center comes out clean. Serve immediately with custard sauce or plain or whipped cream. Makes 1 quart, or 4 to 6 servings.

Coconut Coffee Soufflé: Prepare Baked Coffee Soufflé, adding ½ cup flaked coconut with the coffee.

Nice to know: *If desired, prepare soufflé mixture except for beating and folding in the egg whites in advance; set aside at room temperature. Then about an hour before serving time, beat egg whites, fold into coffee mixture, and bake as directed.*

COFFEE CHARLOTTE SQUARES

- 3 tablespoons instant quality coffee*
- ¾ cup water*
- 30 marshmallows, cut in small pieces
- 1 cup heavy cream
- 12 ladyfingers, split

*Or substitute ¾ cup brewed quality coffee for the instant coffee and water.

Combine instant coffee, water, and marshmallows. Place over low heat and stir until marshmallows are melted. Chill until slightly thickened. Whip cream and fold into coffee mixture.

Arrange ladyfinger halves on bottom of 10- by 6-inch or 8-inch square baking or serving dish. Top with half of the coffee mixture. Cover with another layer of ladyfingers and top with remaining coffee mixture. Chill 8 hours or overnight. Cut in squares to serve. Makes 8 to 10 servings.

COFFEE MERINGUES

Combine ¾ to 1 teaspoon instant quality coffee and 6 tablespoons sugar. Beat 3 egg whites until foamy throughout. Add sugar mixture, 2 tablespoons at a time, beating well after each addition. Then continue beating until mixture will stand in stiff, shiny peaks. To serve as unbaked meringues, drop from teaspoon onto pudding or custard. For baked meringues, drop meringue by spoonfuls onto baking sheet covered with brown paper, forming mounds. Bake in very slow oven (275° F.) about 35 minutes or until delicately browned. Cool before serving. Then place meringues on individual servings of pudding or custard. Makes about 12 small meringues.

MOUSSE ÉLÉGANTE

½ cup semi-sweet chocolate chips
¾ teaspoon instant quality coffee
3 egg yolks
½ teaspoon ground cinnamon
Dash of salt
1 teaspoon vanilla
3 egg whites

Combine chocolate chips and instant coffee in top of double boiler. Stir over hot (not boiling) water until chocolate melts and coffee dissolves. Cool. Then add egg yolks, one at a time, beating well after each addition. Fold in cinnamon, salt, and vanilla. Beat egg whites until soft, rounded peaks will form; fold into chocolate mixture. Spoon into dessert dishes; chill. If desired, garnish with whipped cream. Makes 4 servings.

COFFEE CUSTARD

3 eggs, slightly beaten
6 tablespoons sugar
¼ teaspoon salt
1 teaspoon vanilla
2 tablespoons instant quality coffee
2 cups milk, scalded

Combine eggs, sugar, salt, and vanilla. Dissolve coffee in scalded milk. Gradually add to egg mixture, stirring vigorously. Pour into custard cups. Place in pan of hot water and bake in moderate oven (350° F.) 35 to 40 minutes or until knife inserted in center comes out clean. Chill thoroughly. Loosen edges with sharp knife and unmold on serving dishes. Makes 6 servings.

POT DE CRÈME AU MOKA

- 1 package (4 ounces) sweet cooking chocolate
- 1½ cups light cream
- ¼ cup sugar
- 1 tablespoon instant quality coffee
- 6 egg yolks, slightly beaten
- 1 teaspoon vanilla

Combine chocolate, cream, sugar, and instant coffee in double boiler. Heat over hot water until chocolate is melted. Gradually pour chocolate mixture over the egg yolks, stirring constantly. Return to double boiler; cook over hot water, stirring constantly until mixture is the consistency of a thin pudding, about 7 minutes. Stir in vanilla. Pour mixture into pot de crème cups or small paper soufflé cups. Chill until set. Makes about 2⅓ cups, or 6 to 8 servings.

BRAZILIAN PUDIM MOKA

- 3 cups milk
- 1 cup light cream
- 5 tablespoons instant quality coffee
- 2 teaspoons grated orange rind
- 4 eggs
- 1 egg yolk
- ½ cup sugar
- 1 teaspoon vanilla
- ½ teaspoon salt
- Ground nutmeg
- 1 cup chopped Brazil nuts
- Guava Fluff (page 160) or Regal Chocolate Sauce (page 159)

Combine milk and cream; scald. Stir in instant coffee and orange rind. Cool 10 minutes.

Meanwhile, beat eggs and egg yolk slightly. Then beat in sugar. Gradually add coffee mixture, vanilla, and salt. Strain through fine sieve to remove orange rind. Pour into custard cups. Sprinkle with nutmeg.

Place cups in baking pan; fill pan with hot water to within ¾ inch of tops of cups. Bake in moderate oven (325° F.) 45 minutes or until knife inserted in center comes out clean. Chill thoroughly.

To serve, unmold into serving dishes and sprinkle with Brazil nuts. Serve with Guava Fluff or Regal Chocolate Sauce. Makes about 5 cups or 8 servings.

Guava Fluff: Beat 1 egg white until stiff, shiny peaks will form. Then beat in 3 tablespoons guava jelly. Serve with custards and other desserts. Makes about 1 cup.

COFFEE PECAN CORNUCOPIAS

- 1 package (9½ or 10 ounces) pie crust mix
- 2 tablespoons sugar
- 1 tablespoon instant quality coffee
- Dash of salt
- ½ cup heavy cream
- ⅓ cup chopped pecans

Prepare pie crust mix as directed on package. Roll out thin and cut into eight 4-inch squares. Fold over to form cornucopias, curving narrow end and stuffing wide opening with aluminum foil. Bake in hot oven (425° F.) 10 to 12 minutes or until golden brown. Remove foil and cool on rack.

Meanwhile, dissolve sugar, instant coffee, and salt in the cream. Chill; then whip until soft peaks will form. Fold in chopped pecans. Fill cornucopias with the cream mixture. Sprinkle additional chopped pecans on cream at wide ends of cornucopias, if desired. Makes 8 cornucopias.

ITALIAN COFFEE FOAM

- 4 egg yolks
- ¼ cup sugar
- ⅔ cup Demitasse Coffee (page 16)
- 2 tablespoons brandy

Combine ingredients in the top of a double boiler. Place over hot, not boiling, water and whip until mixture is thick and light. *Do not let mixture boil.* Pour into dessert dishes and serve at once. Makes 4 servings.

COFFEE TORTE SUPREME

- 1/4 cup grated blanched almonds or grated filberts or walnuts
- 6 egg whites
- 1 cup sugar
- 1 1/2 cups grated blanched almonds or grated filberts or walnuts
- 1 tablespoon instant quality coffee
- 1 tablespoon instant quality coffee
- 1/4 cup dark rum or water
- 2 cups heavy cream
- 1/4 cup sugar
- 1 tablespoon instant quality coffee
- 1 teaspoon vanilla
- 1/4 cup grated blanched almonds or grated filberts or walnuts
- 1/2 cup toasted slivered almonds or slivered filberts or broken walnuts

Heavily grease bottom and sides of a 15- by 10- by 1-inch jelly-roll pan. Line with wax paper; then grease the paper. Sprinkle with 1/4 cup grated almonds.

Beat egg whites until foamy throughout. Add 1 cup sugar, 2 tablespoons at a time, beating well after each addition. Continue beating until stiff, shiny peaks will form. Fold in 1 1/2 cups grated almonds and 1 tablespoon instant coffee. Spread evenly in the pan. Bake in a hot oven (400° F.) 15 to 20 minutes or until cake tester inserted in center comes out clean and top is evenly browned.

Sprinkle sugar on a cloth or wax paper placed on racks. Remove torte from pan and invert onto sugared cloth. Remove paper from bottom. Cut torte crosswise into 4 strips, each about 10 by 3 3/4 inches. Blend 1 tablespoon instant coffee into rum; brush or drizzle over each strip or layer of torte. Cool thoroughly. (Torte will shrink slightly as it cools.)

Combine cream, 1/4 cup sugar, 1 tablespoon instant coffee, and vanilla in a small narrow bowl. Whip until soft peaks will form. Stir in 1/4 cup grated almonds. Spread about 1/2 cup whipped cream mixture between each layer of torte. Spread remaining whipped cream mixture over top and sides of torte. Garnish with slivered almonds. Chill 3 to 4 hours or, covered, overnight. Makes 12 servings.

Nice to know: *If desired, torte may be frozen. Thaw about 30 minutes before serving. Or torte may be covered and stored up to 3 days in the refrigerator.*

MOCHA NUT DESSERT

1 package (3 ounces) orange flavor gelatin
2 teaspoons instant quality coffee
1 cup boiling water
1 cup dark corn syrup
1 cup chopped pecans

Dissolve gelatin and instant coffee in boiling water. Stir in corn syrup. Chill until slightly thickened. Then fold in pecans. Pour into individual molds and chill until firm. Serve with a custard sauce or light cream, if desired. Makes 6 servings.

Make It in a Mold

Gelatin's the secret of these light-and-bright desserts—make-ahead's the secret of their popularity with the cook, coffee flavor the secret of their popularity with just about everyone!

COFFEE DELIGHT

1 envelope unflavored gelatin
6 tablespoons sugar
3 tablespoons instant quality coffee
⅛ teaspoon salt
1 cup boiling water
1 cup cold water
Whipped cream or custard sauce

Combine gelatin, sugar, instant coffee, and salt. Add boiling water and stir until gelatin is dissolved. Stir in cold water. Pour into individual molds. Chill until firm—about 3 hours. Unmold. Serve with whipped cream or custard sauce. Makes 4 servings.

FRUITED COFFEE PUDDING

1 envelope unflavored gelatin
¼ cup sugar
1 tablespoon cornstarch
¼ teaspoon salt
¼ cup chopped raisins
2 tablespoons instant quality coffee
1½ cups water
3 eggs, separated
¼ cup sugar
½ cup heavy cream
2 teaspoons brandy extract
6 maraschino cherries, quartered
¼ cup chopped nuts

Combine gelatin, ¼ cup sugar, cornstarch, salt, raisins, and instant coffee in saucepan. Add cold water and place over medium heat, stirring constantly, until gelatin dissolves—about 3 minutes. Beat egg yolks slightly. Add small amount of hot mixture, stirring vigorously. Return to saucepan and cook 3 minutes longer, stirring constantly. Chill until slightly thickened.

Beat egg whites until foamy, add ¼ cup sugar gradually, and beat until soft peaks will form. Whip the cream; then fold in beaten egg whites. Add extract, cherries, and nuts. Stir slightly thickened gelatin mixture; fold into whipped cream mixture. Chill until almost firm. Spoon into sherbet glasses. Makes 6 to 8 servings.

COFFEE GINGERSNAP CREAM

- 1 envelope unflavored gelatin
- ⅓ cup sugar
- Dash of salt
- 1¼ cups hot brewed quality coffee*
- 1½ packages (4½ ounces) cream cheese
- 2 egg whites, stiffly beaten
- 1 teaspoon vanilla
- 9 gingersnaps

*Or use 2 teaspoons instant quality coffee dissolved in 1¼ cups hot water.

Combine gelatin, sugar, and salt. Add hot coffee and stir until gelatin is dissolved—about 3 minutes. Mash cheese until creamy; then gradually add coffee mixture, stirring until smooth. Chill until slightly thickened. Fold in egg whites and vanilla. Pile lightly in sherbet glasses. Break cookies in half and garnish each serving with 3 halves. Chill until firm. Makes 6 servings.

Coffee Gingersnap Pie: Mix 1 cup gingersnap crumbs, 2½ tablespoons sugar, and ¼ cup softened butter or margarine; press on bottom and sides of an 8-inch pie pan. Chill at least 1 hour. Meanwhile, prepare Coffee Gingersnap Cream, omitting gingersnaps; pour into chilled crust.

CHOCO-COFFEE DESSERT

- 1½ teaspoons unflavored gelatin
- ½ cup sugar
- Dash of salt
- ½ cup water
- 2 squares unsweetened chocolate
- 4 egg yolks, slightly beaten
- 1¼ teaspoons vanilla
- 4 egg whites
- 1 cup heavy cream
- 1 tablespoon confectioners' sugar
- 1 teaspoon instant quality coffee
- 16 ladyfingers, split

Combine gelatin, sugar, and salt; set aside. Place water and chocolate in a saucepan over very low heat and stir until chocolate is completely melted. Add gelatin mixture and continue cooking over low heat until gelatin and sugar are dissolved—about 3 minutes. Gradually stir into egg yolks. Then return to saucepan and cook until mixture begins to thicken, about 2 to 3 minutes. Remove from heat. Add 1 teaspoon vanilla. Cool.

Then beat egg whites until soft peaks will form. Fold into the cooled chocolate mixture. Chill until set, about 1 hour. Whip ½ cup of the cream and fold into the chocolate mixture. Combine the remaining ½ cup heavy cream, the confectioners' sugar, instant coffee, and ¼ teaspoon vanilla. Beat until soft peaks will form.

Line bottom and sides of a 9- by 5- by 3-inch loaf pan with wax paper, letting paper extend in 2-inch tabs at each end. Arrange ladyfinger halves on bottom and sides of pan, reserving 6 halves to use on top. Spread about 1½ cups of the chocolate mixture over the ladyfingers. Carefully top with coffee whipped cream mixture. Spread remaining chocolate mixture over the coffee layer. Arrange reserved ladyfingers on top. Chill 6 hours or overnight. Makes 8 to 10 servings.

MOCHA BAVARIAN CREAM

1 envelope unflavored gelatin
1 tablespoon instant quality coffee
¼ cup milk, scalded
½ cup boiling water
1 package (6 ounces) semi-sweet chocolate chips
1 or 2 tablespoons sugar
2 egg yolks
1 cup crushed ice
1 cup heavy cream

Combine gelatin, coffee, milk, and water in an electric blender. Cover and blend on high speed for 40 seconds. Add chocolate chips and sugar. Cover and blend 10 seconds or until smooth. Add egg yolks, ice, and cream. Blend 20 seconds. Pour into serving dishes; chill until set. Makes 6 to 8 servings.

COLD COFFEE SOUFFLÉ

1 envelope unflavored gelatin
¼ cup water
1 tablespoon instant quality coffee
⅛ teaspoon ground cinnamon
6 egg yolks, slightly beaten
4 egg whites
¾ cup sugar
1 cup heavy cream
½ teaspoon vanilla

Dissolve gelatin in water in top of double boiler over simmering water. Then add instant coffee and cinnamon. Blend in egg yolks. Remove from heat.

Beat egg whites until frothy. Gradually beat in sugar; beat until stiff, shiny peaks will form. Blend into gelatin mixture.

Combine cream and vanilla and whip; fold into soufflé mixture. Pour into a 1½-quart soufflé dish or casserole. Chill until set—about 3 hours. Garnish with additional whipped cream, if desired. Makes about 6 cups, enough for 6 to 8 servings, ¾ to 1 cup each.

COCONUT COFFEE RIBBON LOAF

1 envelope unflavored gelatin
¼ cup sugar
⅛ teaspoon salt
1½ teaspoons instant quality coffee*
1¼ cups boiling water*
1¼ cups heavy cream
8- by 4-inch loaf of sponge or white cake
2 tablespoons sugar
2 cups packaged grated coconut, toasted

***Or substitute 1¼ cups hot brewed quality coffee for the instant coffee and boiling water.**

Combine gelatin, sugar, salt, and instant coffee; mix well. Add boiling water and stir until gelatin dissolves—about 3 minutes. Chill until slightly thickened. Whip ¾ cup of the cream and fold into gelatin mixture. Chill until almost firm.

Meanwhile, trim cake as needed to fit 8- by 4-inch loaf pan and split into three layers. Line pan with wax paper. Place first layer of cake in bottom of pan; spread with half the gelatin mixture. Add second layer of cake; spread with remaining gelatin mixture. Top with third layer of cake. Then chill about 3 hours.

Unmold loaf on platter. Whip remaining cream with 2 tablespoons sugar. Spread over top and sides of loaf. Sprinkle with coconut. Chill another hour or more. Makes 8 servings.

Coffee Party: "Come for Afternoon Coffee!"

Whether it's a few friends invited on the spur of the moment or a full-scale affair, an afternoon coffee party is a pleasant way to entertain . . . and a relatively easy one. Most of the food for such a party can be prepared in advance, and other work—such as setting the table—can be done ahead of time, too. When guests are due to arrive, put the coffee on to brew, and you are all set to enjoy your own party!

Bear in mind: If your guests are few, afternoon coffee service can be informal. But if you're having a crowd, you'll be wise to set up a buffet coffee table, so that guests can help themselves and the passing of foods can be kept to a minimum. Borrow—or rent, if necessary—an urn or other large receptacle to hold coffee, preferably one with a warming device to keep the coffee hot. Ask a friend to preside over this, so that you'll be free to greet guests. A party of this sort calls for your best silver, china, and linen. Have the table ready well in advance, decorated with flowers, candles, whatever you choose, with sugar, cream, cups and saucers, spoons, and napkins in place. If you are serving very small sandwiches and cookies, the saucer will do as a resting place for them, but sandwiches or cakes of any size require tea plates and, sometimes, forks as well. (Try to avoid those if you're having a big crowd.) Just before the first guests are due, food can be put on plates and taken to the table. A second friend should be asked to keep these filled, and a cup-and-saucer washer in the kitchen is a must unless you have a far greater supply of china than most people!

CHERRY BREAD

- 2½ cups sifted all-purpose flour
- 3 teaspoons double-acting baking powder
- ½ teaspoon salt
- ¾ cup sugar
- 1 egg, slightly beaten
- 1 cup milk
- ¼ cup maraschino cherry juice
- 2 tablespoons butter, melted
- 1 cup 40% bran flakes
- ¼ cup chopped maraschino cherries
- ¼ cup chopped nuts
- ¼ cup raisins

Sift flour, baking powder, salt, and sugar into mixing bowl. Combine egg, milk, and cherry juice. Add to flour mixture with butter and cereal, stirring only enough to moisten. Add cherries, nuts, and raisins. Pour batter into greased 9- by 5-inch loaf pan. Bake in moderate oven (350° F.) 60 to 65 minutes. Cool thoroughly before slicing. To store, wrap in wax paper or transparent Saran. Makes 1 loaf.

ORANGE NUT BREAD

- 2¼ cups sifted all-purpose flour
- 1 cup minus 2 tablespoons sugar
- 2 teaspoons double-acting baking powder
- ¾ teaspoon salt
- ½ teaspoon baking soda
- ¾ cup chopped nuts
- ½ cup raisins
- ¼ cup ground orange rind
- 1 egg, well beaten
- ½ cup milk
- ½ cup orange juice
- 2 tablespoons shortening, melted

Sift together flour, sugar, baking powder, salt, and baking soda. Add nuts, raisins, and orange rind. Combine beaten egg, milk, and orange juice. Add to flour mixture with melted shortening; mix just until all flour is dampened and fruit and nuts are well distributed. Pour the batter into greased 9- by 5-inch loaf pan. Bake in moderate oven (350° F.) 1 hour. Let cool in pan 10 minutes; then turn out of pan and let stand until cold. Wrap in wax paper or aluminum foil and store overnight before slicing.

To make delicious sandwiches: Cut bread in thin slices and spread with butter, cream cheese, marmalade, or any other desired filling.

Nice to know: *Orange Nut Bread recipe may be doubled to make two 9- by 5-inch loaves. These keep well in freezer.*

DELICIOUS NUT BREAD

- 3 cups sifted all-purpose flour
- 3 teaspoons double-acting baking powder
- 1½ teaspoons salt
- 1 cup firmly packed light brown sugar
- 1 egg, well beaten
- 1⅓ cups milk
- ¼ cup shortening, melted
- 1 cup finely chopped nuts

Sift together flour, baking powder, and salt. Add brown sugar. Combine egg and milk. Add milk mixture and shortening to flour mixture, mixing only enough to dampen flour. Fold in nuts. Pour into 9- by 5-inch loaf pan or two 8- by 4-inch loaf pans, lined on bottoms with wax paper. Bake in moderate oven (350° F.) 1 hour and 5 or 10 minutes for large loaf or about 50 minutes for small loaves. Cool. Wrap in wax paper or transparent Saran and store overnight before slicing.

Date Nut Bread: Prepare Delicious Nut Bread, reducing nuts to ½ cup and folding in 1 cup finely cut dates with nuts.

MOLASSES NUT BREAD

- 3 cups sifted all-purpose flour
- 3 teaspoons double-acting baking powder
- 1½ teaspoons salt
- ½ teaspoon baking soda
- ½ cup firmly packed light brown sugar
- ½ cup molasses
- 1 egg, well beaten
- 1 cup milk
- ¼ cup shortening, melted
- ½ cup finely chopped nuts
- 1 cup raisins

Sift together flour, baking powder, salt, and soda. Add brown sugar. Combine molasses, egg, and milk. Add milk mixture and shortening to flour, mixing only to dampen flour. Fold in nuts and raisins. Turn into a 9- by 5-inch loaf pan or two 8- by 4-inch loaf pans, lined on bottoms with wax paper. Bake in moderate oven (350° F.) for 1 hour and 5 or 10 minutes for large loaf or about 50 minutes for small loaves. Cool. Wrap in wax paper or transparent Saran and store overnight.

CUCUMBER ROUNDS

4 *unsliced* frankfurter rolls
4 tablespoons (about) soft butter or mayonnaise
1 large cucumber

Cut off the ends of each roll; then slice rolls thinly crosswise. Spread one side of each slice with butter or mayonnaise. Also cut thin slices crosswise from cucumber, pared or not as you please. Trim the cucumber slices, if necessary, to match the diameter of the roll. Then place cucumber slices between 2 slices of roll. Makes 40 small "sandwiches."

PETITE PARTY SANDWICHES

1⅔ cups water
⅛ teaspoon peppercorns
½ bay leaf
½ teaspoon dried dill
1 package (3 ounces) lemon flavor gelatin
½ teaspoon salt
Dash of cayenne
3 tablespoons vinegar
12 to 14 petite open-faced sandwiches (see below)

Combine water, peppercorns, bay leaf, and dried dill in a saucepan. Cover and simmer for about 10 minutes. Strain. Dissolve gelatin and salt in the *hot* liquid. Add cayenne and vinegar. Chill until slightly thickened.

Place open-faced sandwiches on a rack and spoon the slightly thickened glaze over the tops, allowing about 2 tablespoons glaze for each. Chill until glaze is firm. Makes about 1¾ cups glaze, or enough for 12 to 14 small sandwiches.

Suggested sandwiches: Turkey pâté or paste and chopped hard-cooked egg on fingers or triangles of whole wheat bread. . . . Sliced egg and shrimp, garnished with caviar or sliced olive, on buttered salty rye bread—either half slices or whole. . . . Sliced ham, asparagus spears, and chopped ripe olives on buttered fingers, triangles, or squares of pumpernickel. . . . Horse-radish and chili sauce topped with tiny shrimp on salty rye. . . . Cream cheese and sliced smoked salmon on pumpernickel.

CHOCOLATE MACAROON MINIATURES

⅓ cup sugar
2 cups packaged grated coconut
1 egg white
1 package (4 ounces) sweet cooking chocolate, melted
¼ cup sifted cake flour
½ teaspoon double-acting baking powder
½ teaspoon vanilla
1 egg white
⅓ cup sugar

Add ⅓ cup sugar, the coconut, and 1 egg white to melted chocolate. Heat thoroughly, stirring occasionally. Sift together flour and baking powder. Blend into coconut mixture. Add vanilla.

Beat remaining egg white until foamy. Beat in ⅓ cup sugar, 2 tablespoons at a time; then beat until soft peaks will form. Fold into coconut mixture. Place 1-inch aluminum foil bonbon cups (see below) on a baking sheet; fill with batter. Bake in a moderate oven (350° F.) 10 minutes. Cool thoroughly on racks. Makes about 7 dozen miniatures.

Nice to know: *The foil bonbon cups are available from stores and suppliers of specialty baking equipment. Or use 1¼- or 1¾-inch (width at bottoms) cupcake pans that have been greased and dusted with cocoa. If desired, place pans on baking sheets. Bake at 350° F. about 10 minutes for smaller cups or 12 to 15 minutes for larger cups. Cool in pans 3 minutes; then remove and cool on racks. Makes 2 to 3 dozen cupcakes.*

SWEET CHOCOLATE SURPRISE BUNS

½ cup milk
¼ cup butter
⅓ cup sugar
½ teaspoon salt
1 package dry yeast
¼ cup warm water
2 eggs, beaten
3½ cups (about) unsifted all-purpose flour
1 package (4 ounces) sweet cooking chocolate
¾ cup orange marmalade

Scald milk. Add butter, sugar, and salt. Stir until butter is softened and sugar is dissolved. Cool until mixture is lukewarm. Meanwhile soften yeast in warm water. Add yeast mixture and beaten eggs to milk mixture. Add 2 cups of the flour and beat well. Add enough of the remaining flour to make soft dough; mix thoroughly.

Place dough on lightly floured board, cover, and let rest 5 minutes. Knead dough 5 minutes. Place in lightly greased bowl, cover with a damp cloth, and allow to rise in a warm place, free from drafts, until dough is doubled in bulk—about 1½ hours.

Meanwhile, chop half of the chocolate; combine with marmalade. Punch down and roll out dough into an 18- by 9-inch rectangle. Spread chocolate mixture on dough to about ½ inch from edges. Roll up tightly, beginning at wide side.

Pinch edges of roll together to seal well. Cut into 1-inch slices and place cut-side up, a little apart, in a lightly greased 13- by 9-inch pan. Cover with a towel and let stand in a warm place, free from drafts, until almost double in bulk, about 40 to 45 minutes. Bake in a moderate oven (375° F.) 25 to 30 minutes. Remove from pan immediately. Melt remaining chocolate over hot water; drizzle over buns. Sprinkle with confectioners' sugar and chopped pecans, or toasted slivered almonds, if desired. Serve warm. Makes about 16 to 18 buns.

Nice to know: *Buns may be stored unglazed. Then reheat and drizzle with chocolate just before serving.*

BAKEROONS

- 2 packages (4 ounces each) sweet cooking chocolate
- 2 egg whites
- Dash of salt
- 1 cup granulated sugar
- 2 tablespoons cake flour
- 2 cups packaged grated coconut
- 2½ cups sifted cake flour
- 1½ teaspoons double-acting baking powder
- ¾ teaspoon salt
- ¼ cup firmly packed light brown sugar
- 2 egg yolks
- ½ cup butter or margarine
- ⅓ cup milk
- 1 teaspoon vanilla

Chop 1 bar of chocolate coarsely. Melt remaining chocolate over hot water; cool slightly. Beat egg whites with dash of salt until foamy. Add ½ cup granulated sugar, a little at a time, beating until stiff peaks will form. Fold in 2 tablespoons flour. Blend in coconut. Measure ¾ cup; set aside.

Sift flour, baking powder, and ¾ teaspoon salt into a large mixing bowl. Add remaining ½ cup granulated sugar, the brown sugar, egg yolks, butter, milk, vanilla, and melted chocolate. Blend; then beat about 1 minute. Stir in chopped chocolate. Measure ⅓ cup; set aside.

Drop measured coconut mixture by teaspoonfuls 2 inches apart onto a greased baking sheet. Top with about ¼ teaspoon measured chocolate batter. Bake in moderate oven (375° F.) 12 minutes. Drop chocolate batter by teaspoonfuls 2 inches apart onto ungreased baking sheets. Top with ⅓ teaspoon coconut mixture. Bake at 375° F. for 10 to 12 minutes. Store in tightly covered containers. Makes 1 dozen coconut cookies with chocolate tops and 3 dozen chocolate cookies with coconut tops.

LEMON SOURS

- 1 cup sifted cake flour
- 2 tablespoons granulated sugar
- ⅛ teaspoon salt
- ⅓ cup butter or margarine, softened
- 2 eggs, slightly beaten
- 1 cup firmly packed dark brown sugar
- ½ cup chopped pecans
- ½ cup packaged grated coconut
- ½ teaspoon vanilla
- Lemon Glaze (see below)

Sift flour, granulated sugar, and salt into mixing bowl. Cut in butter until mixture is like coarse meal. Press firmly over bottom of a greased 9-inch square pan. Bake in a moderate oven (350° F.) 15 minutes or until pastry is a light golden brown.

Meanwhile, combine eggs, brown sugar, nuts, coconut, and vanilla, mixing well. Pour over pastry. Bake 30 minutes longer or until topping is firm. Cool 15 minutes. Prepare Lemon Glaze and spread over top of coconut mixture. Cut into small bars. Cool. Makes about 32 bars.

Lemon Glaze: Combine ⅔ cup sifted confectioners' sugar, 1 tablespoon lemon juice, and 1 teaspoon grated lemon rind, stirring until mixture is smooth.

CHOCOLATE-FILLED SLIMS

- ½ cup butter
- ¾ cup sifted confectioners' sugar
- 2 eggs, unbeaten
- 1½ squares semi-sweet chocolate, melted and cooled
- 1½ cups sifted cake flour
- 2 teaspoons double-acting baking powder
- ½ teaspoon salt
- 2 tablespoons milk
- ½ teaspoon vanilla
- Rich Coffee Frosting (halving recipe on page 83)
- Finely chopped nuts (optional)

Cream butter, sugar, and eggs, and beat until light and fluffy. Stir in chocolate. Sift together flour, baking powder, and salt. Blend half the flour mixture into the butter mixture. Stir in the milk and vanilla. Then add remaining flour mixture, mixing well.

Using a ½-inch semicircular or star tube attachment on a cookie press, form the dough into 2-inch strips on ungreased baking sheet. Bake in a moderate oven (350° F.) 8 to 10 minutes. Cool on rack.

Put cookies together sandwich-fashion, spreading with Rich Coffee Frosting. (If garnishing top, reserve about ¼ cup of the frosting.) Allow the filling to extend a bit beyond the edge of the cookies. Dip the sides and ends in finely chopped nuts, if desired. Garnish tops of cookies with a decorative design (a small star or lettering tube is suggested), using the remaining frosting.

Cookies are best the day they are prepared, but are satisfactory if stored in a tightly covered container overnight. Place wax paper between the layers of cookies to avoid having them stick together. Makes 3 dozen filled cookies.

BRIGHT-EYE COOKIES

- 2 cups sifted all-purpose flour
- ½ teaspoon double-acting baking powder
- 1 cup butter, softened
- ½ cup sugar
- 2 tablespoons water
- 1 teaspoon vanilla
- 1 egg yolk
- 1 egg white, slightly beaten
- 1¼ cups finely chopped nuts
- Jam or jelly

Sift together flour and baking powder. Cream together the butter, sugar, water, vanilla, and egg yolk. Add the sifted ingredients to the butter mixture; mix well. Chill dough thoroughly. Form the dough into balls the size of a walnut; roll in the egg white and then in the nuts. Place on a lightly greased baking sheet and bake in moderate oven (350° F.) for 5 minutes. Remove from oven. Make a slight depression in each ball with a spoon. Then return cookies to oven for 8 to 10 minutes longer. Cool. Fill depression with jam or jelly. Makes about 4 dozen cookies.

Chocolate Bright-Eye Cookies: Prepare Bright-Eye Cookies, adding ⅓ cup cocoa to the flour and baking powder before sifting. Fill depression with chocolate or vanilla icing instead of jam, if desired.

BUTTERSCOTCH PECAN BARS

- ¼ cup granulated sugar
- 1 cup sifted all-purpose flour
- ½ cup butter or margarine
- ½ cup finely chopped pecans
- ½ cup butter or margarine
- 2 cups firmly packed light brown sugar
- 2 eggs, slightly beaten
- 1¼ cups sifted all-purpose flour
- 1½ teaspoons double-acting baking powder
- ¼ teaspoon salt
- ¼ teaspoon rum extract
- ½ cup pecan halves

Combine the granulated sugar and 1 cup flour. Cut in ½ cup butter until mixture is crumbly. Mix in chopped pecans. Press mixture evenly into the bottom of an ungreased 13- by 9-inch pan. (This will make a thin layer.) Bake in moderate oven (350° F.) 15 minutes.

Meanwhile, melt remaining ½ cup butter in a heavy saucepan over low heat. Add brown sugar and bring to a boil, stirring constantly. (Mixture will appear granular and thick.) Cool about 1 minute, stirring constantly. Gradually add eggs, a small amount at a time, beating constantly. Sift together 1¼ cups flour, baking powder, and salt. Add to egg mixture with rum extract and mix well.

Spread evenly over baked layer. Sprinkle with pecan halves. Return to oven and bake 25 to 30 minutes. Cool in pan. Cut into bars. Makes about 36 bars.

COCONUT DREAM SQUARES

- 1¼ cups sifted cake flour
- 1¼ cups firmly packed brown sugar
- ⅓ cup butter
- 2 eggs
- ½ teaspoon double-acting baking powder
- 1 teaspoon vanilla
- 1⅓ cups (about) flaked coconut*
- 1 cup chopped walnuts

*Or use 1 cup packaged grated coconut.

Combine 1 cup of the flour and ¼ cup of the sugar. Add butter and mix until thoroughly blended and smooth. Press firmly into an ungreased 9-inch square pan and bake in moderate oven (350° F.) 15 minutes.

Meanwhile, beat eggs until light. Add remaining 1 cup sugar gradually, beating constantly until mixture is light and fluffy. Sift remaining ¼ cup flour and the baking powder together and fold into egg mixture. Add vanilla, coconut, and nuts and mix thoroughly. Spread on top of baked mixture in pan and return to oven. Bake 20 to 25 minutes longer, or until lightly browned. Cut in squares while warm. Makes about 2 dozen squares.

FLAKE COOKIES

- 1 cup sifted all-purpose flour
- ½ teaspoon double-acting baking powder
- ½ teaspoon salt
- ½ teaspoon baking soda
- ⅓ cup butter*
- ½ cup granulated sugar
- ½ cup firmly packed brown sugar
- 1 egg
- 1 teaspoon vanilla
- ¾ cup crisp oat flakes, 40% bran flakes, or crisp whole wheat flakes
- Brown Sugar Glaze (see page 178)

*Or use ½ cup margarine or other vegetable shortening.

Sift together flour, baking powder, salt, and soda. Cream butter. Gradually add sugars, and continue creaming until light and fluffy. Add egg and vanilla and beat well. Add flour mixture and cereal, mixing just until blended. Shape dough into 1-inch balls with floured hands. Place on ungreased baking sheet. Bake in moderate oven (375° F.) for 10 to 12 minutes. Glaze, if desired. Store in tightly covered container. Makes 2 dozen cookies.

Brown Sugar Glaze: Melt 2 tablespoons butter in saucepan. Stir in ¼ cup firmly packed light brown sugar. Cook and stir over low heat until sugar is moistened and mixture thickens slightly. Remove from heat; cool slightly. Add 1 tablespoon milk and beat until smooth. Then add ½ cup sifted confectioners' sugar and beat until smooth. Spread thinly on cookies.

Chocolate Chip Flake Cookies: Prepare Flake Cookies as directed, adding 1 package (6 ounces) semi-sweet chocolate chips. Omit glaze. Makes 2½ dozen.

Nut Flake Cookies: Prepare Flake Cookies as directed, adding ¾ cup chopped nuts. Makes about 2½ dozen.

Spice Flake Cookies: Prepare Flake Cookies as directed, sifting ¼ teaspoon ground nutmeg and ¼ teaspoon ground cinnamon with the flour, baking powder, salt, and soda.
Nice to know: *Dough may be dropped by teaspoonfuls instead of rolled in balls, if desired.*

SATIN FUDGE BROWNIES

- 1⅓ cups semi-sweet chocolate chips
- 1 package (8 ounces) cream cheese, softened
- ½ cup sugar
- 2 eggs
- 2 teaspoons vanilla
- ½ cup plus 1 tablespoon unsifted all-purpose flour
- ½ teaspoon double-acting baking powder
- ¼ teaspoon salt
- ½ cup chopped nuts

Melt 1 cup chocolate chips in a small saucepan over *low* heat, stirring constantly. Place cream cheese in a large mixing bowl. Beat until smooth. Gradually add sugar, beating constantly. Add eggs; blend well. Blend in melted chocolate and the vanilla. Add flour, baking powder, and salt. Stir until completely blended. Stir in nuts. Spread mixture evenly in a 9-inch square pan which has been lightly greased on bottom. Sprinkle remaining ⅓ cup chocolate chips over the top. Bake in moderate oven (375° F.) 15 minutes. Cool at least 2 hours before serving. Cut in 2-inch squares. Makes 16 brownies.

HONEY CEREAL COOKIES

2 cups sifted all-purpose flour
½ teaspoon double-acting baking powder
1 teaspoon baking soda
½ teaspoon salt
1 cup butter or other shortening
½ cup firmly packed brown sugar
¾ cup granulated sugar
½ cup honey
1 egg
2 cups crisp whole wheat flakes*
2 cups sugar coated crisp rice cereal or honey-flavored puffed wheat
1 cup flaked coconut

*Or use 2 cups rolled oats, if desired.

Sift together flour, baking powder, soda, and salt. Place shortening, sugars, honey, egg, and flour mixture in a large mixing bowl. Blend well. Add cereals and coconut. Mix thoroughly. Drop by teaspoonfuls onto ungreased baking sheet. Bake in moderate oven (375° F.) 8 to 10 minutes or until golden brown. Let stand a few seconds before removing from baking sheet. Cookies will become crisp when cold. Makes about 8 dozen.

PETITS FOURS

1 package white cake mix
1¼ cups water
2 egg whites
Port Wine Glaze (see below) or De Luxe Coffee Glaze (page 84)

Prepare white cake mix with water and egg whites as directed on package. Pour batter into 15- by 10- by 1½-inch pan which has been lined on the bottom with wax paper. Bake in moderate oven (350° F.) about 25 minutes. Cool; trim off edges and cut into four sections, each about 7 by 4 inches. Spread cake with Port Wine Glaze or De Luxe Coffee Glaze and then dip a knife in hot water and cut each section into various shapes as suggested below. If desired, decorate each with bits of candied fruit, nuts, or tiny colored candy. Makes about 50.

Port Wine Glaze: Combine 3 cups sifted confectioners' sugar, 6 tablespoons port wine, 2 tablespoons melted butter, and 5 drops red food coloring. Blend well. Spread over cake. Makes 1⅓ cups or enough to cover a 15- by 10-inch cake.

To make rectangles, cut a section into 3 lengthwise strips, about 1 inch wide. Then cut each strip into 3 pieces, about 2¼ inches long. Makes 9 rectangles.

To make triangles, cut a section into six 2¼-inch squares. Then cut each in half diagonally. Makes 12 triangles.

To make squares, cut a section into 15 pieces, about 1½ inches square. Makes 15 squares.

To make diamonds, mark off a section by inserting a toothpick at center of each long side; then place 2 toothpicks on each short side to mark thirds. Cut cake diagonally from first toothpick on short side to center toothpick on nearer longer side. Continue cutting cake in parallel diagonal strips, cutting from next toothpick to cake corner, and so on. Similarly, cut strips in opposite direction, forming diamonds. Makes 7 diamonds with 10 small triangles at edges, which may be used.

Glorified Packaged Puddings

Take a packaged pudding, add the very special flavor of coffee, plus a liberal helping of kitchen know-how. Result? Everyone will ask, "How do you manage to make things so extra-good?"

COFFEE CREAM PIE

- 1 package (3¼- to 4-ounce size) butterscotch, chocolate, chocolate fudge, coconut cream, or vanilla pudding and pie filling mix
- 1½ to 2 tablespoons instant quality coffee
- 1½ cups milk
- 1 baked 8-inch pie shell

Combine pudding mix with instant quality coffee and milk. Cook as directed on package. Remove from heat and cool 5 minutes, stirring once or twice. Pour into a baked 8-inch pie shell. Chill at least 3 hours before serving. Garnish with whipped cream, nuts, or coconut, if desired.

Nice to know: *If desired, substitute 1 cup brewed quality coffee for the instant coffee and reduce milk to ½ cup.*

SHAKE-A-COFFEE PUDDING

- 1⅔ cups evaporated milk
- ½ cup water
- 1 tablespoon instant quality coffee
- 1 package (3¾- to 4½-ounce size) butterscotch, chocolate, coconut cream, or vanilla instant pudding mix

Combine evaporated milk, water, instant quality coffee, and instant pudding mix in a shaker, quart jar, or other container with a tight lid. Cover and shake briskly 1 minute or just until well mixed. Pour into serving dishes and let stand to set—about 5 minutes. Makes 5 or 6 servings.

COFFEE CREAM PUDDING

- 1 package (3¼- to 4-ounce size) butterscotch, chocolate, chocolate fudge, coconut cream, or vanilla pudding and pie filling mix
- 1½ to 2 tablespoons instant quality coffee
- 2 cups milk

Combine pudding mix with instant quality coffee and milk. Cook as directed on package. Remove from heat and cover surface with wax paper. Cool. To serve, sprinkle with coconut, chopped nuts, or grated chocolate, or top with whipped cream or prepared whipped topping, if desired. Makes 4 or 5 servings.

Nice to know: *This pudding may also be used as a filling for cream puffs or éclairs.*

COFFEE INSTANT PUDDING

- 2 cups milk
- 1 to 1½ tablespoons instant quality coffee
- 1 package (3¾- to 4½-ounce size) butterscotch, chocolate, or vanilla instant pudding mix

Combine milk, instant quality coffee, and instant pudding mix. Beat with rotary beater 1 minute or until well mixed. Pour into serving dishes and let stand until set—about 5 minutes. Makes 4 or 5 servings.

COFFEE NECTAR PUDDING

- 2 cups milk
- ¼ cup heavy cream
- 2 teaspoons instant quality coffee
- 2 tablespoons sugar
- ½ teaspoon aromatic bitters *or* ⅛ teaspoon almond extract
- 1 package (3¾ ounces) coconut cream or vanilla instant pudding mix

Combine milk, heavy cream, instant quality coffee, and aromatic bitters *or* almond extract; mix well. Then add instant pudding mix. Beat with rotary beater 1 minute or until well mixed. Pour into serving dishes and let stand until set—about 5 minutes. Makes 4 or 5 servings.

COFFEE FLUFF

- 1 egg white
- 2 tablespoons sugar
- 1 package vanilla tapioca pudding mix
- ¼ cup milk
- 1 egg yolk
- 2 teaspoons instant quality coffee
- 1¾ cups milk

Beat egg white with sugar until stiff, shiny peaks will form. Set aside. Combine pudding mix, ¼ cup milk, egg yolk, and instant quality coffee; blend thoroughly. Add 1¾ cups milk. Cook as directed on package. Remove from heat and pour gradually over egg white mixture, blending thoroughly. Let stand about 15 minutes; stir just to mix. Serve warm or chilled. Makes 5 servings.

POT DE CRÈME DE LUXE

- 1 package (4 ounces) chocolate pudding and pie filling mix
- ⅓ cup sugar
- 1 tablespoon instant quality coffee
- 1½ cups milk
- 2 egg yolks, slightly beaten
- ⅛ teaspoon peppermint extract
- ½ cup heavy cream

Combine pudding mix, sugar, instant coffee, and milk in saucepan. Cook and stir over medium heat until mixture begins to thicken. Pour a little of the hot mixture into egg yolks and stir quickly to blend. Add to mixture in saucepan and continue cooking until mixture comes to a *full* boil. Stir in peppermint extract. Cover with wax paper and chill thoroughly. Then whip cream and fold into chilled pudding. Spoon into soufflé cups or a serving dish. Chill until set, about 2 hours, or freeze until firm. Garnish with whipped cream and shaved chocolate, if desired. Makes 8 to 10 servings.

COFFEE-SCOTCH POT DE CRÈME

- 1 package (4 ounces) butterscotch pudding and pie filling mix
- ¼ cup sugar
- 1 tablespoon instant quality coffee
- 1½ cups milk
- 2 egg yolks, slightly beaten
- 1 envelope whipped topping mix
- ½ cup *cold* milk

Combine pudding mix, sugar, coffee, and 1½ cups milk in saucepan. Cook and stir over medium heat until mixture comes to a *full* boil. Quickly blend a little hot mixture into egg yolks; then add to mixture in saucepan. Continue cooking until mixture again comes to a *full* boil. Remove from heat. Place wax paper on surface of pudding. Chill at least 1½ hours.

Combine whipped topping mix and ½ cup *cold* milk in a small bowl with narrow bottom. Whip as directed on package. Fold 1 cup prepared whipped topping into chilled pudding. Spoon into soufflé cups or individual serving dishes. Chill until set, about 2 hours, or freeze until firm. Top with remaining prepared whipped topping. Garnish with shaved chocolate or maraschino cherries, if desired. Makes 6 to 8 servings.

LAYERED POT DE CRÈME

- 1¼ cups macaroon crumbs
- ¼ cup sugar
- ⅓ cup butter, softened
- 1 package (4 ounces) butterscotch pudding and pie filling mix
- 1 cup sugar
- 1 tablespoon instant quality coffee
- 4½ cups milk
- 6 egg yolks
- 1 package (4 ounces) chocolate pudding and pie filling mix
- 1 square unsweetened chocolate
- 1 package (3¼ ounces) vanilla pudding and pie filling mix
- 1½ cups heavy cream

Combine crumbs, ¼ cup sugar, and butter and mix well. Press firmly onto bottom of a 9-inch spring-form pan. Chill.

Combine butterscotch pudding mix with ⅓ cup sugar, instant coffee, and 1½ cups milk in saucepan. Cook and stir over medium heat until mixture begins to thicken. Beat 2 egg yolks slightly; quickly stir in a little of the hot pudding. Add to pudding in saucepan and cook until mixture comes to a *full* boil. Cover with wax paper and chill thoroughly.

Then combine chocolate pudding mix, unsweetened chocolate, ⅓ cup sugar, and 1½ cups milk in saucepan. Cook and stir over medium heat until mixture begins to thicken. Beat 2 egg yolks slightly; quickly stir in a little of the hot pudding.

Add to pudding in saucepan and cook until mixture comes to a *full* boil. Cover with wax paper and chill thoroughly.

Combine vanilla pudding with remaining ⅓ cup sugar and 1½ cups milk. Cook and stir over medium heat until mixture begins to thicken. Beat remaining 2 egg yolks slightly; quickly stir in a little of the hot pudding. Add to pudding in saucepan and cook until mixture comes to a *full* boil. Cover with wax paper and chill thoroughly.

Then whip the cream and fold ⅓, about 1 cup, into each of the chilled puddings. Layer puddings in the prepared pan. Freeze 5 hours or overnight. To serve, remove sides of spring-form pan and garnish dessert with additional whipped cream, if desired. Makes 12 servings.

COFFEE FLOATING ISLAND

1 package (3¾ ounces) vanilla instant pudding mix
1½ tablespoons instant quality coffee
⅛ teaspoon salt
4 tablespoons sugar
3 cups cold milk
1 egg white

Combine pudding mix, instant coffee, salt, and 2 tablespoons of the sugar in a mixing bowl. Add milk and beat with rotary beater 1 minute or until well mixed. Pour at once into dessert dishes. Let stand until set—takes about 5 minutes.

Meanwhile, beat egg white until foamy throughout. Gradually add the remaining 2 tablespoons sugar and continue beating until meringue will stand in peaks. Top each serving of pudding with a dollop of meringue. Makes 6 to 8 servings.

REFRIGERATOR CAKE

1 package (4 ounces) sweet cooking chocolate
1 package (5 ounces) vanilla pudding and pie filling mix
2 teaspoons instant quality coffee
1 teaspoon unflavored gelatin
2 cups milk
¾ cup heavy cream
12 ladyfingers, split

Break chocolate into squares; set aside. Combine pudding mix, instant coffee, and gelatin in saucepan. Stir in milk. Cook and stir over medium heat until mixture comes to a *full* boil. Remove from heat, add chocolate, and stir until mixture is smooth. Cool completely (do not chill). Then whip the cream. Beat pudding until smooth; fold in whipped cream.

Line an 8- by 4-inch loaf pan with wax paper, letting it extend an inch beyond rim. Line bottom and sides with most of the ladyfinger halves. Pour in half of the pudding. Top with remaining ladyfingers; then pour on remaining pudding. Chill until set—2 to 3 hours. Lift from pan, remove paper, and slide onto serving plate. Garnish with whipped cream, if desired. Makes 6 to 8 servings.

COFFEE MALLOW HEARTS

- 1 envelope unflavored gelatin
- ¼ cup cold brewed quality coffee
- 2 cups miniature marshmallows
- ¼ cup brewed quality coffee
- 4 commercial cake layers
- 1 package (3¾ ounces) vanilla instant pudding mix
- 1 cup heavy cream
- ¾ cup cold brewed quality coffee

Combine gelatin and ¼ cup cold coffee and let stand 5 minutes. Meanwhile, place marshmallows and ¼ cup coffee in saucepan over low heat and stir until marshmallows are melted. Remove from heat and add gelatin mixture, stirring until dissolved. Cool.

Split each cake layer horizontally, forming 8 thin layers. Using an individual heart-shaped gelatin mold, cut 3 hearts from each thin layer. Press a heart into each of 12 lightly oiled heart-shaped molds.

When gelatin mixture is cool, prepare instant pudding mix as directed on package, using cream and ¾ cup coffee instead of milk called for in directions. Let stand about 5 minutes; then fold in gelatin mixture.

Fill molds with pudding mixture. Lightly press remaining hearts on top. Chill thoroughly. Unmold and garnish with whipped cream, if desired. Makes 12 servings.

Very, Very Cool

Ask the kids what they like best for dessert. The answer will probably be, "Ice cream!" Ask Dad and you're very likely to get the same reply, for ice cream is a favorite with everyone. Here are frozen desserts—ice creams and their kissing cousins—guaranteed to please the whole family with their very special coffee-plus flavors.

MOCHA-FLECK ICE CREAM

- ⅔ cup chocolate syrup
- ⅓ cup unsifted confectioners' sugar
- Dash of salt
- 1 tablespoon instant quality coffee
- 3 tablespoons water
- 2 egg whites
- 2 egg yolks
- 1 square unsweetened chocolate, shaved
- 1 cup heavy cream

Mix chocolate syrup, sugar, and salt. Dissolve instant coffee in water and add to chocolate mixture, blending well. Beat egg whites until stiff. Beat egg yolks until thick and lemon-colored. Add egg yolks to mocha mixture, mixing well. Then fold in egg whites and shaved chocolate. Whip the cream and fold into mocha mixture. Pour into freezing tray or small paper cups. If desired, top with additional shaved chocolate or slivered toasted blanched almonds. Freeze until firm—about 4 hours. Makes about 1 quart.

COCONUT COFFEE MOUSSE

- 1 envelope unflavored gelatin
- ⅔ cup sugar
- ¼ teaspoon salt
- 2 tablespoons instant quality coffee
- 1 cup milk, scalded
- 2 cups heavy cream
- 2½ teaspoons vanilla
- 1 tablespoon butter
- 2 cups packaged grated coconut
- Dash of salt

Mix gelatin, sugar, ¼ teaspoon salt, and the instant coffee. Add the hot milk and stir until gelatin and sugar are dissolved. Chill until slightly thickened. Then whip the cream; fold into gelatin mixture with vanilla. Pour into freezing tray. Freeze until partially frozen. Meanwhile, melt butter in skillet. Add coconut and dash of salt; sauté until coconut is delicately browned. Then beat partially frozen mixture until fluffy and smooth. Fold in sautéed coconut. Return to tray and freeze until firm—about 3 to 4 hours. Makes about 1½ quarts.

RICH COFFEE ICE CREAM

1½ teaspoons unflavored gelatin
6 tablespoons sugar
⅛ teaspoon salt
1 tablespoon instant quality coffee
½ cup water
1½ cups heavy cream
½ teaspoon vanilla

Mix gelatin, sugar, salt, and coffee in saucepan. Add water and stir over medium heat until gelatin and sugar are dissolved. Cool thoroughly. Then whip cream; fold in gelatin mixture and vanilla. Pour into freezing tray.

Freeze about 1 hour or until partially frozen. Then pour into chilled bowl and beat with rotary beater until fluffy and smooth. Return to freezer tray and freeze until firm—3 to 4 hours. Makes 1 quart.

COFFEE TORTONI

4 teaspoons instant quality coffee
1 envelope whipped topping mix
¾ cup *cold* milk
1 teaspoon vanilla
⅛ teaspoon almond extract
2 egg whites
⅛ teaspoon salt
⅓ cup sugar
⅓ cup chopped nuts

Combine instant coffee, whipped topping mix, cold milk, vanilla, and almond extract. Whip as directed on topping mix package. Beat egg whites and salt until foamy. Gradually add sugar, a tablespoon at a time, beating after each addition until well blended. Continue beating until stiff, shiny peaks will form. Blend egg white mixture and chopped nuts into coffee mixture. Spoon into soufflé cups. Sprinkle with additional chopped nuts, if desired. Freeze until firm—at least 4 hours. Makes 12 servings.

GRANITA DI CAFFÈ

½ cup sugar
2 cups hot Demitasse Coffee (page 16)
2 teaspoons vanilla
Whipped cream (optional)

Dissolve sugar in the hot coffee. (You may use more or less sugar to taste.) Cool; then add vanilla. Pour mixture into freezing tray or shallow pan. Freeze until almost firm.

Then spoon into a chilled bowl and beat well. Return to freezing tray and freeze until of the consistency of sherbet. Spoon into sherbet glasses and top with whipped cream, if desired. Makes 4 servings.

COFFEE CHOCOLATE CREAMS

1 cup heavy cream
2 tablespoons sugar
¾ teaspoon instant quality coffee
1 package (4 ounces) sweet cooking chocolate, finely grated

Combine cream, sugar, and instant coffee. Whip until soft peaks will form. Fold in chocolate. Spoon into small soufflé cups. Freeze until firm. Makes 6 servings.

COFFEE-SCOTCH ICE CREAM

⅓ cup regular grind quality coffee
1½ cups milk
1 cup sugar
¼ teaspoon salt
2 egg yolks, slightly beaten
1½ cups heavy cream
2 teaspoons vanilla

Combine coffee and milk in top of double boiler; scald over boiling water. Remove from heat, but leave over hot water. Place ½ cup sugar in a heavy skillet and stir over low heat until sugar is melted and golden brown. Remove from heat. Quickly strain milk through cheesecloth or very fine sieve.

Very gradually add strained milk to the caramelized sugar, stirring constantly.

Add ½ cup sugar and the salt, stirring until dissolved. Gradually stir the hot mixture into egg yolks; then pour egg yolk mixture into top of double boiler. Cook over boiling water, stirring constantly, until mixture coats a metal spoon. Cool thoroughly. Then whip the cream with the vanilla; fold into coffee mixture. Pour into freezing trays or shallow pans. Freeze until almost firm.

Then spoon into a chilled bowl and beat until smooth. Return to trays and freeze until firm. Serve with additional whipped cream and garnish with sliced bananas, if desired. Makes 8 to 10 servings.

FROZEN COFFEE SURPRISE

⅔ cup sugar
1 tablespoon instant quality coffee
⅛ teaspoon salt
1¼ cups milk
½ teaspoon vanilla
½ cup Post Grape-Nuts Cereal
1 cup heavy cream

Dissolve sugar, instant coffee, and salt in the milk and vanilla in mixing bowl. Add cereal. Whip the cream and fold into cereal mixture. Pour into freezing tray or shallow pan. Freeze until partially firm—about 1 hour. Then spoon into a chilled bowl and beat until smooth. Return to tray and freeze until firm—about 1½ hours. Makes about 3½ cups.

EASY COFFEE SMOOTHIE

2 tablespoons instant quality coffee
1 cup water
24 marshmallows
1 cup heavy cream
1 tablespoon Cointreau

Blend instant coffee and water. Bring just to a boil. Add marshmallows and stir over very low heat until melted. Remove from heat and chill until mixture begins to thicken. Whip the cream. Blend whipped cream and Cointreau into thickened coffee mixture. Pour into a freezing tray or shallow pan. Freeze until firm. Makes about 1 quart.

TOFFEE NUT ICE CREAM

- **1 package (4 ounces) butterscotch pudding and pie filling mix**
- **1 tablespoon instant quality coffee**
- **¼ cup firmly packed brown sugar**
- **2 cups milk**
- **1 cup heavy cream**
- **½ teaspoon vanilla**
- **2 drops almond extract**
- **½ cup chopped pecans**
- **1 tablespoon butter**

Combine pudding mix, instant coffee, sugar, and milk in saucepan. Cook and stir over medium heat until mixture comes to a *full* boil. Chill thoroughly (see below). Whip the cream with vanilla and almond extract; fold into chilled pudding mixture.

Pour into freezing tray or shallow pan. Freeze until partially firm—about 1 hour. Meanwhile, sauté pecans in butter until golden brown. Then spoon partially frozen mixture into a chilled bowl and beat with rotary beater until smooth, but not melted. Fold in nuts. Return to tray and freeze until firm —3 to 4 hours. Makes about 1 quart.

Nice to know: *To hasten chilling, pour pudding mixture into freezing tray and place in freezer 30 minutes. Beat slightly with rotary beater before folding in whipped cream.*

Sundae Sauces

By itself, coffee ice cream makes a delicious dessert—but wearing a helping of one of these easy-make, easy-store sauces, a dish of coffee ice cream becomes something very special.

QUICK CHOCOLATE SAUCE

2 teaspoons butter
2 packages (4 ounces each) sweet cooking chocolate*
1 cup evaporated milk

*Or use 1 package (6 ounces) semi-sweet chocolate chips.

Combine all ingredients in a saucepan. Place over low heat and stir until chocolate is melted and mixture is smooth and well blended. Spoon over ice cream, cupcakes, or sponge cake. To store, cover tightly and chill; reheat before serving. Makes about 1½ cups sauce.

1-2-3 FUDGE SAUCE

1⅔ cups (1 tall can) evaporated milk
2 cups sugar
3 squares unsweetened chocolate
1 teaspoon vanilla

Combine milk, sugar, and chocolate in a saucepan. Bring to a boil over medium heat, stirring constantly. Continue cooking 5 minutes, stirring vigorously. Remove from heat. Add vanilla and beat with a rotary beater 1 minute. Serve warm or chilled on ice cream or cake. Makes about 3 cups.

Nice to know: *For a thinner sauce, stir in a little additional evaporated milk or cream.*

HOT BUTTER RUM SAUCE

1 cup maple-blended syrup
2 tablespoons butter
2 tablespoons rum

Combine syrup and butter in saucepan over medium heat, stirring until butter is melted. Add 2 tablespoons rum and blend. Serve warm on ice cream or waffles. Makes 1¼ cups.

Nice to know: *If desired, buttered syrup may be substituted for the syrup and butter in recipe above. Heat syrup thoroughly before adding rum.*

MAPLE-NUT SAUCE

1 cup maple-blended syrup
¼ to ½ cup chopped black walnuts

Combine the syrup and nuts. Cover tightly and chill several hours before serving. (Flavor improves during storage.) Serve on ice cream, cake, or pudding. Makes 1¼ to 1½ cups.

REGAL CHOCOLATE SAUCE

2 squares unsweetened chocolate
6 tablespoons water
½ cup sugar
Dash of salt
3 tablespoons butter or margarine
¼ teaspoon vanilla

Combine chocolate and water in saucepan and place over low heat, stirring until chocolate is melted and mixture is blended. Add sugar and salt. Cook until sugar is dissolved and mixture very slightly thickened, stirring constantly. Add butter and vanilla. Serve warm or cooled. Makes about 1 cup sauce.

EASY FUDGE SAUCE

2 squares unsweetened chocolate
1½ cups sugar
¼ cup butter
1 cup light cream
1 teaspoon vanilla
Dash of salt

Combine chocolate, sugar, butter, and cream in small saucepan. Bring to a boil over medium heat, stirring constantly. Then, without stirring, boil gently for 7 minutes. Remove from heat. Add vanilla and salt. Beat 2 minutes. Makes 2¼ cups.

Nice to know: *Leftover sauce may be stored, covered, in refrigerator. To reheat, place jar in hot water for a few minutes.*

COCONUT PRALINE SAUCE

- ½ cup butter
- 1⅓ cups (about) flaked coconut
- ¾ cup firmly packed light brown sugar
- ⅛ teaspoon salt
- 3 tablespoons light corn syrup
- 1¼ cups evaporated milk
- 1 teaspoon vanilla

Melt butter in saucepan. Add coconut and sauté until golden brown, stirring constantly. Remove coconut and set aside. Combine sugar, salt, and corn syrup with butter remaining in pan. Cook over low heat until mixture bubbles vigorously, stirring constantly. Gradually add milk, bring to a boil, and boil gently 1½ minutes. Remove from heat. Add vanilla and coconut. Serve warm or cold on cake, ice cream, or pudding. To store, cover tightly and chill. Makes about 2½ cups.

COFFEE SNOWBALLS

- 1 package (4 ounces) sweet cooking chocolate, melted
- 1⅓ cups flaked coconut, toasted
- 1 quart coffee ice cream

Combine melted chocolate and coconut. Spread on wax paper and allow to cool. Then roll scoops of ice cream in the chocolate mixture. Serve at once, or store in freezer until ready to serve. Makes about 6 servings.

COFFEE ICE CREAM DELIGHTS

Coffee Eggnog Sundaes: Flavor your favorite custard sauce with brandy or brandy extract instead of vanilla. Pour chilled sauce over coffee ice cream.

Coffee Mallow-Mint Sundaes: Top each serving of coffee ice cream with a generous spoonful of soft marshmallow sauce and garnish with green mint jelly.

Coffee-Date Parfaits: In parfait or other slender glasses, layer coffee ice cream, crisp cereal flakes, and slivered fresh dates. Serve at once.

Coffee Crunch Sundaes: Top each serving of coffee ice cream with crushed peanut brittle, crumbled macaroons, or crumbled chocolate wafers.

Coffee Sauces

Work homemade magic with these special coffee-flavored sauces. They'll help you transform ordinary desserts, such as ice creams, simple puddings, plain cakes, into beg-for-second-helping triumphs.

BITTERSWEET MOCHA SAUCE

- 1 package (4 ounces) sweet cooking chocolate
- 2 tablespoons sugar
- 2 tablespoons water
- 1 tablespoon instant quality coffee
- ¼ teaspoon vanilla
- 3 tablespoons light cream

Melt chocolate with sugar and water in a saucepan over low heat, stirring constantly. Remove from heat. Stir in instant coffee until smooth. Then stir in vanilla and cream. Makes about ¾ cup sauce.

COFFEE SAUCE

- 2 tablespoons instant quality coffee
- 1½ teaspoons cornstarch*
- Dash of salt
- 1 cup light corn syrup
- ¾ cup light cream
- 2 tablespoons butter

*Or use 1 tablespoon all-purpose flour.

Combine instant coffee, cornstarch, and salt in saucepan; blend. Add syrup gradually, stirring constantly. Add cream and butter. Simmer 5 minutes, or until thickened, stirring constantly. Cool. Serve on ice cream, pudding, or cream puffs. Makes 1½ cups sauce.

COFFEE-SCOTCH SAUCE

1 package (4 ounces) butterscotch instant pudding mix
2 to 3 tablespoons instant quality coffee
⅔ cup dark corn syrup
¾ cup evaporated milk*

***Or use ⅔ cup whole milk.**

Combine pudding mix and coffee in a bowl. Blend in syrup. Stir in milk. Chill. Serve on ice cream or cake. Makes about 1⅔ cups sauce.

Nice to know: *Sauce can be stored, covered, in the refrigerator for 1 week.*

ARABIAN NIGHTS SAUCE

1 tablespoon instant quality coffee
½ teaspoon cornstarch
¼ teaspoon ground cinnamon
¼ teaspoon salt
½ cup water
½ cup honey or corn syrup
½ cup chopped dates
1 tablespoon butter or margarine
¼ cup chopped nuts
¼ teaspoon vanilla

Mix coffee, cornstarch, cinnamon, and salt in a saucepan. Then add water, honey, dates, and butter. Bring to a boil over medium heat, stirring constantly. Then cook, stirring constantly, about 1 minute, or until clear. Remove from heat; add nuts and vanilla. Serve warm or cooled over ice cream or plain pudding. Makes 1⅓ cups sauce.

EASY MOCHA SAUCE

1 package (4 ounces) sweet cooking chocolate
3 tablespoons sugar
1 tablespoon instant quality coffee
½ cup evaporated milk
½ teaspoon vanilla

Combine chocolate, sugar, instant coffee, and evaporated milk in saucepan over low heat; stir constantly until chocolate is melted and sauce is smooth. Remove from heat; stir in vanilla. Serve over ice cream or cake. Makes about 1 cup sauce.

Easy Chocolate Sauce: Prepare Easy Mocha Sauce, reducing sugar to 1 tablespoon and omitting instant coffee.

MAPLE COFFEE SAUCE

½ cup maple-blended syrup
½ teaspoon instant quality coffee
1 tablespoon butter
¼ cup chopped pecans

Bring syrup to a boil. Add instant coffee and simmer 3 minutes, stirring constantly. Remove from heat. Stir in butter and nuts. Serve warm on vanilla pudding or on ice cream. Makes about ¾ cup sauce.

DARK MOCHA SAUCE

2 squares unsweetened chocolate
½ cup light cream
¾ cup sugar
3 tablespoons butter
1 tablespoon instant quality coffee
Dash of salt
¾ teaspoon vanilla

Melt chocolate with cream in saucepan over low heat, stirring constantly until mixture is smooth and blended. Add sugar, butter, instant coffee, and salt; continue cooking and stirring 3 to 5 minutes longer, or until slightly thickened. Remove from heat and add vanilla. Serve warm or cooled on ice cream and other desserts. Makes 1⅓ cups sauce.

Mocha Nut Sauce: Prepare Dark Mocha Sauce, adding ½ cup chopped nuts with the vanilla.

Nice to know: *Store, covered, in refrigerator. Before serving, place bowl of sauce in hot water and stir until smooth.*

VITE-FAIT CAFÉ SAUCE

¼ cup instant quality coffee
1 can (15 ounces) sweetened condensed milk
1 tablespoon water

Combine ingredients in a saucepan. Place over medium heat just until coffee is dissolved, stirring constantly. Serve as a sauce over ice cream, cake, or pudding, or use as a syrup in milk shakes and other drinks. Makes about 1½ cups sauce.

"Coffee and . . ."
Special: Sandwiches

You can hide scraps of any good leftover between two slices of bread and call it a sandwich—but if you put effort plus imagination plus know-how into sandwich-making, you'll produce a culinary achievement worthy of star billing at any meal. Here are sandwiches supreme: glazed, open-faced, grilled, French toasted, with a selection of fillings to make any sandwich-lover's mouth water. Pour a cup of coffee, pull up a chair, and fall to—it's not a snack, it's a feast!

TUNA ROLLS

- ½ clove garlic, crushed
- 1 tablespoon butter
- ⅔ cup all-purpose barbecue sauce
- 1 can (9¼ ounces) tuna, drained and flaked
- 3 tablespoons stuffed green olives, sliced thinly
- 2 tablespoons finely chopped parsley
- 4 seeded hard rolls, split and toasted

Sauté garlic in butter until golden brown. Add remaining ingredients, except rolls. Heat thoroughly over medium heat, stirring constantly. Spoon onto hot rolls. Makes 4 servings.

SLOPPY JOES

- 2 tablespoons butter
- ½ cup finely chopped onions
- 1 pound ground beef
- ¾ teaspoon salt
- 1 cup all-purpose barbecue sauce
- 6 buttered hamburger rolls

Melt butter in a skillet; add onions and sauté until tender.

Then add meat and cook about 5 minutes, or until cooked but not browned. Blend in salt and barbecue sauce. Serve on buttered rolls. Makes 6 servings.

BARBECUED STUFFED FRANKFURTERS

10 frankfurters (about 1 pound)
1⅓ cups chive or vegetable cottage cheese
10 thin bacon slices
1 cup all-purpose barbecue sauce

Split frankfurters lengthwise. Open each and stuff with about 2 tablespoons cottage cheese. Wind a slice of bacon around each frankfurter. Bake on a rack in a pan in hot oven (400° F.) 20 minutes. Then pour barbecue sauce over frankfurters. Bake 10 minutes longer. Makes 4 or 5 servings.

To cook on outdoor grill: Split frankfurters only to ½ inch from each end. Stuff each with 2 tablespoons cottage cheese and wind with bacon as directed, securing bacon with a toothpick at each end. Place in a foil pan on a grill over hot coals and cook about 15 minutes, turning frequently until bacon is cooked on all sides. Then brush with barbecue sauce and cook about 5 minutes, or until frankfurters are glazed.

Relish-Stuffed Frankfurters: Prepare Barbecued Stuffed Frankfurters as directed, substituting ⅔ cup pickle relish for the cottage cheese and using about 1 tablespoon relish in each of the frankfurters.

Gherkin-Stuffed Frankfurters: Prepare Barbecued Stuffed Frankfurters as directed, substituting 10 sliced (lengthwise) sweet gherkins for the cottage cheese and using about 1 gherkin in each of the frankfurters.

Olive-Stuffed Frankfurters: Prepare Barbecued Stuffed Frankfurters as directed, substituting 10 sliced stuffed green olives for the cheese and using about 1 olive in each frankfurter.

BEEF BARBECUE SANDWICHES

½ cup all-purpose barbecue sauce
½ cup water
¼ pound sliced roast beef
12 slices rye toast

Heat barbecue sauce and water in saucepan. Arrange meat on slices of toast. Spoon sauce over open sandwiches. Makes 12 open-faced sandwiches, or 6 servings.

CHEESE CRISP SANDWICHES

¼ cup maple-blended syrup
¼ cup butter, melted
8 slices white bread
1 package (8 ounces) sliced process sharp Cheddar cheese

Combine syrup and butter. Brush 4 slices of bread on one side with half the syrup mixture. Place bread on hot griddle, syrup side down. Cover bread with cheese slices. Top with remaining bread. Brush top of bread with remaining syrup mixture. Grill about 3 minutes, or until lightly browned. Turn sandwiches and grill second side 3 minutes or until lightly browned. Serve with additional syrup. Makes 4 sandwiches.

MEAT SANDWICH SUPREME

1 cup sour cream
2 to 3 teaspoons onion salad dressing mix
2 teaspoons prepared horse-radish, well drained
8 slices rye or pumpernickel bread
12 slices cooked roast beef, pork, lamb, or turkey
Lettuce leaves

Blend sour cream, salad dressing mix, and horse-radish. Spread on bread, using about 1 tablespoon for each slice. Arrange meat on bread. Top with remaining dressing, using about 2 tablespoons for each sandwich. Cover with lettuce and remaining bread. Cut sandwiches diagonally into 2 or 4 pieces. Serve with pickle slices, if desired. Makes 4 sandwiches.

For Open-Faced Sandwiches: Use only 4 slices of bread and 6 slices of meat. Prepare dressing mixture, spreading about 1 tablespoon on each slice of bread. Place 2 bread slices on each plate. Arrange meat and lettuce on bread. Top with remaining dressing. Serve with pickle slices. Makes 2 servings.

TOASTY CHEESE SANDWICHES

1 package (8 ounces) process sharp Cheddar cheese (at room temperature)
¼ cup butter
16 slices white bread
Maple-blended syrup

Combine cheese and butter, beating until well blended and fluffy. Spread mixture on all slices of bread. Stack in pairs, cheese side up, to make 8 sandwiches. Place on baking sheet and bake in hot oven (425° F.) 10 to 15 minutes or until puffed and golden brown. Serve with syrup. Makes 8 servings.

OVEN FRENCH TOAST SANDWICHES

1 egg, slightly beaten
¼ cup milk
¼ teaspoon salt
4 slices bread
2 slices boiled ham
2 tablespoons grated Cheddar cheese
Maple-blended syrup

Combine egg, milk, and salt; blend. Dip bread in egg mixture and place on a well-greased baking sheet. Bake in a hot oven (400° F.) 6 minutes. Then turn 2 slices over and top each with a slice of ham and about 1 tablespoon grated Cheddar cheese. Top with remaining bread slices, browned side down. Bake about 6 minutes; then turn and bake another 4 minutes. If desired, serve with syrup. Makes 2 sandwiches.

BACON LOGS

1 egg, slightly beaten
¼ cup milk
¼ teaspoon salt
4 slices bread
12 bacon slices
Maple-blended syrup

Combine egg, milk, and salt. Dip bread quickly in egg mixture and sauté in shallow hot fat, turning to brown both sides. Drain on absorbent paper; then cut each slice into 3 strips. Meanwhile, fry bacon until crisp; drain. Top a strip of bread with a slice of bacon, add another strip of bread and top with bacon. Repeat to make 6 Bacon Logs. Serve with maple-blended syrup.

TOASTED HAM SANDWICHES

- 12 slices bread
- 6 thin slices boiled ham
- Prepared mustard (optional)
- ¼ cup butter or margarine
- 2 eggs, slightly beaten
- ¼ cup milk
- ¼ teaspoon salt
- Maple-blended syrup

Trim crusts from bread. Top half of the bread with ham slices. Spread lightly with mustard; cover with remaining bread. Melt butter in large skillet. Blend eggs, milk, and salt. Dip sandwiches quickly into egg mixture. Sauté in butter, turning to brown both sides. Serve hot with syrup. Makes 6 servings.

Toasted Cheese Sandwiches: Prepare Toasted Ham Sandwiches as directed, substituting 6 slices of mild Cheddar or process cheese for the ham.

Toasted Club Sandwiches: Prepare Toasted Ham Sandwiches as directed, adding 6 slices mild Cheddar or process cheese to sandwiches with the ham.

OVEN-CRISP SANDWICHES

- ¼ cup maple-blended syrup
- ¼ cup butter, melted
- 8 slices raisin bread
- ½ cup softened cream cheese

Combine syrup and butter. Brush 4 slices of bread on one side with half of the syrup mixture. Place on a baking sheet, syrup side down. Spread each slice with cream cheese. Top with remaining bread slices. Brush top of each bread slice with remaining syrup mixture. Bake in a hot oven (400° F.) 10 minutes; then turn and continue baking 8 to 10 minutes or until golden brown. Makes 4 sandwiches.

OPEN GLAZED SANDWICHES

- 6 open-faced sandwiches (see suggestions on page 205)
- Sauterne or Sherry Glaze (page 206)

Place sandwiches on a rack. Cover filling with chilled glaze, using about ⅓ cup for each. Chill until firm. Makes 6 sandwiches, or 3 to 6 servings.

Suggested sandwiches:

Turkey and Cranberry Sauce: Use buttered whole wheat bread. Top with cranberry sauce and sliced turkey. Garnish with whole walnuts, thin orange slices, and sliced ripe olives.

Liver Pâté and Bacon: Use buttered whole wheat bread. Spread with pâté. Sprinkle crumbled fried bacon around the edges. Garnish center with egg slice and olive slice.

Crab Meat and Grapefruit: Use buttered rye bread. Top with diced celery, flaked crab meat, and grapefruit sections. Garnish with green pepper strips.

Roast Beef and Tomato: Use buttered rye bread. Spread with prepared horse-radish. Top with sliced roast beef and wedges of tomato. Garnish with chopped capers.

Smoked Salmon and Cream Cheese: Use buttered pumpernickel bread. Top with smoked salmon slices. Use pastry tube to make border design of cream cheese. Garnish with finely chopped chives and a dash of freshly crushed peppercorns.

Sliced Egg and Chicken Breast: Use pumpernickel bread and spread with butter mixed with a dash of curry powder. Top each slice of bread with 1 sliced egg and sliced breast of chicken. Garnish with sliced olives.

Shrimp and Cucumber: Use buttered rye bread. Top with sliced cucumber and jumbo shrimp. Garnish with a lemon slice, if desired.

Liver Pâté and Caviar: Use buttered whole wheat bread. Cover with liver pâté and sprinkle with finely chopped chives. Place lemon slice in center and top with caviar.

Roast Beef and Roquefort Cheese: Use whole wheat bread. Spread with butter mixed with Roquefort cheese. Top with rolled slices of roast beef and garnish with shredded radishes.

SHERRY GLAZE

¼ teaspoon thyme
1½ cups water
1 package (3 ounces) lemon flavor gelatin
1 tablespoon lemon juice
½ cup dry sherry

Simmer thyme in water for about 3 minutes. Strain. Dissolve gelatin in hot liquid. Add lemon juice and sherry. Chill until slightly thickened. Makes about 2 cups glaze.

SAUTERNE GLAZE

⅛ teaspoon sweet basil
1 cup water
1 package (3 ounces) lemon flavor gelatin
½ teaspoon salt
1 tablespoon lemon juice
1 cup sauterne

Simmer the sweet basil in the water for about 3 minutes. Strain. Dissolve gelatin and salt in the hot liquid. Add lemon juice and wine. Chill until slightly thickened. Makes 2 cups.

NEW-STYLE WESTERN SANDWICH

3 eggs
1 tablespoon minced onion
1 can (2¼ ounces) deviled ham
Dash of Tabasco or Worcestershire sauce
¼ teaspoon salt
Dash of pepper
Butter
4 sandwich rolls, split, toasted, and buttered

Beat eggs slightly. Add onion, ham, sauce, salt, and pepper together in a bowl. Melt butter in a skillet and add egg mixture. Cook over medium heat, drawing mixture in from sides toward center with a spatula until mixture is set. Serve at once on warm rolls. Makes 4 sandwiches.

EGG SANDWICH FILLING

6 hard-cooked eggs, chilled
6 tablespoons mayonnaise
1 teaspoon onion salad dressing mix
1 teaspoon grated onion
4 to 6 drops Worcestershire sauce
1 tablespoon finely chopped ripe olives

Chop eggs coarsely. Add remaining ingredients and blend well. Chill thoroughly. Makes 2 cups filling, enough for 8 sandwiches.

CHICKEN SANDWICH FILLING

- 1 can (12 ounces) chicken, coarsely chopped (about 2 cups)
- 1 cup mayonnaise
- 1 tablespoon onion salad dressing mix
- ¼ cup lemon juice
- ¼ cup grated onion
- 1 cup finely chopped celery

Combine all ingredients and blend well. Cover and chill thoroughly. Makes about 3 cups filling, enough for 12 sandwiches.

COTTAGE CHEESE SANDWICH FILLING

- 1 pound cream-style cottage cheese
- 1 teaspoon onion salad dressing mix
- 2 teaspoons chopped chives
- 2 teaspoons chopped pimiento

Press cottage cheese through a fine sieve. Add remaining ingredients and blend well. Makes 2 cups filling, enough for 8 sandwiches.

SANDWICH LOAVES

- 1 unsliced loaf white sandwich bread
- 1 unsliced loaf whole wheat sandwich bread
- Chicken Sandwich Filling (see above)
- Cottage Cheese Sandwich Filling (see above)
- Egg Sandwich Filling (page 206)
- 4 packages (8 ounces each) cream cheese (at room temperature)
- ¼ cup (about) milk or cream
- 1 tablespoon onion salad dressing mix

Trim crusts from bread, using sharp knife. Slice each loaf lengthwise into 5 even slices.

Prepare the first sandwich loaf by spreading a white slice

with about ¾ cup chicken filling. Top with a whole wheat slice; spread with 1 cup cottage cheese filling. Top with a white slice; spread with 1 cup egg filling. Top with a whole wheat slice; spread with about ¾ cup chicken filling. Top with a white slice. Chill slightly.

For second loaf, repeat the above steps, starting and ending with the whole wheat slices of bread. Chill slightly.

Meanwhile, soften cheese with electric mixer or fork, adding milk until mixture is creamy and smooth. Add salad dressing mix; blend well. Use 2 cups of cheese mixture to frost top and sides of each loaf. Chill in refrigerator 3 hours or longer. Serve cold. Slice and serve in whole or half slices. Makes 20 luncheon-size servings, or 40 finger sandwiches.

FRENCH TOASTED CHICKEN SANDWICHES

- 1 cup finely chopped cooked or canned chicken
- ½ cup minced celery
- ¼ cup chopped sweet pickle
- 1 teaspoon salt
- Dash of pepper
- ¼ cup mayonnaise
- 12 thin slices white bread
- 3 eggs, beaten
- ½ cup milk
- 1 teaspoon sugar
- ¼ teaspoon salt
- Butter or margarine

Combine chicken, celery, pickle, seasonings, and mayonnaise and mix well. Make 6 sandwiches with the bread. Mix eggs, milk, sugar, and salt. Dip each sandwich into egg mixture, being sure to coat each side completely. Sauté sandwiches slowly in butter in hot skillet on both sides until filling is thoroughly heated and sandwiches are golden brown. Serve with cranberry sauce, if desired. Makes 6 servings.

Coffee Break: England

English die-hards may still break for tea in the afternoon, but for morning "elevenses" everybody has coffee—and, of course, something very good, very British, to go with it!

SCONES

2 cups sifted all-purpose flour
2½ teaspoons double-acting baking powder
1 teaspoon salt
2 tablespoons sugar
⅓ cup shortening
2 egg yolks
½ cup light cream
1 egg white, slightly beaten
2 tablespoons sugar
¼ teaspoon ground cinnamon

Sift flour with baking powder, salt, and 2 tablespoons sugar into mixing bowl. Cut in shortening. Beat egg yolks well and add cream. Add to flour mixture and stir until soft dough is formed (20 strokes). If dough seems dry, add an additional tablespoon of light cream.

Turn out on lightly floured board and knead 20 turns. Roll dough into circle ¾ to 1 inch thick, and cut into 8 wedges. Place wedges on ungreased baking sheet. Brush tops lightly with egg white; sprinkle with mixture of 2 tablespoons sugar and the cinnamon. Bake in a hot oven (425° F.) 12 minutes or until browned. Makes 8 large scones.

POUND CAKE

Important. Prolonged creaming of butter and sugar is essential in making a good pound cake. Butter should be creamed until very soft and light and sugar added gradually, beating at least 10 minutes in mixer or longer by hand. Then eggs should be thoroughly beaten in, one at a time.

- 2¼ cups sifted cake flour
- 1 teaspoon double-acting baking powder
- ½ teaspoon salt
- 1 cup butter
- 1¼ cups sugar
- 1¼ teaspoons vanilla
- ¼ teaspoon ground mace
- 4 eggs
- ¼ cup milk

Sift flour with baking powder and salt. Cream butter until *very soft and fluffy*. Add sugar, 2 tablespoons at a time, creaming thoroughly after each addition. Add vanilla and mace, blending well. Beat in eggs, one at a time, beating thoroughly after each addition. Add flour mixture alternately with milk, beginning and ending with flour and beating after each addition until smooth.

Pour batter into a 9- by 5-inch loaf pan which has been lined on the bottom with wax paper. Bake in a slow oven (325° F.) 1 hour and 15 to 20 minutes or until cake tester inserted in center of cake comes out clean. Cool about 15 minutes in pan. Then turn out, remove paper, and turn right side up to cool thoroughly. Wrap in transparent Saran or aluminum foil and store overnight before slicing—this makes cake more moist and easier to slice.

For 10-inch tube cake: Double all ingredients except mace. (Continue to use ¼ teaspoon ground mace.) Bake in a greased and floured 10-inch tube pan in slow oven (325° F.) for 1 hour and 30 to 35 minutes or until cake tester inserted into cake comes out clean. Cool at least 15 minutes before removing from pan.

Wine Jelly Sandwiches: Store Pound Cake overnight; then cut in ¼-inch slices. Spread wine jelly between slices. Cut each sandwich in thirds to make dainty finger sandwiches. Makes about 4 dozen finger sandwiches.

COCONUT SHORTBREAD COOKIES

- 1 cup butter or margarine
- ½ cup sugar
- 1 egg
- 3 cups sifted all-purpose flour
- Dash of salt
- 1 cup packaged grated coconut

Cream butter, add remaining ingredients, and mix well. Chill dough about 1 hour. Roll about ⅓ of the dough at a time ¼ inch thick on lightly floured board. Cut into squares or fancy shapes. If desired, prick tops with fork to make designs. Bake on ungreased baking sheets in moderate oven (375° F.) 10 to 12 minutes or until lightly browned. Cool. Store in loosely covered container. Makes about 3 dozen cookies.

WELSH CHEESECAKES

- 1 cup minus 2 tablespoons unsifted all-purpose flour
- ⅛ teaspoon salt
- ¼ teaspoon double-acting baking powder
- 1½ teaspoons sugar
- ¼ cup butter
- 1 egg yolk
- 1 tablespoon lemon juice
- ⅓ cup (about) plum, raspberry, or apricot jam
- ½ package (2 cups unsifted) lemon flake cake mix
- 2 tablespoons all-purpose flour
- 1 egg
- ¼ cup water
- 1 teaspoon grated lemon rind
- 1 egg white, slightly beaten
- 1 teaspoon lemon juice
- 1 teaspoon salad oil
- 1½ cups sifted confectioners' sugar
- ¼ cup toasted slivered almonds

Mix 1 cup minus 2 tablespoons flour with salt, baking powder, and 1½ teaspoons sugar. Rub in butter with a spoon. Add egg yolk and 1 tablespoon lemon juice. Mix to form a smooth dough. Turn out onto a well-floured board and shape into a flat oval. Roll out very thin and cut into 2¼-inch rounds. Place rounds in bottoms of greased miniature cupcake tins, pressing into bottom and sides of pans. Place ½ teaspoon of jam in center of each. Chill.

Combine cake mix, 2 tablespoons flour, egg, water, and lemon rind. Mix until well blended. Spoon cake mixture over jam, filling pans about ¾ full (about 1 heaping teaspoon of cake batter in each). Bake in a slow oven (325° F.) 20 to 25 minutes or until lightly browned. Remove cakes from pan immediately. Cool on racks.

Meanwhile, combine egg white, 1 teaspoon lemon juice, and salad oil. Gradually add confectioners' sugar, mixing well after each addition. Beat until smooth and creamy. Spoon glaze over tops of cakes. Sprinkle with toasted almonds. Makes about 36 miniature cakes.

TIPSY SQUIRE

- 1½ cups cold milk
- ½ cup cold light cream
- 2 teaspoons sherry extract
- 1 package (3¾ ounces) vanilla instant pudding
- 6 ladyfingers or 12 strips day-old sponge cake
- ⅔ cup flaked coconut, toasted
- ½ cup toasted slivered blanched almonds
- 1 cup thinly sliced drained canned peaches

Combine milk, cream, and sherry extract in a mixing bowl. Add pudding mix and beat slowly with egg beater just until mixed, about 1 minute. Let stand to set—takes 5 minutes.

Meanwhile, crumble ladyfingers into serving bowl. (If sponge cake is used, soak the cake in peach juice, if desired, before crumbling into the dish.) Cover with alternate layers of coconut, almonds, peaches, and pudding, making three layers of each. Top with a layer of coconut. Serve with whipped cream and additional toasted coconut, if desired. Makes 6 to 8 servings.

DUNDEE CAKE

- 2¼ cups sifted cake flour
- 1 teaspoon double-acting baking powder
- ¼ teaspoon salt
- ½ teaspoon ground nutmeg
- ½ teaspoon ground cinnamon
- ¾ cup butter
- 1¼ cups sifted confectioners' sugar
- 4 eggs
- ½ cup orange juice
- ½ cup white raisins
- ½ cup seedless raisins
- 1 cup currants
- ½ cup chopped mixed candied fruit
- 1 cup finely slivered almonds
- ¼ cup finely chopped almonds
- 2 tablespoons light corn syrup
- 2 tablespoons water

Sift flour with baking powder, salt, and spices. Cream butter, gradually add sugar, and cream until light and fluffy. Add eggs, one at a time, beating well after each addition. Then add flour mixture alternately with orange juice, beginning and ending with flour and beating after each addition until smooth. (Batter will look somewhat curdled.) Fold in fruit and slivered almonds.

Spread in well-greased 9-inch tube pan. Bake in moderate oven (350° F.) 30 minutes; then sprinkle chopped almonds over top of cake and bake 30 to 35 minutes longer.

Simmer syrup and water together for 1 minute; brush over top of cake to hold almonds in place and to give a gloss. Cool cake 15 minutes in pan; then turn out on rack to finish cooling. When cold, wrap in foil and store at least overnight in refrigerator before serving.

Coconut Dundee Cake: Prepare Dundee Cake, substituting 1⅓ cups flaked coconut or 1 cup packaged grated coconut for the white raisins.

Nice to know: *Cake slices best when it is chilled, but tastes best at room temperature. Cake may be wrapped first in cheesecloth that has been soaked in fruit juice or wine, then in foil, and stored in refrigerator for a week or more.*

LAMINGTONS

- 1⅔ cups sifted cake flour
- ¾ teaspoon double-acting baking powder
- ¼ teaspoon salt
- ¾ cup butter
- 1 cup sugar
- 1½ teaspoons grated lemon rind
- 3 eggs, unbeaten
- ¼ cup milk
- 1½ cups packaged grated coconut
- Glossy Chocolate Glaze (page 214)

Sift flour with baking powder and salt. Cream butter until very soft and fluffy. Add sugar, 2 tablespoons at a time, creaming thoroughly after each addition. (This will take at least 10 minutes in an electric mixer or longer by hand.) Add grated lemon rind, beating well. Beat in eggs, one at a time, beating thoroughly after each addition. Add flour mixture alternately with milk, beginning and ending with flour and beating after each addition until smooth. Fold in ¾ cup of the coconut.

Pour batter into a 9-inch square pan, which has been lined on bottom with wax paper. Bake in a slow oven (325° F.) 50

to 55 minutes. Cool about 10 minutes in pan. Then turn out, remove paper, and turn right side up to cool thoroughly.

Cut cake into 16 squares. Brush crumbs from cake squares. Holding a square of cake on a fork over bowl of glaze, spoon Glossy Chocolate Glaze over top and sides of each piece of cake. Roll each cake square in the remaining coconut to coat the top and sides of each piece. Store covered at room temperature or in refrigerator. Makes 16 squares.

Glossy Chocolate Glaze: Combine 3¼ cups sifted confectioners' sugar, ⅓ cup cocoa, and ½ teaspoon salt in bowl. Gradually add 6 to 8 tablespoons hot water, stirring until smooth. Stir in 1 teaspoon vanilla. (While frosting the cakes, add additional small amounts of hot water to keep glaze thin enough to spoon easily over cakes.) Makes about 1⅓ cups.

COTTAGE PUDDING

- 2 cups sifted cake flour
- 2 teaspoons double-acting baking powder
- ½ teaspoon salt
- 3 tablespoons butter or other shortening
- 1 cup sugar
- 1 cup milk
- ½ teaspoon vanilla

Sift flour with baking powder and salt. Cream butter, add sugar gradually, and cream together well. Add flour alternately with milk, a small amount at a time, beating after each addition until smooth. Add vanilla. Bake in greased 8-inch square pan in moderate oven (350° F.) 50 to 60 minutes or until cake tests done. Serve hot with lemon, chocolate, or cherry sauce. Makes 9 servings.

Nice to know: *If desired, recipe may be doubled and baked in a 13- by 9-inch pan in a moderate oven (350° F.) 55 minutes.*

SCOTCH CAKES

- 1 egg
- ½ cup firmly packed brown sugar
- 1 tablespoon butter, melted
- ½ teaspoon salt
- ¼ teaspoon vanilla
- ½ cup quick-cooking rolled oats
- ½ cup flaked coconut

Beat the egg; add brown sugar gradually, mixing well. Stir in remaining ingredients. Spoon into medium muffin pans, greased on bottoms and sides, filling ¾ full. Bake in moderate oven (375° F.) about 15 minutes. Makes 8 to 10 cakes.

STEAMED CHOCOLATE PUDDING

- 1 package (6 ounces) semi-sweet chocolate chips
- ½ cup butter
- ¼ cup sugar
- 1 egg, beaten
- 1 teaspoon vanilla
- 1 cup sifted all-purpose flour
- 1 teaspoon double-acting baking powder
- ½ teaspoon salt
- ⅓ cup milk
- ¼ cup raisins (optional)
- ½ cup chopped pecans (optional)
- ½ cup heavy cream

Partially melt ½ cup chocolate chips over very low heat. Remove from heat and stir until smooth. Cream butter until softened. Gradually add sugar, creaming until light and fluffy. Add egg and vanilla; beat until well blended. Sift together flour, baking powder, and salt. Add flour mixture alternately with milk to butter mixture, beating until well mixed. Blend in melted chocolate chips, raisins, and nuts.

Spoon batter into custard cups, filling about ⅔ full. Then place on a rack in ½ inch of water in an electric frypan that has been preheated to 220° F. Cover frypan and steam 30 minutes. Add additional water, if necessary.

Meanwhile, melt remaining chocolate chips; cool. Whip the cream. Blend cooled melted chocolate into the whipped cream; chill until serving time. Serve with the hot pudding. Makes 8 servings.

Nice to know: *Pudding may be held in the frypan, with the heat turned off, about 30 to 45 minutes before serving.*

Coffee Party: "Come for a Weight-Watchers' Luncheon!"

Black coffee is a dieter's delight—a delicious hot pick-me-up that hasn't a calorie in a gallon! Even if cream and sugar are a must with you, a teaspoon of sugar adds only 18 calories, a tablespoon of light cream, 30. When weight-watchers get together for lunch—and the help-each-other plan can be a fine morale booster for dieters—the meal becomes a party if you serve these delicious calorie-conscious dishes. Top off the meal with black coffee, and you and your guests can feel both satisfied and smug!

LEMON SNOW

(About 9 calories per serving without sauce)

1 envelope dietetic lemon flavor gelatin
1 cup hot water
1 teaspoon lemon juice
⅛ teaspoon grated lemon rind
Dash of salt
1 egg white
Low-Calorie Custard Sauce (page 217)

Dissolve gelatin in *hot* water. Add lemon juice, lemon rind, and salt. Chill until slightly thickened. Place bowl in ice and water and beat with rotary beater until mixture is fluffy and thick. Beat egg white until soft peaks will form; fold into whipped gelatin. Pour into sherbet glasses or bowl. Chill until firm. Serve with the sauce, if desired. Makes 4 servings.

Orange Snow: Prepare Lemon Snow, using dietetic orange flavor gelatin instead of lemon, reducing hot water to ½ cup, and using ½ cup orange juice and ⅛ teaspoon grated orange rind instead of lemon juice and rind. (About 22 calories per serving without sauce.)

COFFEE SPONGE

(About 9 calories per serving)

1 envelope dietetic orange flavor gelatin
1 teaspoon instant quality coffee
1 cup hot water
Non-caloric sweetener (to equal 2 teaspoons sugar)
Dash of ground nutmeg
1 egg white

Dissolve gelatin and coffee in hot water. Add sweetener and nutmeg. Chill until slightly thickened. Place in larger bowl of ice and water. Whip with rotary beater until fluffy and thick. Beat egg white until soft peaks form; fold into gelatin mixture. Pour into molds. Chill until firm. Unmold; garnish with prepared whipped topping, if desired. Makes 4 servings.

LOW-FAT BRAN MUFFINS

(About 105 calories per muffin)

¾ cup sifted all-purpose flour
2½ teaspoons double-acting baking powder
¼ teaspoon salt
2 tablespoons sugar
1 egg, well beaten
¾ cup skim milk
1 tablespoon shortening, melted
1½ cups 40% bran flakes

Sift flour with baking powder, salt, and sugar. Combine egg and skim milk; add to flour mixture. Add shortening and mix only enough to dampen flour. Fold in cereal. Spoon into lightly greased muffin pans, filling each ⅔ full. Bake in hot oven (425° F.) 15 to 20 minutes. Makes 8 muffins.

LOW-CALORIE CUSTARD SAUCE

(About 59 calories per serving)

1 envelope dietetic vanilla pudding mix
⅛ to ¼ teaspoon ground nutmeg
1¼ cups milk

Add pudding mix and nutmeg to milk in small saucepan, stirring until well blended. Then cook and stir until mixture comes to a boil. Chill. Before serving, stir or beat until creamy. Serve on Lemon or Orange Snow (page 216). Makes 1⅓ cups or 4 servings.

ORANGE FREEZE

(About 37 calories per serving)

- 1 cup orange juice
- 2 envelopes dietetic vanilla pudding mix
- 1 envelope dietetic orange flavor gelatin
- 1/8 teaspoon salt
- 1/2 cup hot water
- 2 egg whites

Combine juice and pudding mix in a small saucepan, stirring until well blended. Cook and stir until mixture comes to a boil. Remove from heat.

Dissolve gelatin and salt in *hot* water. Combine with pudding mixture and chill until mixture thickens. Pour into freezing tray. Freeze until mixture forms ice crystals around edge and is thick in center.

Spoon into a chilled bowl and beat with rotary beater until smooth. Beat egg whites until stiff, shiny peaks will form. Fold into pudding mixture. Return to freezing tray and freeze until firm, stirring occasionally during first 30 to 45 minutes. Let stand at room temperature 15 minutes before serving. Serve plain or with unsweetened fruit. Makes 6 servings.

MIRACLE CHERRY PUDDING

(About 77 calories per serving)

- 1 can (1 pound 1 ounce) unsweetened pitted red cherries
- 2 envelopes dietetic vanilla pudding mix
- Dash of salt
- Non-caloric sweetener (to equal 1/4 cup sugar)
- 1/8 teaspoon almond extract
- Few drops red food coloring

Drain cherries, reserving 3/4 cup of the liquid. Combine cherries and 1/2 cup of the liquid in a saucepan. Bring to a boil. Meanwhile, combine pudding mix, salt, sweetener, and remaining 1/4 cup liquid. Stir to form a smooth paste. Gradually add to boiling fruit, stirring to blend. Then cook and stir until mixture comes to a boil. Add almond extract and food coloring. Pour into serving dish and let stand 2 to 3 hours or until set. Makes 4 servings.

TRIFLE

(About 123 calories per serving)

- 2 envelopes dietetic vanilla pudding mix
- 2 cups skim milk
- ⅓ cup low-calorie strawberry preserves
- 3 ladyfingers, split
- ⅓ cup sherry
- ¼ cup chopped nuts
- 1 pear, peeled and thinly sliced

Add pudding mix to milk in small saucepan. Beat with rotary beater to blend. Bring to a boil over medium heat, stirring constantly. Remove from heat and cool thoroughly.

Spread preserves on ladyfinger halves. Cut in half crosswise and place 2 pieces in each of 6 sherbet glasses or dessert dishes. Spoon sherry over ladyfingers, using about 1 tablespoon for each serving. Top with nuts and pear slices.

When pudding is thoroughly cooled, beat until smooth. Spoon over pear slices. Chill 2 to 3 hours. Makes 6 servings.

Orange Trifle: Prepare Trifle as directed, omitting the preserves, reducing the nuts to 2 tablespoons, and substituting ¾ cup orange sections (about 2 oranges) for the pears. (About 96 calories per serving.)

DIETERS' CHEESE PIE

(About 158 calories per serving)

- 1 cup graham cracker crumbs
- 1 tablespoon butter, melted
- 2 envelopes dietetic lemon flavor gelatin
- 2 cups hot water
- 1½ cups (12 ounces) uncreamed pot cheese
- 1½ teaspoons lemon juice
- ½ teaspoon grated lemon rind
- 1½ teaspoons vanilla
- ¼ teaspoon salt
- Non-caloric sweetener (to equal 8 teaspoons sugar)
- 2 cans (8½ ounces each) dietetic pineapple tidbits, drained and crushed

Combine crumbs and butter. Press evenly on bottom and sides of a 9-inch pie pan. Bake in a moderate oven (350° F.) 10 minutes. Cool. Dissolve gelatin in *hot* water. Chill until slightly thickened. Beat cheese until smooth. Add remaining ingredients and fold into thickened gelatin. Pour into crust and chill until firm. Makes 8 servings.

COFFEE WHIP TOPPING

(About 86 calories per cup)

- 3 tablespoons water
- 1½ teaspoons lemon juice
- ¼ teaspoon vanilla
- 3 tablespoons instant nonfat dry milk
- ¾ teaspoon instant quality coffee
- Non-caloric sweetener (to equal 2 teaspoons sugar)

Pour water, lemon juice, and vanilla into small deep bowl. Sprinkle with the instant nonfat dry milk. Beat with rotary beater to consistency of stiff whipped cream. Fold in instant coffee and sweetener. Chill 30 minutes before serving. Serve instead of whipped cream on desserts. Makes about 1 cup.

SEA FOOD RIBBON SALAD

(About 41 calories per serving)

- 4 envelopes dietetic lemon flavor gelatin
- 3 cups hot water
- 1⅛ teaspoons salt
- 4 teaspoons vinegar
- 1 cup tomato juice
- ⅛ teaspoon pepper
- ½ cup cottage cheese
- ½ cup flaked crab meat
- 1 teaspoon grated onion

Dissolve 2 envelopes of the gelatin in 2 cups of the *hot* water. Add ⅛ teaspoon of the salt and 2 teaspoons of the vinegar. Chill until slightly thickened.

Then dissolve remaining 2 envelopes gelatin in 1 cup *hot* water. Add remaining 1 teaspoon salt, 2 teaspoons vinegar, the tomato juice, and pepper. Chill until slightly thickened.

Into first mixture, fold the cottage cheese. Pour ⅓ of mixture into an 8- by 4-inch loaf pan and chill until almost firm. Fold crab meat and onion into the tomato mixture. Pour half over cottage cheese mixture. Chill until almost firm. Continue layering the two mixtures, chilling each layer until almost firm before adding the next. (Mold will have five layers in all.) When last layer has been added, chill mold until firm. Unmold. Makes 8 servings.

BUTTERSCOTCH COOKIES

(About 41 calories per cookie)

- 1½ cups sifted all-purpose flour
- 1 teaspoon double-acting baking powder
- ⅛ teaspoon salt
- ⅓ cup butter or other shortening
- 3 tablespoons brown sugar
- 3 envelopes (1 package) dietetic butterscotch pudding mix
- 1 egg
- 1 tablespoon water
- ½ teaspoon vanilla

Sift flour with baking powder and salt. Cream butter and sugar; add pudding mix gradually, mixing thoroughly. Add egg and beat until mixture is light and fluffy. Add water and vanilla. Then add flour mixture and mix well. Place dough on wax paper and shape into a roll about 2 inches in diameter. Wrap in wax paper and chill overnight, or until firm enough to slice. Cut into ⅛-inch slices. Bake on ungreased baking sheet in a moderate oven (375° F.) 8 to 10 minutes. Makes about 3 dozen cookies.

For party-size cookies: Shape dough into two rolls, about 1 inch in diameter. Chill; bake about 8 minutes. Makes about 100 cookies. (About 15 calories per cookie.)

LOW-CALORIE SALAD DRESSING

(About 21 calories per tablespoon)

- 3 tablespoons vinegar
- 1 envelope garlic or Italian salad dressing mix
- 2 tablespoons salad oil
- ⅔ cup tomato juice

Place vinegar in cruet; add salad dressing mix and shake well. Add oil and tomato juice; shake again. Makes 1 cup.

Continental Breakfast

Breads so flaky-light they practically float off the plate, delicious sweet butter, cup after cup of steaming creamy-rich coffee . . . is it heaven? No, it's breakfast, European style!

BRIOCHE

- 1 package active dry yeast
- ⅓ cup warm water
- 1 teaspoon sugar
- 1 cup sifted all-purpose flour
- 3 cups sifted all-purpose flour
- ½ cup soft butter
- 2½ tablespoons sugar
- 1 teaspoon salt
- 2 eggs, slightly beaten
- ½ cup milk, scalded and cooled
- ½ cup soft butter
- 2 eggs, slightly beaten
- 2 eggs, slightly beaten
- 1 egg, well beaten

Soften yeast in warm water. Add 1 teaspoon sugar and 1 cup flour. Mix and knead until smooth. Form dough into a ball and place in a bowl. Add lukewarm water to cover. Let rise until ball floats in water—about 1 hour.

Place 3 cups flour in a large bowl. Add ball of dough, ½ cup butter, 2½ tablespoons sugar, salt, 2 eggs, and milk. Mix until dough loses its stickiness. Knead on lightly floured board until smooth. Return to bowl.

Add ½ cup butter and 2 eggs. Stir vigorously with wooden spoon or work with hands until dough loses its stickiness. Then knead on board until very smooth. Return to bowl.

Add 2 eggs. Beat with spoon or work with hands until dough loses its stickiness; then knead on board until very smooth and silky. Place in greased bowl, turning dough to grease all sides. Cover; let rise in warm place, free from drafts, until doubled in bulk. Then punch down, shape into ball, and place in a greased bowl. Cover tightly with foil. Chill overnight.

Set aside 1/6 of the dough for topknots. Divide remaining dough into 18 to 24 pieces, shaping each into a smooth ball. Place in well-greased brioche pans on baking sheets or in muffin pans. Shape reserved dough into the same number of smaller balls. Dampen fingers and make a deep depression in each large ball and place a small ball in depression. Or with pointed scissors, snip an "X" in top of large ball, dampen with water, and place small ball in the cut opening. Cover with towel; let rise until doubled in bulk—about 1 hour.

Brush beaten egg on brioche. To keep topknots upright, cut brown paper the size of baking sheet or muffin pan and place lightly on top of brioche. Bake in hot oven (400° F.) 10 minutes, remove paper, and bake another 5 or 10 minutes or until browned. Remove from pans immediately. Serve warm with soft butter. (To reheat, place brioche in brown paper bag in warm oven about 10 minutes.) Makes 18 to 24 brioche.

Nice to know: *It is important to knead dough until it is no longer sticky and is silky smooth each time.*

CROISSANTS

- ¾ cup hot water
- ½ cup sugar
- 1 tablespoon salt
- ¼ cup shortening
- 1 cup warm water
- 2 packages active dry yeast
- 1 egg, beaten
- 5¼ cups sifted all-purpose flour
- Melted margarine or butter

Combine hot water, sugar, salt, and shortening. Cool to lukewarm. Measure warm water into a large mixing bowl. Sprinkle yeast over water; stir until dissolved. Stir in the lukewarm water mixture. Add egg and 2½ cups flour. Beat until smooth. Stir in remaining flour and beat one minute. (Dough will be soft.) Place dough in greased bowl; brush top with soft shortening. Cover tightly with wax paper or aluminum foil. Store in refrigerator until doubled in bulk, or until needed. (Dough may be kept 1 week in refrigerator.)

Divide dough into 3 equal pieces. Roll out each piece into

a circle about ¼ inch thick and about 9 inches in diameter. Brush lightly with melted margarine or butter. Cut each circle into 8 wedges. Stretch wide end of wedge slightly; then roll firmly, starting at wide end. Seal points firmly. Place about 2 inches apart on greased baking sheet with point underneath. Curve to form crescents. Cover. Let rise in warm place, free from drafts, until doubled in bulk—about 1 hour. Brush lightly with melted margarine or butter. Bake in hot oven (400° F.) about 15 minutes. Makes 24 croissants.

Pan Rolls: Divide dough in half. Form each half into a roll about 12 inches long. Cut each half into 16 equal pieces. Form into smooth balls. Place in 2 greased 8-inch shallow round or square pans about ¼ inch apart. Cover. Let rise in warm place, free from drafts, until doubled in bulk—about 1 hour. Brush lightly with melted margarine or butter. Bake in moderate oven (375° F.) about 20 minutes. Makes 32 pan rolls.

Fan Tans: Divide dough into 3 equal pieces. Roll each piece into 11- by 9-inch oblong. Brush lightly with melted margarine or butter. Cut into 7 equal strips, about 1½ inches wide. Pile strips one on top of the other. Cut into 6 equal pieces, about 1½ inches long. Place cut-side up in greased medium muffin pans. Cover. Let rise in warm place, free from drafts, until doubled in bulk—about 1 hour. Brush lightly with melted margarine or butter. Bake in hot oven (400° F.) about 20 minutes. Makes 18 Fan Tans.

CAFÉ AU LAIT

Prepare Demitasse Coffee (page 16). Meanwhile, heat an equal amount of milk. Then pour equal amounts of coffee and hot milk into cups or mugs—some prefer to pour coffee and milk simultaneously, using both hands, so they arrive in the cup together. This drink is especially good with doughnuts or other quick breads.

Quick Café au Lait: Measure 1¼ teaspoons instant quality coffee into a cup. Add ⅔ cup hot milk or ⅓ cup *each* hot milk *and* hot water, stirring to dissolve coffee. Makes 1 serving.

Gifts from Your Kitchen

The gift that you make in the heart of your home, your kitchen, is uniquely a gift from you—in a way which nothing that you buy, no matter how lavish, can ever be. A part of you—your time, your effort, your thoughtfulness—goes with the present as a special compliment to the person for whom it is intended. The cookies and candies and coffee-specials in this section are a pleasure to make, a joy to give. They'll ensure that any gift-giving occasion will be eagerly welcomed.

Here's an Idea: Send along a thoughtful bonus with your gift—include the recipe. Type or write it legibly on a file card, being sure to include such information as length of cooking time, temperature, and a complete list of ingredients. Attach with cord to the neck of a bottle, with tape to the top of a box. If you'd like to add a "professional" touch, inexpensive recipe cards can be ordered from small printers or from gift shops or mail-order gift houses. They carry printed headings, such as *From the kitchen of Mary Jones,* or *One of my favorites—Mary Smith,* along with a decoration—something like a drawing of an old-fashioned stove, or of a spoon and mixing bowl. There's plenty of space for you to write or type in the recipe. Attractive labels printed in the same manner are also available to dress up gift boxes, bottles, or jars.

Here's an Idea: If you want to give a more substantial gift, let the present from your kitchen serve double duty by packing it in a container that the recipient can use for another purpose.

Plastic refrigerator boxes and jars, which come in many shapes and sizes, colored or clear, make pretty use-again gift holders. Fudge left in the pan into which you pour it will stay fresh—and the pan will be used long after the fudge is only a pleasant memory. Candy arranged on an attractive plate (keep it in place with a see-through wrap of clear plastic), cookies packed in a cookie jar, Coffee Butter (page 229) in a fat little jam pot that can come to breakfast all year around, sauces and syrups in pitchers that can be sent, without apology, to the table—these are only a few double-purpose gift ideas. Let your imagination go on from there!

Here's an Idea: All through the year, save commercial containers in which to pack your made-at-home coffee gifts. Many of the everyday items you buy come in attractive packages which can be kept clean and ready—labels removed, of course—on your pantry shelf, awaiting the next gift-giving occasion. Many brands of salad dressings come in pretty bottles. Instant coffee and mayonnaise, to name two, supply nicely shaped jars. Coffee cans may be covered in gay paper (the self-adhesive kind is easy to use) and offer multiple value: being metal and easy to fill with snugly fitting lids, they are particularly good flavor-savers and crispness-keepers for such items as cookies, and will keep candy fresh longer than a cardboard box could. If you want to send more than one can will hold, stack them two or three high, tape together, and top with a perky bow.

Here's an Idea: If directions are needed for the use or storage of your gift, be sure they accompany it. For instance, foods which need to be refrigerated should carry a tag or label, with a phrase such as "Please keep in the refrigerator." When serving hints might be a help, send those, too. For example, if you're giving Coffee Cooler Syrup (page 230) as a gift, suggest that it can be used for delicious sundaes and sodas. Tag your gift of Coffee Butter (page 229) with the suggestion that it will make good waffles taste even better and turn toast into a special treat.

COFFEE FONDANT

- **2 cups sugar**
- **1 tablespoon instant quality coffee**
- **1 tablespoon light corn syrup**
- **Dash of salt**
- **1 cup water**
- **3 tablespoons butter**
- **½ teaspoon vanilla**
- **Pecan halves**

Combine sugar and coffee in a large saucepan; mix well. Add corn syrup, salt, and water. Place over low heat and stir constantly until sugar is dissolved and mixture comes to a boil. Cover and cook 3 minutes; then remove cover and continue boiling, without stirring. Occasionally wipe sides of pan with damp cloth to remove sugar crystals. Cook until a small amount of syrup forms a soft ball in cold water (or to a temperature of 240° F.). Remove from heat. Add butter but *do not stir*. Pour fondant onto a cold wet platter. Cool to lukewarm (110° F.). Add vanilla.

Work with wooden paddle or spatula until creamy. Knead until smooth. Let stand, uncovered, until cold. Then shape into a ball, wrap in wax paper, and store in tightly covered container in refrigerator or other cool place to ripen for at least 24 hours before using. Fondant may be kept for 2 or 3 days; if it begins to dry out, cover with damp cloth. Then form into small patties, pressing a pecan half into top of each. Makes about 1 pound fondant, or 4 dozen patties.

Mocha Fondant: Prepare Coffee Fondant, increasing corn syrup to 2 tablespoons and water to 1¼ cups and decreasing butter to 2 tablespoons. After kneading the lukewarm fondant, form into a ball and make an indentation on top. Melt 1½ squares unsweetened chocolate and pour about ¼ of the melted chocolate into indentation in fondant. Knead until chocolate is blended. Repeat until all chocolate is used. Then continue as directed above.

COFFEE-FLAVORED COCONUT

- **1 heaping tablespoon instant quality coffee**
- **¼ cup water**
- **1 to 1½ cups flaked, packaged grated, or shredded coconut**

Dissolve coffee in the water in a pint jar. Add coconut and shake thoroughly. Then spread the coconut on a baking sheet and dry in a slow oven (300° F.) about 30 minutes. Use as a garnish or topping for ice cream, cake frostings, puddings, and other desserts. Makes 1 to 1½ cups.

Mocha-Flavored Coconut: Combine ½ teaspoon cocoa and ½ teaspoon instant quality coffee (omit water); then shake with coconut as directed above. Do not bake.

COFFEE FUDGE

- 3 cups sugar
- ⅛ teaspoon salt
- ½ cup light cream
- 2 tablespoons light corn syrup
- 1 cup milk
- 2 tablespoons instant quality coffee
- 3 tablespoons butter or margarine
- 1 teaspoon vanilla

Combine sugar, salt, cream, corn syrup, and milk in saucepan. Bring to a boil, stirring constantly. Continue boiling, without stirring, until a small amount of mixture forms a very soft ball in cold water (or to a temperature of 234° F.). Add coffee, stirring just enough to blend. Continue boiling without stirring until mixture again forms a very soft ball in cold water (or to a temperature of 234° F.). Remove from heat. Add butter and vanilla but *do not stir*. Cool to lukewarm (110° F.); then beat until mixture begins to thicken and lose its gloss. Spread in a lightly buttered 8-inch square pan. When cold, cut into pieces. Makes 1½ pounds or about 36 pieces.

Chocolate Chip Coffee Fudge: Prepare Coffee Fudge, adding 1 package (6 ounces) semi-sweet chocolate chips and ½ cup chopped nuts just before fudge is spread in pan.

Coconut Coffee Fudge: Prepare Coffee Fudge, adding 1 cup flaked coconut just before fudge is spread in pan. Spread in pan; then sprinkle with ⅓ cup coarsely chopped candied cherries.

Coconut Honey Coffee Fudge: Prepare Coffee Fudge, substituting 2 tablespoons honey for the corn syrup and adding 1 cup flaked coconut just before the fudge is spread in pan.

COFFEE BUTTER

- 3 tablespoons sugar
- 2 or 3 teaspoons instant quality coffee
- 1 tablespoon water
- ½ cup butter
- ¼ teaspoon vanilla

Combine sugar, instant coffee, and water in a small saucepan. Place over low heat and stir constantly about 1 minute or until sugar is dissolved. Cool slightly. Meanwhile, cream butter until soft and fluffy. Gradually add the sugar mixture to the butter. Add vanilla and blend thoroughly. Use as a spread for toast or pancakes. Makes about ⅔ cup.

Quick Coffee Butter: Cream ½ cup butter until soft and fluffy. Mix 2 tablespoons maple-blended syrup and 2 or 3 teaspoons instant quality coffee; then gradually blend into butter. Makes about ⅔ cup.

COFFEE 'N' CHIP BARS

- 2¼ cups sifted all-purpose flour
- ½ teaspoon double-acting baking powder
- ¼ teaspoon salt
- 1 cup butter
- 1 cup firmly packed light brown sugar
- 1½ tablespoons instant quality coffee
- ¼ cup water
- 1 teaspoon almond extract
- 1 package (6 ounces) semi-sweet chocolate chips
- ½ cup chopped nuts

Sift flour with baking powder and salt. Cream butter. Gradually add sugar, creaming thoroughly. Dissolve coffee in water; add to butter mixture. Add extract and blend well. Gradually add the dry ingredients, blending thoroughly. Stir in chocolate chips and nuts. Press into a well-greased 15- by 10- by 1-inch jelly roll pan. Bake in a moderate oven (350° F.) for 20 to 25 minutes. Cool; then cut in bars. Makes about 3½ dozen.

COFFEE WALNUT SANDIES

- 1¼ cups unsifted all-purpose flour
- ½ cup sugar
- 1 tablespoon instant quality coffee
- ¼ teaspoon salt
- ¾ cup butter
- ¾ cup chopped walnuts

Mix flour, sugar, coffee, and salt in mixing bowl. With a pastry blender, cut in butter until the size of small peas. Press dough together. Shape into small balls; then roll in walnuts. Place on ungreased baking sheets about 2 inches apart. Flatten with bottom of a glass dipped in sugar. Bake in a slow oven (300° F.) 20 minutes or until very lightly browned. Cool slightly before removing from baking sheets. Cool thoroughly on racks. Store in loosely covered containers. Makes 3 dozen.

COFFEE BOURBON BALLS

- 2 cups fine vanilla wafer crumbs
- 1 cup unsifted confectioners' sugar
- 1 cup chopped walnuts
- ¼ cup instant quality coffee
- 3 tablespoons corn syrup
- ⅓ cup bourbon
- Dash of salt
- Additional confectioners' sugar

Combine all ingredients, except additional sugar, and mix thoroughly. Roll into balls, using a rounded teaspoon of mixture for each. Store in a tightly covered container for several days. Then, before serving, roll in confectioners' sugar. Makes about 50 balls.

MOCHA PEANUT CLUSTERS

- 1 package (6 ounces) semi-sweet chocolate chips
- 16 large marshmallows, quartered
- ⅓ cup butter or margarine
- 1 tablespoon instant quality coffee
- 2 cups salted peanuts

Combine chocolate, marshmallows, and butter in top of double boiler. Cook over hot water, stirring occasionally, until melted and smooth. Mix in instant coffee. Remove from heat and stir in peanuts. Drop from a teaspoon onto wax paper. Cool until firm. Makes about 3 dozen clusters.

COFFEE COOLER SYRUP

- ¼ cup instant quality coffee
- ½ cup water
- 2 cups corn syrup
- ¼ teaspoon salt
- 2 teaspoons vanilla

Dissolve coffee in water. Blend in corn syrup and salt. Simmer 5 minutes. Remove from heat and add vanilla. Cool. Serve on ice cream or pancakes or in beverages. Store, tightly covered, in refrigerator. Makes 2 cups.

Coffee Almond Sundae: Pour Coffee Cooler Syrup over coffee ice cream. Sprinkle with salted almonds.

Coffee Cooler Soda: For each serving, pour ½ cup Coffee Cooler Syrup into a tall glass. Add 2 tablespoons heavy cream; then stir in a little chilled club soda. Add 1 or 2 scoops coffee ice cream and fill with club soda, stirring gently to mix.

MOCHA COCONUT CONFECTIONS

1 package (6 ounces) semi-sweet chocolate chips
2 tablespoons instant quality coffee
⅓ cup water
3 tablespoons light corn syrup
3 cups sifted confectioners' sugar
1 cup chopped walnuts
1¼ cups vanilla wafer crumbs
1 cup flaked coconut

Place chocolate chips in a small saucepan over very low heat. Remove from heat when almost melted; stir until smooth. Dissolve instant coffee in the water. Blend corn syrup, sugar, and coffee mixture into chocolate. Add walnuts. Then stir in vanilla wafer crumbs and ½ cup of the coconut. Shape mixture into 1-inch balls. Roll in remaining coconut. Store in tightly covered container 2 days to blend the flavors. Makes about 5 dozen confections.

MOCHA TRUFFLES

1 package (6 ounces) semi-sweet chocolate chips
⅔ cup butter
1 egg yolk
1¼ cups unsifted confectioners' sugar
1 tablespoon rum
1 teaspoon instant quality coffee
Chocolate cookie crumbs

Melt chocolate chips over hot water. Cool. Meanwhile, cream butter. Add egg yolk and sugar; blend well. Add chocolate, rum, and instant coffee, mixing well. Chill until firm enough to handle. Form into small balls, about ½ inch in diameter. Roll in cookie crumbs. Chill several hours. Makes about 4 dozen confections.

MOCHA BALLS

- 1 tablespoon instant quality coffee
- ¼ cup water
- 2 cups vanilla wafer crumbs
- 2 cups unsifted confectioners' sugar
- 1⅓ cups (about) flaked coconut
- 2 tablespoons cocoa
- 2 tablespoons milk
- Additional confectioners' sugar

Dissolve the coffee in the water. Combine the wafer crumbs, confectioners' sugar, coconut, and cocoa. Add the milk and coffee and mix well. Shape into balls about ¾ inch in diameter. Roll the balls in additional confectioners' sugar. Chill. Makes 4 to 5 dozen confections.

Coffee Break: Paris

Choose a table at a sidewalk café, order coffee and something deliciously rich to go with it—and watch the world go by. Can't travel? Do the next best thing; make these French treats at home!

CHOCOLATE PIE FRANÇAIS

- 3 packages (4 ounces each) sweet cooking chocolate
- 3 tablespoons hot water
- ⅔ cup softened butter
- 2 tablespoons all-purpose flour
- 1 tablespoon sugar
- 4 egg yolks, well beaten
- 4 egg whites
- 1 unbaked 9-inch graham cracker crust

Melt chocolate in hot water in top of double boiler. Remove from heat. Add butter, flour, and sugar, blending until butter melts. Gradually add egg yolks, stirring constantly. Blend until smooth. Beat egg whites until stiff, shiny peaks will form. Fold into chocolate mixture. Pour into graham cracker crust. Bake in hot oven (425° F.) for 15 minutes. (Pie will be soft in the center but will set on cooling.) Top with sweetened whipped cream, if desired. Makes 10 to 12 servings.

PEACHES CONDÉ

- 3½ cups milk
- 3 tablespoons butter
- ½ cup sugar
- ¼ teaspoon salt
- 1¼ teaspoons vanilla
- 1⅓ cups packaged pre-cooked rice
- 2 egg yolks
- 2 tablespoons milk
- 1 can (1 pound 13 ounces) peach halves, undrained
- ¼ cup brandy
- 3 tablespoons (about) chopped candied fruit
- 2 tablespoons coarsely chopped pistachio nuts

Combine 3½ cups milk, butter, sugar, salt, vanilla, and rice in a saucepan. Bring to a boil. Cook over medium heat 20 minutes, stirring frequently. Combine egg yolks and 2 tablespoons milk; beat slightly. Gradually add to hot rice mixture, stirring vigorously. Chill.

Meanwhile, combine peaches and brandy in a saucepan. Bring to a boil; then chill thoroughly. Combine chilled rice mixture and 3 tablespoons of the peach syrup mixture. Spoon into serving dish. Arrange peach halves around rice. Garnish each peach half with candied fruit and pistachio nuts. Top with whipped cream, if desired. Makes 6 servings.

COCONUT RICE IMPERIAL

1½ cups milk
⅔ cup packaged pre-cooked rice
¾ teaspoon salt
1 envelope unflavored gelatin
2 tablespoons cold water
2 egg yolks
½ cup sugar
½ teaspoon orange extract
1¼ teaspoons grated orange rind
1⅓ cups (about) flaked coconut
1 cup heavy cream
Sweetened raspberries, strawberries, or other fruit

Scald milk in saucepan. Add rice and salt, mixing just to moisten all rice. Cover, remove from heat, and let stand about 5 minutes, fluffing occasionally with a fork. Meanwhile, soften gelatin in cold water.

Combine egg yolks and sugar. Add a few spoonfuls of the hot rice mixture to egg yolks and sugar. Mix well. Then add egg yolk mixture to rice in saucepan. Add the softened gelatin, extract, orange rind, and coconut; mix well. Chill until mixture begins to thicken.

Whip the cream and fold into thickened rice mixture. Pour into 1-quart mold. Chill until firm. Serve with fruit. Makes 8 servings.

REGAL CHOCOLATE MOUSSE

1 package (4 ounces) sweet cooking chocolate
⅓ cup water
¾ cup sugar
⅛ teaspoon salt
3 egg yolks, well beaten
1 teaspoon vanilla
2 cups heavy cream
1 pint vanilla ice cream

Place chocolate and water in top of double boiler. Heat over hot water, stirring vigorously until chocolate is melted. Add sugar and salt. Continue to cook, stirring constantly until sugar is dissolved. Slowly stir into egg yolks. Cool; then add vanilla.

Whip the cream and fold into cooled chocolate. Pour into a greased 2-quart mold. Freeze until partially frozen. Press ice cream into center of chocolate mixture. Smooth chocolate over ice cream to make bottom flat. Freeze until firm. Unmold. Makes 8 to 10 servings.

NAPOLEONS

- 1 package (3¼ ounces) vanilla pudding and pie filling mix
- 1 cup milk
- Pastry for 9-inch pie shell or ½ package pie crust mix
- ¼ cup heavy cream
- ¾ cup unsifted confectioners' sugar
- 1½ to 2 tablespoons water
- 1 square semi-sweet chocolate
- 1 to 1½ teaspoons water

Combine pudding mix and milk in saucepan. Cook and stir over medium heat until mixture comes to a *full* boil. Cover surface of pudding with wax paper and chill—about 1 hour.

Meanwhile, roll pastry into a 14- by 10-inch rectangle. Cut into 3 equal strips, 14 by 3⅓ inches each. Carefully place on a baking sheet. Prick with a fork. Bake in hot oven (425° F.) about 12 minutes or until golden brown. Set aside to cool.

Whip chilled pudding until light and fluffy. Then whip the cream; fold into pudding. Spread 2 of the cooled pastry strips with the pudding mixture. With filling side up, stack one on top of the other.

Then blend confectioners' sugar and 1½ to 2 tablespoons water; carefully spread on remaining pastry layer so that glaze does not run over sides. Melt the chocolate over hot water. Gradually add 1 to 1½ teaspoons water. Immediately make thin lines of chocolate across the length of the glazed pastry, about ½ inch apart. Using a sharp knife or spatula, draw across the lines from side to side at intervals to give a rippled effect. Place on top of stacked layers. Chill about 2 hours.

Using a sharp knife and quick cutting strokes, cut into six equal portions. Makes 6 servings.

DE LUXE VANILLA CHEESECAKE

- ¾ cup finely crushed graham cracker or zwieback crumbs
- 1 tablespoon sugar
- 2 tablespoons butter, melted
- 1 package (3¼ ounces) vanilla pudding and pie filling mix
- ½ cup sugar
- 1 cup milk*
- 3 packages (8 ounces each) cream cheese, softened
- 3 eggs, separated
- 1 tablespoon lemon juice
- 1 teaspoon vanilla
- ¼ teaspoon ground nutmeg (optional)
- ¼ teaspoon salt

*Or use 1 can (6 ounces) evaporated milk plus water to make 1 cup.

Combine crumbs, 1 tablespoon sugar, and butter; mix well. Grease sides of a 9-inch spring-form pan to 1 inch from the top. Sprinkle about 2 tablespoons crumb mixture on sides of pan. Press remaining crumb mixture firmly on bottom of pan.

Combine pudding mix, ½ cup sugar, and milk in a saucepan. Cook and stir over medium heat until mixture comes to a *full* boil. Remove from heat. Cover surface of pudding with wax paper.

In large bowl, beat cream cheese until fluffy, using low speed of electric mixer or beating by hand. Add egg yolks; beat well. Add lemon juice, vanilla, nutmeg, salt, and cooked pudding; blend well. Beat egg whites until they will form soft peaks; fold into cream cheese mixture. Pour into prepared spring-form pan.

Bake in a hot oven (425° F.) 30 minutes or until center is set when lightly touched and top is golden brown. (Cake becomes firmer when cooled.) Cool to room temperature; then store in refrigerator. Remove from refrigerator 30 minutes before serving. Makes 10 to 12 servings.

Nice to know: *If desired, spread top of hot cheesecake with mixture of 1 cup sour cream and ¼ cup unsifted confectioners' sugar. Return to hot oven (425° F.) for 1 minute. Topping should be shiny but not brown. Cool to room temperature; then store in refrigerator.*

PROFITEROLES

¼ cup butter
½ cup boiling water
½ cup sifted all-purpose flour
2 eggs
2 cups Coffee Whipped Cream (page 82)
Easy Fudge Sauce (page 193)

Add butter to water in saucepan and bring to a boil. Reduce heat; add flour all at once, stirring rapidly. Cook and stir until mixture thickens and leaves sides of pan—about 2 minutes. Remove from heat. Add eggs, one at a time, beating well after each addition. Then beat until mixture is satiny and breaks off when spoon is raised.

Using a pastry bag with ⅜-inch opening, force mixture into 1-inch mounds onto ungreased baking sheet. Or, drop mixture by teaspoonfuls on ungreased baking sheet. Bake in hot oven (425° F.) until golden brown—about 17 minutes. When cool, cut off tops, fill with Coffee Whipped Cream, and replace tops. Use 4 or 5 puffs for each serving and serve with hot Easy Fudge Sauce. Makes 3½ dozen puffs, or 8 to 10 servings.

GÂTEAU D' RIZ

1½ cups sugar
3 tablespoons water
2 cups milk
2 cups water
½ teaspoon salt
1⅓ cups packaged pre-cooked rice
3 eggs, well beaten
1 teaspoon vanilla
Custard sauce or whipped cream

Combine 1 cup of the sugar and 3 tablespoons of water in a small saucepan. Simmer and stir over very low heat until sugar dissolves and syrup turns golden brown. Brush a thin even coating over the inside of a fluted 1½-quart mold. Set aside.

Combine milk, 2 cups water, ½ cup sugar, and the salt in a saucepan. Cover and bring to a boil. Stir in rice. Cover, remove from heat, and let stand 10 minutes. (Not all of the liquid will be absorbed.)

Meanwhile, combine eggs and vanilla. Gradually add some of the hot rice mixture to the eggs, stirring rapidly. Then add egg mixture to remaining rice in saucepan. Pour into the syrup-coated mold. Bake in a hot oven (400° F.) 40 to 45 minutes, or until center is firm. Remove from oven, invert onto a serving plate, and remove mold at once. Serve warm with custard sauce or whipped cream. Makes 8 servings.

The Instant Coffee Story

One day, just after the turn of the century, an Englishman living in Guatemala was waiting for his wife in the garden of their home. A servant had just set out the impressive silver service which—in the English tradition of keeping home-away-from-home standards high—the wife had brought with her.

Idly, the man savored the delicious aroma of fresh coffee as he watched the steam rise from the lovely silver pot. Then his attention focused on the spout of the pot. He saw a fine, dark powder forming there. The powder, it seemed to him, must be the condensation of the coffee vapors.

That gave him an idea. He began experiments by which he hoped eventually to produce for commercial consumption coffee which could be made in the cup, simply by adding hot water to the dark powder. He was successful and, in 1909, put the first instant coffee on sale.

Today, there are more than 300 different instant coffee brands on the market. Maxwell House, the largest of the instant coffee producers, has been responsible for many of the improvements which have changed the wartime soluble coffee powder into the all-coffee aromatized product now available.

Instant coffee processing begins with a precise blend of green coffees, selected to provide a pleasing balance of body with flavor and aroma. After cleansing and blending, these green coffees are ready for roasting.

Each roaster handles about 1,500 pounds of coffee; continuous roasting is at rates as high as 11,000 pounds per hour. The color of the roast is prescribed and can be matched almost precisely. The operator matches the color of the roast against a set standard, and experts recheck samples of each batch against the standard, using scientific equipment for measuring the depth of color. Moisture content is carefully controlled.

After it is cooled, the roasted coffee for the instant process is ground. The grind is much coarser than for regular coffee, designed for easy extraction and handling. This helps prevent the coffee's breaking down and creating "fines"—small particles.

The fundamental difference between regular and instant coffee is that the percolator or extraction step in making the brew is done in the plant, under scientifically controlled conditions, instead of in the home. But instead of the usual kitchen coffeepot, the plant's percolators are two stories tall. More, there is a battery of six of these percolators in each production unit, mounted side by side.

Water—which must meet purity specifications—is pumped through a heat exchanger, where it is heated to a temperature of more than 300° F. before it goes, under pressure, into the percolators.

There is a bin above each percolator, with a capacity of about 3,000 pounds of ground coffee. Loading the percolators is a simple process. The bottom plug valve is opened. Gravity moves the coffee down from the bin into the percolator.

An operator controlling the entire extraction process maintains a constant watch on the temperature. From the percolators, the coffee extract goes to a cooler, which maintains a temperature that guarantees maximum flavor and aroma.

Cooled, the coffee extract goes to a tank where the specific gravity and temperature are measured to determine concentration of extract. From there, the extract is pumped up six floors to the dryer.

This dryer is an enormous vessel, one of the distinguishing characteristics of any instant coffee plant. Air, heated by an adjoining furnace, is introduced at the top of the dryer. The extract is piped into the dryer by spray nozzles. Droplets of pure coffee extract—exactly like coffee made in a home percolator—are carried downward in the air stream through the dryers, with the water evaporating as it goes. This action converts the droplets into hollow spheres or "flavor buds."

Near the bottom, the coffee spheres are separated from the

air stream and fall into a cone in the dryer. The coffee is ready, then, for further quality checks before it is packaged and shipped.

The spent (used) coffee grounds are moved into a storage tank. From the bottom of this tank, grounds are conveyed to a press, where moisture is reduced. The grounds are then fed into a boiler for burning as fuel. Spent coffee grounds supply all the steam load or heat for instant coffee processing. One day's supply of spent grounds could provide the power load equivalent needed for a city of 1,500 homes.

Indeed, the whole process of instant coffee making is, from start to finish, one of rigid control, efficiency—and, now, of automation. For example, the Instant Maxwell House Coffee plant at Hoboken, N. J., is an eye-opening revelation of how automation has influenced the food industry. At capacity, fewer than 200 men operate this, the largest instant coffee plant in the world.

Tricks with Instant Coffee

Used in cooking, instant quality coffee supplies delicious, true coffee flavor to dishes of many kinds. But did you know that you can improve other flavors with instant quality coffee in lesser amounts? Next time you make cocoa with a ready-mix, try adding a scant ¼ teaspoon of instant quality coffee for each cup. You'll get a delightful, better-than-ever beverage. . . . The identical trick works wonders with chocolate frosting made from a mix, too. Add a teaspoon of instant quality coffee to the dry ingredients before adding butter and/or liquid. Result? A deeper, richer, elusive flavor that puts your mix-made frosting in a class by itself. . . . Delicate *Coffee Whipped Cream* (page 82) or Coffee Topping (page 84) are flavor-plus additions for plain desserts. . . . *Instant Parfaits:* Layer *Coffee Whipped Cream* alternately with chocolate cookie crumbs in parfait glasses, beginning and ending with the cream; top with a cherry or a nut meat. Far variety, use gingersnap crumbs. . . . *Instant Sundae:* To ½ cup finely chopped walnuts or pecans, add 1 teaspoon instant quality coffee; mix well, sprinkle over three or four servings of vanilla or chocolate ice cream. . . . *Quick Coffee Ice Cream:* Blend 2 rounded teaspoons instant quality coffee with 1 quart slightly softened vanilla ice cream. Spoon into a freezing tray and freeze until firm. Makes 4 or 5 servings. . . . *Other tricks:* Try instant quality coffee sprinkled on: whipped cream-topped desserts, meringue-topped pies, puddings and custards, sugar cookies, ice cream, frosted cakes. . . . Mix instant quality coffee with sugar to taste—about ½ teaspoon instant quality coffee with ½ cup sugar is a good starting point; then add more coffee or sugar as desired. Use mixture as a roll-in for fudge balls or French chocolates, cookie balls, and doughnuts.

QUICK COCONUT COFFEE CRUST

- 1 tablespoon instant quality coffee
- 1 tablespoon water
- 2 cups flaked coconut
- ¼ cup butter, melted

Dissolve instant coffee in water. Blend with remaining ingredients. Evenly press over bottom and sides of an 8- or 9-inch pie pan. Chill until firm—about 1 hour. Fill with your favorite chiffon, cream, or ice cream filling. (Use 3 cups filling for 8-inch pie and 4 cups filling for 9-inch pie.)

COFFEE CRUMB TOPPING

- 1 tablespoon instant quality coffee
- ¾ cup unsifted confectioners' sugar
- ½ teaspoon ground cinnamon
- ⅛ teaspoon ground nutmeg
- 2 tablespoons butter, melted

Thoroughly mix all ingredients except butter. Then add butter, stirring with a fork until mixture is well blended. Sprinkle over coffee cake just before baking. Makes enough topping for a 9-inch round or square coffee cake.

Coffee Break: Italy

The Italians have a way with pastries different from any other. Try these wonderful nibble-with-coffee delights and treat yourself to a coffee break Mediterranean style!

ITALIAN CAFÉ AU LAIT

Prepare 2 cups Demitasse Coffee (page 16). Meanwhile, heat 2 cups milk. Then pour the hot Demitasse Coffee and the hot milk into a heatproof pitcher containing 1 well-beaten egg. Makes about 4 cups, or 6 servings, about 5 ounces each.

ITALIAN COFFEE

½ cup instant quality coffee
4 cups boiling water
12 twists of lemon peel

Measure coffee into a carafe or serving pot. Stir in boiling water. Cover and let steep 5 minutes over low heat. Serve in demitasse cups with a twist of lemon peel. Makes 4 cups, or 12 servings, about 3 ounces each.

FLORENTINES

⅓ cup sifted all-purpose flour
Dash of salt
¼ teaspoon baking soda
¼ cup butter
⅓ cup firmly packed brown sugar
2 tablespoons light corn syrup
1 egg, well beaten
½ teaspoon vanilla
⅔ cup packaged grated coconut
2 squares semi-sweet chocolate

Sift flour with salt and soda. Cream butter; gradually add sugar, creaming until light and fluffy. Add corn syrup and egg and beat well. Stir in flour mixture, vanilla, and coconut. Drop teaspoons of mixture about 2 inches apart on greased baking sheet. Spread into 1½-inch rounds, ⅛ inch thick. Bake in moderate oven (350° F.) about 8 minutes or until golden brown. Cool on baking sheet 1 minute. Then loosen from sheet with spatula, placing sheet over low heat if wafers are difficult to loosen.

Heat chocolate over hot water until partly melted; then remove from heat and stir rapidly until entirely melted. Drizzle chocolate in lacy pattern over wafers. Let stand until chocolate is firm. Makes about 4 dozen.

For 4-inch rounds: Drop scant tablespoons of batter on greased baking sheet. Spread into 2½-inch rounds, ⅛ inch thick. Makes about 2 dozen.

Ice Cream Filled Wafers: Prepare 4-inch Florentines, omitting the chocolate drizzle. Just before serving, spoon softened ice cream onto half of the wafers. Top with remaining wafers and serve with Regal Chocolate Sauce (page 193).

Nice to know: *Wafers may be stored overnight in a tightly covered container with wax paper between layers.*

ITALIAN CHEESE PIE

- 1½ pounds ricotta cheese
- 6 tablespoons sugar
- ¼ teaspoon salt
- 1 teaspoon vanilla
- 4 eggs, well beaten
- 1 package (4 ounces) sweet cooking chocolate, coarsely chopped
- 1 jar (4 ounces) mixed candied fruit, finely chopped
- 2 cups unsifted all-purpose flour
- ½ teaspoon baking soda
- ⅛ teaspoon salt
- ¼ cup shortening
- 1 egg, slightly beaten
- ⅓ cup milk

Add cheese, sugar, ¼ teaspoon salt, and vanilla to the 4 eggs; blend until almost smooth. Stir in chocolate and fruit. Set aside.

Sift flour, soda, and ⅛ teaspoon salt into a mixing bowl. Cut in shortening. Combine 1 egg and milk; add to flour mixture, mixing until blended. Knead on a floured board about 5 minutes or until dough is smooth and flour is completely blended. Roll out very thin and place in two 8-inch glass pie plates or one 11-inch glass pie plate. Fill with cheese mixture. Cut remaining dough into 1-inch strips and arrange on top of pie. Bake in a moderate oven (350° F.) until lightly browned—about 40 minutes for 8-inch pie or about 50 minutes for 11-inch pie. Cool before serving. Makes about 12 servings.

CHESTNUT PASTRIES

- 1 pound fresh chestnuts
- 1 package (4 ounces) sweet cooking chocolate, grated
- Dash of salt
- ¼ teaspoon ground cinnamon
- 2 tablespoons currants
- ½ teaspoon vanilla
- ½ cup finely chopped nuts
- ½ cup honey
- 4 cups sifted all-purpose flour
- 2 eggs
- ⅓ cup salad oil
- Dash of salt
- ½ cup plus 2 tablespoons water
- 1 cup honey
- ½ cup water
- Additional finely chopped nuts
- Confectioners' sugar

Slit the shells of the chestnuts on the convex side with a sharp knife. Place in a saucepan and cover with water. Bring to a boil, reduce heat, and boil gently 20 minutes. Remove from heat. Then remove chestnuts one by one from water and peel while still hot. Mash or press through a sieve.

Combine chestnuts, grated chocolate, dash of salt, the cinnamon, currants, vanilla, ½ cup nuts, and ½ cup honey and mix well. Cook over boiling water, stirring occasionally, for 10 minutes or until filling becomes sticky. Set aside to cool.

Place flour in mixing bowl and make a well in the center. Add eggs, oil, dash of salt, and ½ cup plus 2 tablespoons water, making a dough by folding flour into ingredients in well. (Add more water if necessary to make a soft but not sticky dough.) Divide into 3 parts. Roll out each part very thinly and cut into 2-inch circles. Place 1 heaping teaspoon of filling in the center of each circle, moisten the edge with water, fold over, and seal with the tines of a fork. Fry in 2½ inches of hot oil (400° F.) until golden brown—about 30 seconds. Drain. Cool.

Bring 1 cup honey and ½ cup water to a rolling boil in a small saucepan. Drop pastries, a few at a time, into boiling mixture to coat thoroughly, about 20 seconds. Place on a cake rack to drain. Sprinkle with chopped nuts. Cool, then dust with confectioners' sugar. Store in a loosely covered container. Makes about 5 dozen pastries.

Nice to know: *Pastries will keep at least 5 weeks in loosely covered container. If pastries are soft after storage, heat in a very slow oven (250° F.) for a few minutes.*

TOASTED COCONUT TORTONI

- 1 package (3¼ ounces) vanilla pudding and pie filling mix
- ¼ cup sugar
- 1 cup evaporated milk
- 1 cup water
- 1 cup heavy cream
- 1 teaspoon vanilla
- 1 cup packaged grated coconut

Combine pudding mix, sugar, milk, and water in saucepan. Cook and stir over medium heat until mixture comes to a *full* boil. Pour into freezing tray or shallow pan. Place in freezer 30 minutes to chill quickly.

Combine cream and vanilla in bowl. Beat until cream will hold soft peaks. Fold into chilled pudding mixture. Return to freezing tray and freeze 1 hour or until partially frozen. Meanwhile, spread coconut in a shallow pan; toast lightly in a moderate oven (350° F.), stirring often—takes 5 to 10 minutes. Cool.

Spoon mixture into large chilled bowl. Beat until smooth but not melted. Fold in ¾ cup coconut. Return mixture to freezing tray or spoon into paper soufflé cups; sprinkle top with remaining coconut. Freeze until firm—about 4 hours. Makes 1 quart or 6 to 8 servings.

TORTONI DE LUXE

- 1 cup packaged grated coconut
- 3 tablespoons Cointreau
- 2 egg whites
- 2 cups heavy cream
- ½ cup sugar
- ¼ teaspoon salt
- ½ teaspoon vanilla

Combine coconut and Cointreau in a small bowl and mix until Cointreau is absorbed. Place egg whites and cream in a large bowl and beat until slightly thickened. Gradually add sugar and continue beating until mixture is fairly stiff. Fold in salt, vanilla, and coconut. Spoon into a 1½-quart mold, two freezing trays, or 10 small paper soufflé cups. Freeze until firm—about 2 to 3 hours. Garnish with additional Cointreau-flavored coconut, if desired. Makes about 10 servings.

QUICK COCONUT MACAROONS

- 2 cups (7-ounce package) packaged grated coconut
- ¾ cup sweetened condensed milk
- 1 teaspoon vanilla
- ¼ teaspoon almond extract
- Dash of salt

Combine all ingredients and mix well. Drop by teaspoonfuls 1 inch apart on greased baking sheets. Bake in slow oven (325° F.) about 15 minutes or until golden brown. Remove from baking sheets at once. Makes 2½ dozen.

Nice to know: *For larger macaroons, use about 2 tablespoons of the mixture for each cookie and spread with spatula or back of spoon into 3-inch circles. Bake 15 to 20 minutes. Makes about 1 dozen.*

COCONUT EGG YOLK COOKIES

- ¾ cup butter
- 1 cup sugar
- 4 egg yolks
- 2 cups sifted all-purpose flour
- ⅔ cup packaged grated coconut
- 2 teaspoons almond extract
- 1 teaspoon vanilla

Cream butter until softened; gradually add sugar, creaming well. Beat in egg yolks. Then add flour and coconut; continue beating until flour and coconut are blended. Stir in almond and vanilla extracts. Drop by tablespoonfuls onto ungreased baking sheets. Sprinkle with additional grated coconut, if desired. Bake in moderate oven (375° F.) 12 to 15 minutes or until cookies are browned around the edges. When cool, drizzle with favorite glaze and sprinkle with additional coconut, if desired. Makes about 3 dozen cookies.

Nice to know: *If desired, batter may be divided in half and each half shaped into a rectangle about 6 inches long. Freeze 1 hour; then slice ¼ inch thick and bake as for drop cookies.*

The Coffee Story: From Plantation to You

As the popularity of coffee spread and increased throughout the world the demand for it, of course, kept pace. Cultivation of coffee was tried in many places, and the soil and climate of Latin America were found to be particularly favorable. The first coffee plant reached the new world—the island of Martinique in the West Indies—in 1725. From that one seedling came the great coffee plantations that spread over many Latin American countries—and a change in the entire economy of the Western Hemisphere.

Coffee grows only in the Torrid Zone, closely following the equator around the world. Altitude is important, making the lovely mountain areas of Brazil, Venezuela, Colombia, the Central American countries, and Mexico ideal coffee-growing land. The rich, volcanic-ash soil is perfect for cultivation of the finest varieties of coffee, and the abundant rainfall is important, both in quantity and in its seasonal appearance.

The coffee plant is an evergreen shrub with long, narrow, shiny leaves, which grow in pairs, opposite each other, on the stem. Started in a nursery, the plants are set out as foot-tall seedlings, in rows about 10 feet apart, like an apple orchard. Some varieties grow best on flat lawns, others on sloping hillsides. The coffee trees, at maturity, are kept pruned to a height of 12 to 15 feet. Careful cultivation, adequate shade, and sufficient fertilization produce coffee trees that start bearing commercially usable fruit about their sixth year. Close to the equator, the plants are usually grown under other, higher trees to provide such shade.

Signaling the beginning of the bearing cycle, the mature coffee trees burst into a profusion of exquisite, fragrant five-petal white flowers, very much like orange blossoms in both appearance and aroma. Later, the fruit—called cherries—appears. At first the cherries are green. Six months after the blooming period, they are ready for picking.

In climates close to the equator, the trees blossom several times a year—often there are blossoms, green cherries, and ripe cherries on the same tree at the same time. In subtropical climates, however, there is only one blossoming season.

Much coffee is grown on small farms, but most of it comes from large plantations—called *fincas* in Spanish-speaking countries or *fazendas* in Portuguese-speaking Brazil. A *finca* or *fazenda* is a small, practically self-sufficient community. Because so much labor is required to grow coffee, the owner must make it possible for his workers to live on the premises. He must provide houses, a church, a meeting place, a school for the children. And, because workers require recreation—and because these are Latin Americans, to whom any excuse is right and proper for a *fiesta*, festivals, or fairs—place for such must be provided, too.

When the crop is ready, everybody—men, women, and children—participates in the picking, for no time must be lost between ripening of the coffee berry and the start of processing. Harvesting is a tremendous task—Brazilian *fazendas*, for example, vary from 400,000 to 2 million coffee trees!

The coffee bean, which is used in the roasting and grinding processes that result in the coffee we buy, is actually the pit or seed of the coffee cherry. The fruit is made up of an outer skin, then a layer of sweet pulp, then a thin, parchment-like shell surrounding each of the two beans which form the pit. Those two beans make up what is called "green coffee."

After being picked by hand from the trees, the coffee cherries are prepared for market by either a dry or a wet method. The dry method, used in Brazil, involves spreading out the ripe cherries on concrete patios, where they dry in the sun over a 15- to 20-day period, during which they are turned by rakes several times a day to ensure even drying, and heaped and covered at night to protect them from moisture. The dry cherries are hulled by machine to remove the dried husk and inner skins, and the green beans are graded according to size and shape.

In countries where there is a more plentiful supply of water, the wet method is used. The ripe cherries are hulled mechanically and the beans, in their parchment shell, are fermented in cement tanks for 24 to 36 hours. Then they are poured into concrete sluiceways and thoroughly washed in constantly changing water. After that, they are dried on concrete patios, but for a shorter time than the dry method takes. Finally, the parchment shell is milled off, imperfections removed by hand, and the green coffee is ready for shipping to the seaport —by truck, by riverboat, by railroad, or, sometimes still, by mule pack. In each case, the coffee is sacked in grass or burlap bags for shipment to world markets—132 pounds to the bag in Brazil, 154 pounds in most other countries.

There are more than a hundred kinds and varieties of coffee. They are, however, divided into two species with Latin names, "Coffea robusta" and "Coffea arabica." Coffea robusta is grown primarily in the coastal regions of Africa. There are two major classifications within the species Coffea arabica—"Brazils" and "Milds." The former refers to coffee grown only in Brazil, the latter to all coffees grown elsewhere in the world. In early days, Brazil produced only harsh-flavored coffees. Later, other places—Colombia, Central America—began to produce coffee, using different methods of preparation, that tasted mild and smooth by comparison—hence the term, Milds. Brazil accounts for almost 50 per cent of the world's coffee production, and is of great importance from the volume standpoint; the Mild coffee countries gain their importance from the quality and flavor of their product.

Thirty-four million bags of coffee are produced annually for export. Twenty-eight and a half million of them are grown in Latin America. Twenty million bags of Latin American coffee are used each year in the United States alone.

When you buy coffee, you choose the brand, most probably, on the basis of taste—the one that makes the cup of coffee that tastes best to you and your family. The whole of the highly technical, complex coffee business is based on that nebulous factor of taste—something which cannot be measured or determined by scientific means. The aim of the seller of coffee, then, is to produce a brand that appeals to the taste of more people than his competitors' brands.

To achieve that goal, the coffee producer subjects the green coffee beans to a long and complicated process of cleaning, roasting, blending, and grinding.

New York's lower Manhattan, centered around the Wall Street area, is the heart of the world's largest coffee market. Here are located the most important shippers' agents, coffee importers, and green-coffee jobbers, as well as the green-coffee buying offices of this country's large coffee roasters.

Coffees are sold through green-coffee brokers, who visit the buying offices of the roasters as well as those of green jobbers. These brokers, or shippers' agents, have coffees from every coffee-producing section of the world for sale. Generally, the coffees offered by these men are owned by exporters and stored in countries where the coffee was grown.

Maxwell House, for example, does not have buying offices of its own in the coffee-producing countries, but instead has understandings with exporting and importing firms whose principal business is to fill the Maxwell House requirements. Coffees from Brazil, Colombia, Venezuela, Salvador, Guatemala, Mexico, Costa Rica, and British East Africa are used by the company, which has roasting plants throughout the United States, and one in Canada—so the problem of supply is a complex one.

Most of the Brazilian coffee used by Maxwell House is imported by the company directly from Brazil, and is referred to by the name of the port from which it is shipped—for example, when shipped from the port of Santos, it is called "Santos," from Rio de Janeiro, it is referred to as "Rio" coffee.

Coffee is free of import duty, but the Food and Drug Administration inspects all imports of coffee for infestation and contamination.

In its journey from the plantation to the roasting plant, coffee passes through seven stages of transportation. It begins by traveling from the drying ground or cleaning plant to the railroad or other type of transport that, in turn, carries the coffee to the city of export. There it is taken to a warehouse at the point of shipment, then moved from the warehouse to a steamer for its overseas trip. At the port of destination, it is taken from the steamer to the receiving warehouse. Last, the coffee is moved from the warehouse to the roasting plant.

Until the middle of the nineteenth century, the transportation of coffee was a hazardous business. There were pirates and privateers who roved the main sea routes to prey on merchant ships. Even when the pirates had been wiped out and the era of the steamship had arrived, there were still problems. Most coffee plantations are some distance from the ocean, so that the coffee must be sent to the seaport, sometimes a long and tedious journey.

But the movement of coffee does not require safe and swift transportation alone—there must be expert, skillful handling of the shipment as well, all along the way, for the condition of the coffee when it reaches its destination depends on proper loading, stowage, and unloading.

When the coffee reaches its destination, it is unloaded according to a prearranged plan. Sections of the pier are marked off, and on each section a different grade of coffee is placed. This assures the importer an opportunity to inspect the newly arrived coffee.

Coffee, in its green state, is prepared for the consumer in plants equipped to blend, roast, and grind the coffee beans to suit varying tastes of coffee drinkers. Research has established that the best results are obtained when coffee is roasted the shortest possible time at the lowest possible temperature, and roasting equipment is geared to meet these requirements. The best way to understand how coffee is transformed from the green-bean stage to the ground coffee that you buy is to follow a shipment of coffee beans through the roasting process.

The green beans, on arrival at the roasting plant, are dumped down a chute and carried, by gravity, through a receiving bin located above a green-coffee cleaner. The cleaner removes all lint, strings, and other foreign material that is lighter than the coffee beans. Heavier foreign materials, such as stones, are removed after the coffee is roasted.

Once cleaned, the coffee is carried by a conveyor to a blending machine, where various types of coffees, from many places, are blended according to the producer's formula so that the coffee you buy under your favorite brand name will always have the same flavor from cup to cup, pound to pound.

From the blender, the coffee passes to a storage bin to await roasting. Taken from the bin, it is roasted, then cooled, then cleaned again by a pneumatic separator. Next, the coffee is ground, and again placed in bins from which it is taken to be packaged and weighed. Each lot, at packaging time, is tested and sampled to make sure it conforms to the brand standards.

Coffee roasting would be a simple process if all coffees were alike. However, different kinds of coffees have varying characteristics. It is said that roasting coffee is work that almost anyone can do—but few can do well. Here an important factor, the human element, enters the picture. This human element, governing the blending and roasting, determines the flavor of the coffee you buy—that nebulous, unmeasurable factor of taste which makes one brand taste better to you than any other and determines the one that you buy.

Here's something to think about while you are making tomorrow morning's fragrant, wake-up pot of coffee: Each time you buy coffee, you bring home the entire year's production of one tree, for each coffee tree's annual yield comes down, in the final roasted, ground form in which you buy it, to just 1 pound. If your family uses a pound of coffee a week, there are 52 trees, somewhere on Latin America's *fincas* and *fazendas*, that are "yours."

Index

A

B